CHANNELS OF POWER

CHANNELS OF POWER

The UN Security Council and U.S. Statecraft in Iraq

Alexander Thompson

CORNELL UNIVERSITY PRESS ITHACA AND LONDON

First published 2009 by Cornell University Press
First printing, Cornell Paperbacks, 2010

Printed in the United States of America

Library of Congress Cataloging-in-Publication Data

Thompson, Alexander, 1972–
Channels of power : the UN Security Council and U.S. statecraft in Iraq / Alexander Thompson.
p. cm.
Includes bibliographical references and index.
ISBN 978-0-8014-4718-1 (cloth : alk. paper)
ISBN 978-0-8014-7637-2 (pbk. : alk. paper)
1. United States—Foreign relations—Iraq. 2. Iraq—Foreign relations—United States. 3. United Nations. Security Council—History. 4. United Nations—Iraq. 5. Persian Gulf War, 1991. 6. Iraq War, 2003– I. Title

E183.8.I57T46 2009
956.7044'22—dc22

2008045815

Cornell University Press strives to use environmentally responsible suppliers and materials to the fullest extent possible in the publishing of its books. Such materials include vegetable-based, low-VOC inks and acid-free papers that are recycled, totally chlorine-free, or partly composed of nonwood fibers. For further information, visit our website at www.cornellpress.cornell.edu.

Cloth printing 10 9 8 7 6 5 4 3 2 1
Paperback printing 10 9 8 7 6 5 4 3 2 1

Contents

Preface

For several months leading up to the March 2003 invasion of Iraq, all eyes were on Washington—but they were also on New York. The United Nations (UN) played a central role in the international diplomacy and politics of the Iraq war and is still implicated during the postwar reconstruction and democratic consolidation period. The United States has coveted the UN's stamp of approval, especially in the form of Security Council mandates, throughout the episode. And for good reason: the presence or absence of such mandates has been a critical variable in determining both the reaction of the international community to the policies pursued and their ultimate success.

In the end, President George W. Bush chose to invade Iraq without authorization from the UN, trading off the political costs of acting alone for the perceived benefits of exercising unfettered power. This latest chapter is a microcosm of a long conflict that began with Saddam Hussein's invasion of Kuwait in 1990 and continued through years of sanctions, weapons inspections, and the use of force in varying degrees. U.S. policy has vacillated between multilateral and unilateral strategies, with some actions channeled through the UN and some not.

Surprisingly, these patterns have not been accounted for in the scholarly literature. As I followed the string of confrontations and the literature surrounding them, I noticed that almost all existing articles and books have sought to describe or explain particular events, with little effort to unite the entire history of the Iraq–United States conflict under a common framework. This book provides a theoretically driven account of why the United States has so often channeled its power through the Security Council in conducting policies toward Iraq and why, at certain key junctures, it has not. It aims to explain both the reasons for and the consequences of U.S. actions.

The Iraq case is an example of a broader and increasingly important phenomenon. Today, even the most powerful states routinely direct their coercive foreign policies—from trade retaliation to humanitarian intervention to regime change—through international organizations (IOs). On its face, this is puzzling, since institutional entanglements tend to limit options and constrain power.

I explain this behavior by treating IOs as information providers. Standing, independent organizations impose costly constraints and provide neutral assessments of the policies of coercing states, thereby generating politically important information that leaders and publics can use to screen desirable from undesirable actions. Under certain conditions, coercers have incentives to subject their actions to such scrutiny and limitations because doing so lowers the political costs of exercising power. In other cases, the costs of working through an IO are too high and other options—forms of unilateralism or ad hoc multilateralism—are chosen.

The role of IOs in security affairs has never been more important. Military intervention without some effort to gain multilateral approval is now virtually obsolete, a remarkable feature of contemporary international relations that merits both theoretical and policy attention. The widespread hostility to the 2003 Iraq invasion vividly illustrates the importance attached to multilateral organizations, especially the Security Council, when it comes to the use or threat of force. This book helps us understand the relationship between power and institutions in the international system generally, while shedding particular light on the Security Council's unique and dramatically expanding role. One clear implication is that the fates of the world's only superpower and of its preeminent security institution have never been more closely linked. Each needs the other to retain influence.

I am indebted to many individuals and institutions. This project began as my doctoral thesis at the University of Chicago, which was funded through fellowships from the MacArthur and Mellon Foundations. Though little of the dissertation has survived years of revisions and events in the real world, it was nevertheless the intellectual seed that grew into this book. My dissertation committee—Duncan Snidal, Charles Lipson, Charlie Glaser, and Lloyd Gruber—were frank and critical but always constructive in their criticism. Each of them provided invaluable guidance that made my research more rigorous and interesting. Duncan in particular has been my leading advocate, advice-giver, and professional role model since I entered graduate school in 1995. His comments on my work are always detailed and incisive—and just plain smart. This book, along with the rest of my work, is much better thanks to him.

The PIPES workshop at Chicago was my intellectual home for several years, and the regular participants, both faculty and graduate students, shaped my thinking in important ways. Several provided comments on parts of the dissertation presented there, including Jasen Castillo, Dan Drezner, David Edelstein, Michael Freeman, Seth Jones, Jennifer Mitzen, Brian Portnoy, Susie Pratt, Alex Wendt, and Joel Westra.

The political science department at Ohio State provided fertile ground to nurture the seed into a book. I am fortunate to be surrounded by such a vibrant and diverse group of international relations scholars. Several of my colleagues have commented on parts of the book, including Rick Herrmann, Randy Schweller, Daniel Verdier, and Alex Wendt. Daniel and Alex have been especially supportive and generous with their time. I also received book advice, both practical and intellectual, from Ted Hopf, Marcus Kurtz, John Mueller, and Don Sylvan. I had many research assistants at Ohio State over the years—too many to name, unfortunately. Burcu Bayram, Erin Graham, Eric Grynaviski, and Clément Wyplosz went beyond their normal duties to offer comments and analysis for parts of the manuscript.

My department chairs at Ohio State, Paul Beck, Kathleen McGraw, and Herb Weisberg, made sure I had the time and resources for research and writing. A Faculty Seed Grant from the College of Social and Behavioral Sciences at Ohio State was very helpful during the early stages of the manuscript. The Mershon Center at Ohio State provided two separate grants to fund my book-related research, and I am grateful to its director, Rick Herrmann, and the faculty grant committees for supporting this project.

I have also received comments on papers related to the book from various colleagues in the field, including Daniel Blake, Robert Brown, Martha Finnemore, Peter Gourevitch, Darren Hawkins, David Lake, Lisa Martin, Jim McCormick, Elizabeth Saunders, Ken Schultz, Mike Tierney, and Kate Weaver. I apologize to those I may have left out.

Writing the book would not have been possible without the time and cooperation of many current and former government and international organization officials who allowed me to interview them, sometimes at great length. With only a few exceptions, their names do not appear in the book in order to protect confidentiality, but their individual and collective contribution to my understanding of important decisions and events covered in this book is immeasurable.

Working with Cornell University Press has been a pleasure. I am grateful to Roger Haydon for seeing value in the manuscript and for guiding the project with a judicious hand. Two anonymous reviewers provided unusually extensive and insightful comments that made the book much better than the initial manuscript. I hope to thank them in person some day! The editing and production staff at Cornell—Candace Akins, Susan Barnett, Sara Ferguson, Priscilla Hurdle, and Scott Levine—have been efficient and patient with this first-time book author. Jamie Fuller did a thoughtful and careful job copyediting the manuscript.

Many of my most important debts are more personal. My parents always encouraged me to focus on my education and gave me the confidence and flexibility to pursue a career in academia. Alex Hybel turned me on to international relations as an undergraduate and was the first to see my potential as a scholar. My neighbors on Tulane Road improved my quality of life immeasurably and helped me keep everything in perspective. Finally, I could not have written this book without my wife, Jennifer. She has stood by my side for years of graduate school and untenured professor status, putting up with evenings alone and a preoccupied husband—all while pursuing her own career and being an amazing mother to our two girls. This book is dedicated to her, with love.

CHANNELS OF POWER

1

THE POWER OF INTERNATIONAL ORGANIZATIONS

Iraq's invasion of Kuwait in August of 1990 triggered a two-decade confrontation with the United States entailing various tools of statecraft, including repeated efforts at diplomacy, economic sanctions, coercive weapons inspections, frequent bombing, and two wars. Most of these policies were conducted through the United Nations (UN), with the Security Council taking the lead by facilitating debate, repeatedly condemning Iraq's behavior, and authorizing actions in response. However, while the Security Council has been politically relevant at every phase, the United States has sometimes chosen to bypass it—instead acting unilaterally or with a "coalition of the willing." From a high point in 1991, when the Council's role in the Gulf War seemed to signal a new world order of great power cooperation and multilateralism, to a low point in 2003, when the launching of the second war led to accusations of UN impotence and an anti-American backlash, the question of how the United States would channel its power has gripped both policymakers and observers of international relations.

To shed light on U.S. statecraft toward Iraq, I offer a theoretical framework designed to answer an issue of broader scholarly and policy interest: Why do powerful states so often channel coercive foreign policies through international organizations (IOs)? This question exposes an intriguing puzzle for students of international politics. Governments that lack resources or expertise often require IO assistance for material and technical reasons, and weak states rely on international forums to increase their political clout and bargaining power. Developing countries, for example, have relied on institutions such as the Organization of the Petroleum Exporting Countries, the UN Conference on Trade and

Development, the UN General Assembly, and a variety of regional economic and security organizations to enhance their political positions and to aggregate resources. They do so out of necessity.

Powerful states, by contrast, rarely *need* IOs to achieve specific objectives. On the contrary, since turning to an international institution complicates policy-making and entails some loss of autonomy, we might expect the powerful to avoid such entanglements, especially in the pursuit of important national interests. Yet this is often not the case: even superpowers routinely channel coercion, including the use of force, through IOs despite viable alternatives that offer more flexibility and control—namely, unilateralism and ad hoc coalitions.

International institutions have played a prominent if uneven role in statecraft since the Second World War. In about half of all interstate conflicts since World War II (as counted in Sarkees 2000), a multilateral organization authorized the deployment of military forces. Even in the highly competitive environment of the Cold War, the United States turned to the UN for the Korea intervention and sought cover from regional organizations to take action in Cuba (1962), the Dominican Republic (1965), Grenada (1983), and Panama (1989).[1] Since the Cold War, powerful states have increasingly turned to IOs when using force. The United States has achieved endorsements from the UN Security Council (UNSC) or the North Atlantic Treaty Organization (NATO), or both, for virtually every military intervention since 1990, including those in Iraq, Somalia, Bosnia, Rwanda, Haiti, Zaire, Kosovo, and Afghanistan.[2] The British have behaved similarly and pushed hard—in the end, to no avail—for a Security Council resolution authorizing the 2003 Iraq war. Russia and France have also sought UN or regional cover (for example, from the Commonwealth of Independent States, the Organization for Security and Cooperation in Europe, and the Economic Community of West African States) for interventions in the former Soviet "near abroad" and francophone Africa, respectively. For India, UN consent has become a virtual sine qua non for foreign troop deployments. Other middle powers, including Germany, Japan, and Canada, simply will not intervene without an IO mandate.

The Security Council has come to play a uniquely important role in this regard. Even in cases where it failed to endorse intervention policies, as in Kosovo and Iraq (2003), there was a concerted effort to gain such approval. UNSC enforcement

---

1. The relevant bodies were the Organization of American States (OAS) in the first three cases and the Organization of East Caribbean States in Grenada. Despite U.S. efforts, the OAS ultimately did not endorse the Panama intervention.

2. The endorsement for the Afghanistan intervention in 2001 was not explicit, though the relevant Security Council resolutions (1368 of September 12 and 1373 of September 28) were widely understood as indirectly approving of a U.S.-led intervention in retaliation for the September, 11, 2001, terrorist attacks. For a discussion, see Byers (2002). In any case, the United States did not depend on UNSC authorization as a legal basis for the war, invoking instead its inherent right of self-defense.

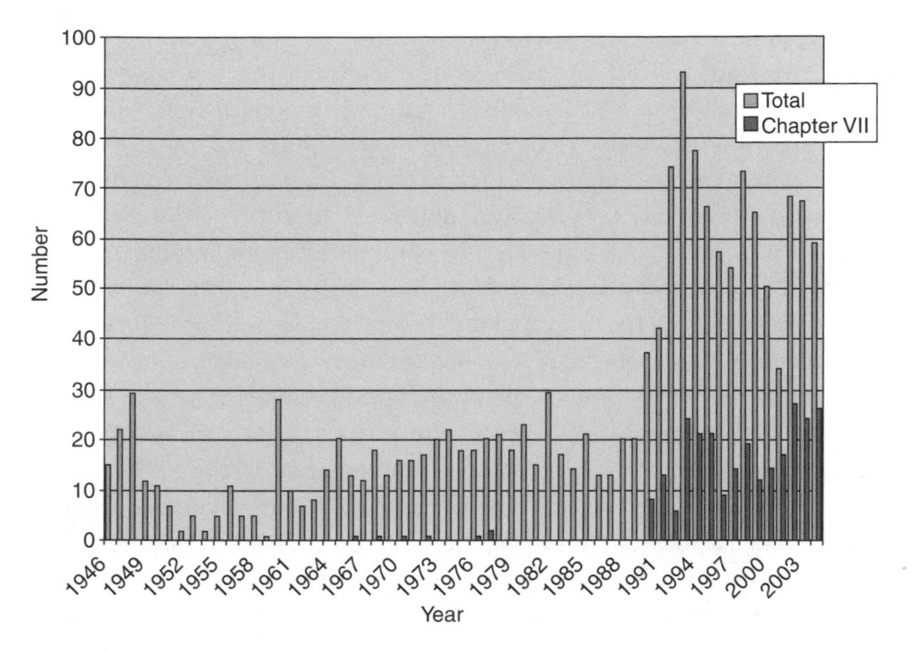

FIGURE 1.1. UN Security Council resolutions, 1946–2004

powers, embodied in Chapter VII of the UN Charter, have been employed with dramatically increased frequency: More than two hundred Chapter VII resolutions were passed between 1990 and 2004, compared with only four during the Cold War, and in recent years an increasing share of resolutions overall invoke Chapter VII.[3] Figure 1.1 displays these trends. Moreover, the Security Council's practice of authorizing coalitions of states to conduct coercive actions—evidenced by the U.S. intervention in Haiti in 1994, the NATO-led forces in Bosnia in the mid-1990s, and the Australian-led International Force for East Timor in 1999—is now well established and increasingly common.[4] As one former diplomat and prominent UN scholar concludes, "the most important development in Council decision-making since 1990 has been its disposition to authorize the use of force" (Malone 1998, 22).

Indeed, military intervention without some effort to gain IO approval is increasingly rare. Nevertheless, states are sometimes willing to proceed without

3. For an overview of these trends, see Wallensteen and Johannson 2004. Data on Chapter VII resolutions are available from the Uppsala Conflict Data Program at http://www.pcr.uu.se/research/UCDP/UCDP_toplevel1.htm. They have been updated by this author. Many invocations of Chapter VII have come in the context of peacekeeping missions that do not qualify as straighforward coercive interventions. However, these peacekeeping and "peacebuilding" operations are increasingly complex and often evolve toward a mixture of consent and coercion, sometimes with extensive authority to use force. See Fenton (2004); Roberts (2004); and Ku and Jacobson (2003, 24).

4. This is a conclusion of the so-called Brahimi Report, commissioned by Secretary-General Kofi Annan to study UN peacekeeping practices. UN Doc. A/55/305–S/2000/809, 21 August 2000.

such approval—Russia's 2008 intervention into Georgia is a recent case in point—and thus a mixture of unilateral and multilateral behavior exists today as in the past. A satisfying explanation of why states rely so much on IOs must also account for this variation.

Despite the obvious importance of these trends, the literature in international relations (IR) lacks a clear explanation of why and how states channel coercion through IOs. In this book I provide a theoretical framework for understanding this behavior and for explaining the singular role played by the Security Council. I also extend the framework's logic to address the additional question of how coercing states choose between unilateralism and multilateralism and how they choose among institutional alternatives—ad hoc multilateralism, regional organizations, or the UN—in the latter case. I offer evidence based primarily on detailed case studies of the United States-led wars against Iraq in 1991 (the Gulf War) and 2003 (the Second Iraq War), and the experience of coercive disarmament during the interwar years. Not only are these cases intrinsically important and policy-relevant, but they also offer variation in the role of IOs, thereby facilitating useful—and partially controlled—comparisons.

My conclusions implicate both theory and practice. By exploring the relationship between statecraft and international organizations, the book contributes to important theoretical debates over the role of institutions in international politics. By examining recent trends in international affairs, and by doing so from the perspective of the world's most influential state, the book also sheds light on policy matters of enormous consequence and relevance. There is little question that U.S. policies will significantly determine the future shape of world politics.

Alongside its contribution to academic and policy debates, this book provides the first theoretically unified account of what can be reasonably described as the "Twenty Years' Crisis" between the United States and Iraq, launched in the summer of 1990 and still ongoing. Adopting that phrase as his book title, E. H. Carr (1946) argued that the Second World War could not be explained independent of the intellectual and political reaction to its predecessor. Similarly, from a historical and social scientific perspective, it is useful to treat the two Iraq wars and the intervening years as a single event; each component is better understood in the context of the period's totality.

IOs and Information Transmission: The Argument

I explain coercion through IOs by exploring the political advantages of channeling action through a formal, standing organization. Building on institutionalist literatures in IR, economics, and the study of American politics, I present a theoretical framework for explaining why and under what conditions states turn to IOs in the conduct of statecraft. I conceptualize IOs as agents of the international community—including both leaders and their publics—that serve to constrain and assess the policies of potential coercing states, thereby generating information that can be used by the international community to distinguish desirable from undesirable actions. Coercers have incentives to accept the scrutiny and limitations that come with working through IOs because doing so mitigates the political downside of exercising power and makes international support more likely.

My argument centers on the dynamics of strategic information transmission. When a coercing state works through an IO, this sends information to foreign leaders and their publics, information that can determine the level of international support—material or political, direct or tacit—offered to the coercing government. Two parallel processes, involving two types of information and two intended audiences, are involved. First, the costs of channeling a policy through an IO allow the coercer to signal benign intentions vis-à-vis third-party states (that is, nontargets), a signal directed primarily at foreign leaders. I refer to this as "intentions information." In the context of coercion, especially by powerful states, these foreign leaders may feel threatened and are able to achieve some assurance and control through IO involvement. This signaling is possible because IOs impose costs on a state exercising power. I conceptualize these costs as falling into four categories: freedom-of-action costs, influence costs, delay, and scrutiny costs.

Second, the endorsement of an IO sends policy-relevant information to foreign publics, who are "rationally ignorant" (Downs 1957) of international affairs and seek information shortcuts to determine the consequences of coercion and whether it is justified. I refer to this as "policy information." This second audience can be as important as the first since leaders are often constrained by domestic politics from supporting another state's use of force. The imprimatur of an IO allows other leaders to appeal to their publics by framing the policy as one that produces broadly favorable consequences that serve collective international interests. While IR scholars have considered the strategic role of domestic publics for coercing states (Mingst 2003; Schultz 2001; Fearon 1994) and have explored more generally the problems facing leaders as they reconcile domestic and international imperatives,[5] the importance of *foreign* publics in shaping state behavior has been largely overlooked. My argument thus presents a new twist on the two-level-games research agenda. In some cases, publics abroad matter even more to

5. The best examples come from the literature on "two-level games" (Putnam 1988). See also Drezner (2003); Milner (1997); and Evans, Jacobson, and Putnam (1993).

leaders than their public at home; the former often pose a significant obstacle to taking coercive actions even in cases where the latter rally in support.

Increased support from the international community is desirable for a coercing state since it determines the political costs of a given policy and may affect its long-term success. Even weak states have means of imposing costs on their more powerful counterparts by actively frustrating opposed policies or through longer-term strategies of noncooperation and "soft balancing."[6] The ongoing struggle in Iraq illustrates all too well the downside of acting without widespread political backing, and it is notable that the United States subsequently adopted a more multilateral approach—centered on the International Atomic Energy Agency and the UNSC—in confronting Iran over its nuclear program.

Not all institutions are equally capable of performing these informational functions, however. The effect of IO involvement is especially important when the organization is more *politically independent,* a function of various institutional characteristics. Most important among these characteristics is the distribution of interests among the institution's membership; this distribution determines the membership's degree of neutrality, that is, the extent to which the membership is representative of the broader international community rather than reflective of the coercing state's interests (Thompson 2006a). In general, the decisions of more heterogeneous and representative institutional agents are more informative to their principals, an insight that has been applied to the informational role of committees in the U.S. Congress (Krehbiel 1991).

In the case of military intervention, a neutral IO is less likely to share the preferences of the coercer in terms of the means, timing, and goals of a policy and is thus more likely to be viewed as credible in the eyes of the international community. Decision-making rules within the IO are also important, as they determine the ability of other IO members to modify or block action by another state. If a higher share of the membership is needed to achieve authorization, and especially if others possess veto power, even the most powerful state may be compelled to forfeit its preferred outcome (Voeten 2001). In sum, political independence renders IOs both more willing and more able to constrain the coercive policy and to withhold approval if necessary, thereby rendering a stamp of approval more meaningful when it is conferred.

Coercing states thus face a trade-off: as they turn to more independent institutions, the constraints and the variance in outcomes increase but so do the political benefits. Going beyond the question of why states sometimes work through IOs, this logic helps explain *how* states channel coercive policies, that is,

6. This is a variant of the concept of "soft power." See Nye (2004). On soft balancing against the United States, see Pape (2005); Paul (2005); and Walt (2005).

how they "forum shop" among institutional alternatives. I argue that the Security Council is the most independent and thus the most informative IO; its approval produces the greatest political benefits, which explains why it is so coveted, but its involvement comes at a potentially high cost. Since they tend to be less neutral and are dominated by their powerful members, regional organizations are less informative but potentially less constraining for the coercer. Finally, ad hoc multilateral coalitions impose few costs on a coercer but render only minimal political benefits. How a coercing state negotiates these trade-offs depends on its sensitivity to international political costs on the one hand and its desire for flexibility on the other. Exploring the implications of institutional variation in this way helps us understand the strategies of modern statecraft and to move beyond the simplistic unilateralism-versus-multilateralism dichotomy that dominates both journalistic and academic discussions.

While my theoretical claims are relevant to the actions of any coercing state, limiting the analysis to powerful states has the advantage of helping to isolate political variables from the straightforward capacity issues that motivate their weaker counterparts. The United States provides an ideal subject in this regard; its overwhelming resources and ability to act alone cast the puzzle of IO-based action in sharpest relief. I confine my discussion to coercive military interventions, thereby excluding standard peacekeeping and purely humanitarian missions conducted with the consent of the parties involved. However, the framework's logic is not limited to military coercion and could be fruitfully applied to various realms of statecraft. When they make decisions about how foreign aid is distributed, how trading relationships are managed, how foreign capital is regulated, and how diplomacy is conducted, governments confront the question of what role IOs should play. To the extent that these policies are coercive, they fall within the theoretical scope of the information argument presented in this book.

Statecraft and IOs

While the institutionalist literature in IR has flourished for the last three decades, it has remained underdeveloped on two fronts. First, for much of this period scholars interested in institutions and cooperation eschewed the study of intergovernmental organizations in favor of broader theoretical constructs such as regimes, governance, and multilateralism,[7] leaving to international law scholars the analysis (often

---

7. Examples include Young (1994); Ruggie (1993); Keohane and Nye (1989) (originally published in 1977); Keohane (1984); and Krasner (1983).

descriptive and normative) of formal IOs.[8] This is beginning to change as scholars recognize that, in the words of Michael Barnett and Martha Finnemore, "International organizations have never been more central to world politics than they are today" (2004, 1). Second, the nexus between institutions and power remained understudied by theorists preoccupied with defending the importance of one or the other.[9] This book addresses both gaps by adding to our knowledge of formal IOs in international politics while explicitly considering their role in power politics.

A handful of recent IR works shed light on why powerful states subject themselves to institutional entanglements in the security sphere. G. John Ikenberry (2001) argues that powerful states can build institutions in order to exhibit "strategic restraint," a form of self-binding that lowers the costs of maintaining world order by reducing fears of domination. Similar logics of hands-tying help explain U.S. promotion of multilateral organizations after World War II and Germany's strategy of assuring its allies through institutional entanglement in NATO and European integration (Wallander 1999; Katzenstein 1997). In the same spirit, David A. Lake (1999) shows that states sometimes go beyond mere cooperation to create "hierarchical" security relationships that protect against opportunism while simultaneously capturing the efficiency benefits of multilateral cooperation. Such works employ the logic of credible commitments and build on a wide-ranging literature in political science on how political actors can benefit from tying their hands through institutions—including central banks, independent judiciaries, legislatures, and IOs—in order to make promises and thus to gain from exchange and cooperation (Martin 2000; North and Weingast 1989; Elster 1979). While powerful actors have the most to lose through such constraining arrangements, they also have the most to gain given their ability to break commitments with impunity in their absence.

Building on principal-agent theory, a new wave of literature seeks to understand why states (as principals) delegate various types of authority to international organizations (as agents). While credible commitment is one possible rationale, there are many others, including the need for specialized expertise, the efficiency gains of centralized information provision, the resolution of collective decision-making dilemmas, the ability to clarify incomplete or ambiguous agreements, and the provision of dispute settlement (Hawkins et al. 2006a; Nielson and

8. For a critique of the literature along these lines, see Verbeek (1998); and Abbott and Snidal (1998).

9. Important exceptions include Drezner (2007); Gruber (2000); and Krasner (1991). To be sure, IR institutionalists have always recognized that power is an important underlying variable influencing state interests and regime formation (Martin 1992b; Keohane 1984, 64). However, as with the rationalist study of institutions in political science more generally, power has rarely played a central analytical role (Moe 2005).

Tierney 2003; Pollack 2003). Under certain conditions, states have incentives to grant authority to even the most formal and legalized institutions (Goldstein et al. 2001; Abbott and Snidal 1998). However, these scholars typically assume that power and delegation do not mix; the most influential states are least likely to favor reliance on independent IOs (Hawkins et al. 2006b, 22; Smith 2000; Kahler 2000, 665–66). It is also interesting to note that work on IO delegation generally concentrates on political economy, the environment, human rights, and other nonsecurity matters. This book extends insights from this literature to issues of power politics, including military coercion.

These largely rationalist treatments of the role of IOs in modern statecraft are complemented by important works in the social constructivist vein. John G. Ruggie (1993) points to a principled commitment among states to act multilaterally as a general characteristic of international politics under American hegemony. Finnemore (2003) provides a more elaborate theory and addresses the issue of military intervention directly. She argues that different historical eras are governed by systemwide norms regulating the use of force; contemporary norms dictate that interventions be conducted multilaterally, preferably through formal organizations such as NATO and the UN. This logic is consistent with a broader view that certain norms structure international society and thus guide state behavior, even in security affairs (Tannenwald 2008; Thomas 2001; Price 1997).

I agree that international politics are meaningfully conditioned by a pro-multilateralism norm and that this norm underpins most IOs, enhancing their political importance. Nevertheless, norm-based arguments cannot explain the wide variation in behavior exhibited by states—sometimes statecraft is channeled through IOs and sometimes it is not—and thus do not shed light on various *strategic* issues that are so central to the study of international politics.

These studies on commitment, delegation, and norms help us understand why powerful political actors have an interest in establishing and enmeshing themselves in institutions at the international level. IOs are usually treated endogenously, that is, as outcomes to be explained. However, the mere existence of institutions and a general desire to use them do not guarantee that they will be involved in any given case. In the anarchy of world politics, states, especially powerful ones, have the option of choosing one institution over others—or of bypassing them altogether. Viewing IOs as already existing and in need of *activation* in the context of particular episodes leads to a different set of questions. Why do states sometimes channel policies through IOs while operating without them at other times? How do states choose among IO alternatives in a given episode? How does institutional involvement affect the reactions of other states? Asking these sorts of questions reorients the institutions literature toward a focus on "statecraft," the strategic exercise of power and influence by states.

The United Nations and the Legitimation of Force

In the more specific context of military intervention, the decision by states to channel their policies through IOs has traditionally been explained in terms of the *legitimacy* conferred on a state's policy by IO approval, which leads to greater international support. Since Inis Claude's influential article on the "collective legitimization" function of the UN, countless scholars and policymakers have pointed to the legitimation function of IOs, especially the UN (e.g., Haass 1994; Luard 1984; Claude 1966). International law scholars have traditionally viewed IOs in a similar way, as capable of conferring legitimacy on the use of force (Caron 1993; Schachter 1984; Chayes 1974). More sophisticated versions of the legitimation logic can be found in social constructivist work in IR. As noted above, constructivists argue that states may choose a multilateral approach because the international community deems it more normatively appropriate than unilateralism and is thus more likely to support the policy (Hurd 2007, 2002; Mitzen 2005; Finnemore 2003; Barnett 1997).

The United Nations and the Security Council in particular are singled out as possessing unique normative power at the global level. Ian Hurd (2007, 76) demonstrates various ways that "states have sought to associate themselves with the Council as a means to legitimize their actions, decisions, and identities." Regarding military intervention, Finnemore (2003, 81) argues that it must conform to "appropriate procedures for intervening such as the necessity of obtaining a Security Council authorization for action." Other IO scholars (Boyer, Sur, and Fleurence 2003, 282) aptly refer to "the unique legitimacy of the Security Council to decide and to direct the use of force." They echo former secretary-general Kofi Annan, who also frequently stressed the UN's "unique legitimacy" and its singular ability to generate international support.

However, while there is a virtual consensus that this legitimation effect matters—even the father of realism, Hans Morgenthau (1985, 34), recognized the benefits of exercising power legitimately—the term is used loosely, and we lack theoretical understanding of how IO legitimation occurs. In most work to date, there is little effort to specify why IO approval is viewed as important by other states and why it changes their perceptions of and reactions to another state's policy.[10] Claude (1966, 374), for example, provides no explanation for *why* the UN has such a powerful effect, offering only that UN approval is important because statesmen attach importance to it. Barnett (1997, 540) echoes Claude's logic when he argues that the UN "has this legitimacy and [moral] authority by virtue of the fact that member states invest legitimacy in it." In the best effort to

10. For a more extensive critique of the legitimation literature, see Voeten (2005).

supply theoretical underpinnings, Hurd (2007) points to the political benefits of successfully invoking the Security Council's "symbolic" power, a function of its subjective legitimacy and authoritative position, and traces the sources and effects of this legitimacy across the UN's history.

While the constructivist literature helps explain the appeal of IO approval, it confronts the puzzle of how substantial perceived legitimacy arises given the lack of democracy, transparency, and accountability of most IOs, including the UN (Keohane 2006; Dahl 1999). The legitimation literature also does not adequately account for why resort to IOs is so uneven across states and across episodes. Legitimation arguments tend to focus on the benefits of working through IOs while ignoring the costs and are thus not well suited to capturing the strategic dynamics of state behavior when it comes to statecraft and IOs. Moreover, alternative causal mechanisms that would produce an observationally equivalent outcome—IO approval leading to greater international support—are overlooked in most work on legitimation.

While not denying the role of norms and legitimation, IR scholars approaching these questions from a rational choice perspective have recently joined the intellectual discussion by suggesting some alternative mechanisms. Borrowing from the comparative politics literature on "elite pacts," Eric Voeten (2005) argues that Security Council pronouncements function as focal points that help the international community solve a coordination dilemma when it comes to constraining the behavior of the U.S. superpower. Adopting a principal-agent perspective, Terrence Chapman and Dan Reiter (2004) argue that UNSC approval helps the U.S. public (as principal) monitor the president (as agent) when it comes to the proposed use of force, leading to larger opinion "rallies" in the case of approval. The theoretical reach of these arguments is limited, however, with an exclusive focus on the Security Council in the first case and an exclusive focus on domestic effects in the latter. Moreover, as in the constructivist literature, the *trade-offs* involved in channeling policies through the UN and other IOs are not sufficiently explored, thereby limiting the usefulness of extant accounts for understanding the phenomenon from the perspective of political strategy and statecraft.

In this book I outline a set of causal mechanisms, based largely on rationalist assumptions, for explaining why IO involvement leads to increased international support and thus why states have incentives to channel coercion through them. By identifying the costs involved, I also theorize the conditions under which states turn to IOs rather than operate alone or with an ad hoc coalition. Finally, I offer a theoretical account for why some IOs matter more than others and why Security Council approval, in particular, is so influential. One goal is thus to unravel the well-documented but still mysterious legitimation effect of the UN.

By suggesting why the Security Council has emerged as uniquely important when it comes to the use of force, I also improve our understanding of that body's role in international relations. Just as the end of the Cold War unleashed the Council by removing the obstacle of bipolarity, so has it unleashed a flood of books on the UNSC (Cronin and Hurd 2008; Hurd 2007; Malone 2006, 2004, 1998; Matheson 2006; Fenton 2004; Glennon 2001; Sarooshi 1999; Russett 1997). In the wake of the 2003 Iraq war, debates about the Council's effectiveness and role have raged among academics and policymakers. Much of this work amounts to case studies of particular episodes, legal analyses of the Council's proper place in world affairs, and arguments for or against the usefulness of the Council. What this literature lacks is a positive theoretical framework for explaining the Security Council's role across cases. My information transmission theory begins to fill this gap.

Case Selection and Outline

To explore the politics of military coercion through IOs, I focus on the role of the Security Council during the period of crisis between the United States and Iraq. This includes four empirical chapters, one on the Gulf War, one on the disarmament efforts of the interwar years, and two on the Second Iraq War. Though these episodes are clearly interrelated, each is also treated as a case study in its own right, and each makes a distinct contribution to the project as a whole. Taken together, these chapters offer the virtues of in-depth case studies and the advantages of comparative analysis. I have consulted a wide variety of sources for evidence. In addition to secondary literature produced by academics and other researchers, I rely on contemporaneous press accounts of events and a wide range of primary sources, including dozens of personal interviews with current and former officials of various governments and the UN, as well as government and IO documents.

There are several justifications for the case selection. First, from the standpoint of research design, the cases offer variation in the role of an IO while holding constant many other factors, such as the central actors involved, the military balance, and the post–Cold War setting. This variation is especially interesting because it does not correlate with obvious changes at the domestic level, such as the president or political party in power—two Republican presidents pursued both the most multilateral (George H. W. Bush) and the most unilateral (George W. Bush) strategies, and a Democratic president (Bill Clinton) pursued a combination of these. Second, exploring cases where the United States is the coercive protagonist affords the greatest opportunity to isolate political variables. The most obvious material explanations for multilateralism, such as burden sharing and resource aggregation, are least likely to motivate the world's only "hyperpower." Third, the Iraq wars and the disarmament period clearly fall within the scope of my theoretical argument, as they involve coercive actions with no consent from the targeted state. While my information logic likely can be extended to cases of mixed coercion and consent and to other issue areas, it should first be explored in the context of the most straightforwardly appropriate case of military intervention.

Perhaps more important, these cases are also appealing from the standpoint of policy debates and current history. For students of IR and foreign policy, the Iraq wars stand as intrinsically important cases. The application of novel theory often casts historically important events in a new light. Moreover, the foreseeable future of international politics—and specifically the nature of intervention—will be shaped by decisions made by the United States, and thus understanding U.S. behavior is of heightened importance for students of international affairs. The current standoffs with Iran and North Korea, to which I return in the concluding chapter, are illustrative: while largely driven by U.S. decisions, their outcome will affect the entire international community. Finally, no IO is more important in international security affairs than the Security Council, which is at once the most controversial and the most authoritative multilateral institution when it comes to the use of force. While its unique role has been noted and described by countless observers, the origins and implications of this prominence deserve far more scholarly attention.

The next chapter outlines the theoretical argument, including hypotheses and observable implications, and defines key concepts. Chapter 3 is an in-depth case study of the Gulf War episode (1990–91), where coercive measures were conducted with explicit UNSC authorization. It investigates why U.S. policymakers chose to work through the Security Council, how this decision served to transmit politically important information to the rest of the world, and what impact this had on reactions from the international community, including both leaders and publics. The goal is to test several observable implications of the information transmission argument by uncovering causal processes and by considering how the international community might have reacted in the absence of UN involvement. The chapter also includes considerations of alternative explanations—both materialist and ideational—for these outcomes.

Chapter 4 covers the disarmament regime of the interwar years, including the role of the UN Special Commission (UNSCOM) and efforts to coerce Iraq into compliance through economic sanctions and the threat—and occasional implementation—of force. This period culminated in 1998 with Operation Desert Fox, a substantial bombing campaign conducted by the United States and

Britain, which received lukewarm international reactions and effectively brought interwar disarmament to an end. The chapter serves three purposes in relation to the project as a whole. First, because it contains several episodes of coercion with varying degrees of Security Council support, it provides multiple observations relevant to the main theoretical arguments on the relationship between IO approval and international political costs. Second, the chapter traces the evolution of U.S. policy and of positions on the Security Council, especially among the Permanent Five (P5), from the end of the Gulf War to the first stages of the Second Iraq War. As interests on the Council diverged, the price of working through the UN increased concomitantly, thereby changing the United States' calculus and steering policy in a unilateral direction. Third, the chapter supplies an empirical bridge between the two wars without which their relationship is not easily understood. This is important since one goal of the book is to provide a coherent account of U.S. behavior and the UNSC's role in Iraq during this period.

Chapters 5 and 6 analyze the statecraft surrounding the Second Iraq War, launched in 2003 without explicit authorization from the Security Council. Chapter 5 begins with the attacks of September 11, 2001, and outlines Washington's ensuing decision to reinvigorate the confrontation with Iraq. The main goal of Chapter 5 is to explain, in light of the book's theoretical arguments, why a series of diplomatic initiatives and coercive tactics were pursued largely through the UN for much of 2002. Chapter 6 focuses on why the United States eventually chose to deviate from the UN path to launch the invasion of Iraq with a modest coalition of the willing. I show how the constraints imposed by the UN process caused the George W. Bush administration to veer toward unilateralism and demonstrate the substantial international political costs that resulted from acting without IO approval.

To facilitate comparison, the presentation of the Second Iraq War case (in chapters 5 and 6) parallels that of the Gulf War case (chapter 3) in many ways. There are two important differences, however. First, because the United States initially chose to pursue a UN-based strategy and later abandoned it, the later case speaks to a wider range of theoretical predictions than the earlier one, in which the UN was involved throughout. I must explain why policymakers chose the IO path *and* why they chose to abandon it—hence the division into two chapters. Second, substantial data on international public opinion are available for the 2003 war, which allows for a more extensive analysis of the reactions of foreign publics and the transmission of policy information than is possible for the Gulf War case. These data show that a Security Council endorsement would have substantially boosted favorability toward the war in many politically important countries. They also show that publics—before and after the war—did not view as credible U.S. justifications for the war based on the threats of weapons of mass destruction and terrorism.

A concluding chapter addresses various implications of the argument and findings. First, I reflect on the choice between unilateralism and multilateralism in U.S. foreign policy, arguably the most important issue facing American foreign policymakers today. I suggest that what I label "knee-jerk unilateralism" and "doe-eyed multilateralism" are equally ill advised; policymakers must choose among options based on a realistic assessment of the relevant political trade-offs (many of which are identified in this book). Viewed in this light, the unilateralism-multilateralism debate makes less sense in the abstract but can have important implications in concrete policy situations. Second, chapter 7 extends the argument beyond the United States to consider the role of the Security Council and security IOs more generally from the perspective of middle powers. Such states are doubly advantaged by multilateral institutions: not only do they rely on them to endorse peacekeeping, humanitarian, and other interventions, but they also use them to constrain the United States and to ensure that non-superpowers retain some control over international security affairs. In these respects, IOs offer middle powers the chance to wield more influence than they otherwise would.

Finally, I suggest that we reorient our thinking about the Security Council and, in turn, the possibilities for its reform. After being universally lauded for its role in the Gulf War, the Council was widely condemned in 2003—by the Left and some legal scholars for failing to stop the United States, and by the Right and Bush administration supporters for failing to take on Saddam Hussein aggressively. My theoretical framework sees IOs as serving the different—and distinctly *political*—function of providing information during episodes of coercion. In this respect, the Security Council performed equally well in both wars: it provided valuable information to the international community on U.S. intentions and on the consequences of prospective policies. Governments responded accordingly. We could greatly improve our understanding of the role of the Security Council in international affairs by explicitly treating it as a political institution as well as a legal one.

2

COERCION, INSTITUTIONS, AND INFORMATION

Coercion lies at the heart of statecraft. To study statecraft, according to David Baldwin (1985, 9), is to study how policymakers "get others to do what they would otherwise not do." In short, statecraft is the exercise of power. While the term "coercion" has been employed in various ways, I define it as efforts to convince a target to take a certain course of action—to initiate a new action or to halt an existing one—by imposing or threatening to impose costs. Conceived this way, coercion parallels Thomas Schelling's (1966) conception of "compellence."[1]

This book addresses what Schelling (1966, 3) refers to as diplomacy "based on the power to hurt." This power to hurt derives mainly from economic and military tools of statecraft but also from purely diplomatic tools,[2] and in most substantive applications it makes little sense to distinguish among the traditional categories of diplomatic coercion, economic coercion, and military coercion. In practice they are often combined; in theory they display similar dynamics. The theoretical argument of this book focuses primarily on military coercion, since

1. While some scholars (e.g., Byman and Waxman 2002; Schelling 1966) prefer to treat "deterrence"—convincing a target not to take an action it otherwise would—as a form of coercion, others distinguish between coercion and deterrence (Schultz 2001; Pape 1996; George and Simons 1994). We should not make too much of the distinction since most deterrent strategies can be understood in compellent terms, and vice versa. For a discussion of these conceptual issues, see Baldwin (1979, 188–92).

2. Diplomacy alone has the power to hurt if valuable cooperation is withdrawn from a target state or if rhetorical strategies succeed in isolating it.

the threat and limited use of military force are constant and overriding features of the cases at hand, though economic and diplomatic coercion play a role and are addressed as well.

Schelling is careful to distinguish between coercion, where at least some force is held in reserve, and "brute force," which involves the infliction of "pure damage." No bargaining takes place when brute force is applied, whereas coercion is fundamentally about bargaining. One might wonder, then, whether this study of the United States-Iraq saga is really about coercion since the use of military force is involved, including two wars. However, while we often associate coercion with mere threats of force and tools short of force (diplomatic and economic), the application of force is indeed part of a coercive strategy insofar as the target still has opportunities to back down or grant concessions. As Robert Pape (1996, 12) notes, "the universe of coercion includes nearly all attempts by states to force others to accept a change in the status quo, including virtually all wars." The only exceptions, according to Pape, are faits accomplis and wars of extermination. Addressing the distinction between coercion and brute force, Byman and Waxman (2002, 3–6) argue that coercion is involved so long as force is limited and the target has options.

By these definitions, most policies conducted by the United States against Iraq between 1990 and 2003 can be rightly described as coercive. Once the Gulf War was launched in January of 1991, there were obviously elements of a brute force strategy, although the approach was still coercive insofar as Iraq's political and military response influenced U.S. strategy. In other words, even during conflict there is often implicit and explicit bargaining.[3] Once the Second Iraq War was launched in 2003, it is fair to say that coercion was replaced by brute force. Since my arguments apply to the coercive elements of U.S. policy, I focus much less empirical attention on the conduct of the wars themselves than on the political activity leading up to them.

I am interested in political strategy, not military strategy. If military strategy is the matter of how armed forces are used to achieve war-fighting objectives (see Paret 1986, 3), political strategy is the matter of how a state's diplomatic tools are employed to achieve policy objectives. A key question in this regard is whether the state chooses to act unilaterally or multilaterally and, if the latter option is chosen, whether actions are conducted with an ad hoc coalition or through a standing IO. In cases where more than one relevant IO is available, the choice among them is an important element of political strategy as well. The well-worn

3. Indeed, on February 22, 1991, after five weeks of bombing, President Bush gave Iraq an offer to begin withdrawing by noon the next day or else face a ground war. Saddam Hussein rejected the offer, and the ground invasion was launched two days later.

question of unilateralism versus multilateralism is indeed crucial—and decidedly more complicated than the traditional dichotomy suggests.

In the study of statecraft, the matter of *how states channel their power* represents the most important political question—and arguably the one of most interest for theory and policy. This chapter outlines a theoretical framework for understanding these choices and presents specific hypotheses and observable implications suitable for empirical assessment.

The next section introduces the role of nontarget states in coercive episodes and outlines the potential international political costs of military coercion. Two subsequent sections introduce the role of institutions as providers of information and explain why formal IOs, because of their independence, are uniquely capable of providing credible information. I then turn to two specific pathways of information transmission to the international community: signaling intentions to state leaders and sending policy information to domestic publics. The final section considers issues of institutional variation and the forum-shopping decisions of coercers, with a focus on the unique role of the UN Security Council.

The Politics and Costs of Coercion

The extant literature on coercion focuses mostly on the relationship between "sender" (the state initiating action) and "target" (the state at which the action is aimed) in an effort to explain the dependent variables of success or effectiveness. Third parties and institutions are discussed only insofar as multilateral cooperation is seen as an important ingredient of success.[4] Many of the most important political aspects of coercion are ignored, especially when it comes to the sender side of the equation. I address this void by looking at a different variable: the international political costs of coercion. These costs are partly a function of the coercion process itself, especially the role granted to IOs, and their specter may influence the sender's behavior—its decisions regarding whether and how to take action—in important ways.

Whether and how a state pursues a particular coercive strategy depends on its expectations of costs and benefits. The most obvious potential costs are material, whether in the form of damage to the economy—as in the opportunity costs of a trade war—or the expense of launching a military campaign. Just as important, though, are various political considerations, many of which extend beyond

4. For example, Mearsheimer (1983, 14) explicitly omits consideration of such political factors. The literature on economic sanctions is also illustrative. See Miers and Morgan 2002; Drezner 2000; and Martin 1992a.

relations with the state being targeted by coercion. In particular, coercing states face the problem of minimizing the international political costs that might be imposed by third-party states, that is, states that are not themselves the target of coercion. Since coercion is associated with domination and expanded influence, especially when conducted by the powerful, a coercer potentially threatens nontarget states.

Whenever a state attempts to influence another against its will, it risks incurring both short- and long-term costs imposed by other states. In the short term, "active" sanctions can be applied.[5] The coercer may suffer from direct retaliation and countercoalitions by third parties attempting to balance the perceived threat (Walt 1987). A similar effect may be achieved through negative issue linkage: the coercer finds its relations with other states suffering in other issue areas as a political statement or as indirect retaliation by third parties. As Pape (2005, 17) suggests, challenges to powerful states need not be direct; others "can delay, complicate, or increase the costs of using the extraordinary power." Manipulation of trading terms and other forms of economic statecraft, intentional noncompliance in shared regimes, and the recall of ambassadors are examples of active but indirect strategies. Finally, other states can respond by imposing social punishments through shaming or loss of prestige (Johnston 2001).

In the long term, the coercer risks damage to its reputation and to its soft power (Nye 2004) if it is perceived as using force arbitrarily or excessively. This leads to more passive sanctions over time. If diplomatic relations with third parties are undermined for reputational reasons, the coercer may find cooperation and the achievement of other foreign policy goals more difficult in the future.[6] Robert Keohane and Joseph Nye (1989, 236) argue, for example, that excessive unilateralism on the part of the United States can "disrupt cooperative international relationships and cast doubt on American motivations." Reputation costs are highest when states act in defiance of formal legal commitments and IOs (Abbott and Snidal 2000; Simmons 2000). Ward Thomas (2001, 36) points to the loss of "moral status" that can result from engaging in inappropriate or selfish behavior, which can diminish a state's influence with nonstate actors and within intergovernmental organizations. Expectations of these political costs play an important role in determining whether and how a state will coerce.

The historical record shows that even powerful states can suffer politically from coercion—especially when they choose to ignore relevant institutions and

5. The terms "active" and "passive" sanctions are borrowed from Thomas (2001, 35–36).

6. It should be noted that reputation matters in terms of linkages across issues and with different actors, not just across time with the same actor (i.e., the case of repeated play). See Yarbrough and Yarbrough (1997, 136–37).

rules. The French and especially the British paid substantial costs for the 1956 Suez intervention, which was conducted without UN approval and on dubious legal grounds (Thomas 1967, 39). According to one account of the aftermath,

> Britain suffered her greatest humiliation since the war in the Far East. A run on the pound occurred, which the USA proposed to allow to continue until the interventionists (including France and Israel) agreed to withdraw. Throughout the Middle East, Britain's influence and authority were undermined, not least in Iraq, where the pro-British government was overthrown. The United States, in a providentially opportunist and systematic move, filled the vacuum created by the demise of Anglo-French fortunes in the Middle East. Concurrently, in Europe, the Soviet Union had the benefit of the diversion of the Suez affair when putting down the Hungarian uprising. (Connaughton 1992, 32)[7]

Even superpowers suffer politically as a result of unilateral coercion. The Soviet Union discovered this with its 1979 intervention in Afghanistan, which halted détente with the West and complicated relations with China, leaving Mikhail Gorbachev scrambling for an exit strategy when he took power in 1985. For the United States, according to one National Security Council (NSC) official, the August 1998 bombing of an al Qaeda camp in Afghanistan and an alleged chemical weapons plant in Khartoum "aggravated bilateral relationships all over the place" and made them "more difficult to manage."[8] U.S. employment of "Super 301" measures to unilaterally coerce its trading partners also engendered substantial political backlash, making it easier for foreign governments to rebuff American demands during the Uruguay Round of trade negotiations and in various regional talks (Bayard and Elliott 1994, 320–21). The situation following the 2003 Iraq war illustrates the potential for costly linkages, as the United States had considerable difficulty garnering cooperation for postwar peacekeeping and reconstruction.

Such reactions are most likely to arise when policies are conducted unilaterally. In a variety of issue areas, working through IOs can inoculate a coercer against many of these international political costs by sending information about intentions and policies to leaders and publics.

In an effort to isolate the strategic dynamics of coercion, I address cases involving powerful coercers, where the motivations for invoking institutions are

---

7. On the "predatory currency manipulation" inflicted on Britain by the United States, see Kirschner (1995, 81–83).

8. Author's interview with a senior staff member of the National Security Council, Washington, D.C., May 17, 1999.

mostly political and have less to do with the material ability of the coercer to succeed. Weak states contemplating coercion are perforce primarily concerned with immediate material costs and issues of capacity, since these may prevent the coercion from succeeding. Powerful states are relatively more concerned with *political* costs and may work through IOs in an attempt to mitigate them. In other words, in a world without politics powerful states would almost always operate alone, avoiding the complications of multilateralism and institutions.

Like most models of coercion, my model focuses on one primary sender.[9] However, in contrast with most studies of coercion, which concentrate on the relationship between the sender and the target, in my study the most relevant actors are the sender and third-party states. The political costs of coercion in a given case are defined by the reactions of third parties.

Institutions and Information

The relationship between power and institutions at the international level has not been sufficiently explored by IR theorists busy arguing that either one or the other is more important. As noted in chapter 1, a relatively new literature explains why powerful states have incentives to create and bind themselves in institutions in order to capture the benefits of credible commitments (Hawkins et al. 2006b; Ikenberry 2001; Abbott and Snidal 2000; Lake 1999). My puzzle is distinct: I ask why states work through institutions while exercising power *in particular foreign policy episodes,* not why they create or maintain institutions over time. Institutions are exogenous in my analysis. In this respect, my question is closer to Lisa Martin's (1992a) investigation of how institutions benefit a state pursuing an economic sanctions policy.

In contrast to these studies, I find the information transmission role of institutions to be more important than their ability to solve the time-inconsistency problems associated with commitment, which are less relevant in the context of a single coercive episode. While costly constraints imposed by institutions are important in my account, they serve primarily to transmit information rather than to solve commitment problems.[10]

9. Even when a large coalition is forged, most coercive episodes are characterized by one dominant, entrepreneurial sender who persuades other states to join the effort. See Martin (1992a). When the UNSC authorizes collective enforcement, the resulting action is typically conducted unilaterally or by a coalition led by a powerful member (Koskenniemi 1996, 461).

10. While IOs increase the costs of backing out of commitments to a particular course of action, they typically cannot solve this problem when it comes to powerful states. The U.S. decision to abandon the UN prior to the 2003 war against Iraq is a good example.

IR scholars have had a rather limited view of strategic information transmission, relying almost exclusively on signaling games where a state's "type"—private information regarding preferences and thus intentions—is the source of uncertainty (e.g., Sartori 2005; Kydd 2000; Fearon 1997). I also focus on how states can reveal information about their type. However, my argument places equal weight on a different kind of information that can be strategically transmitted: information regarding policy consequences, or the relationship between policy choices and their effects. IOs specialize in providing these two types of information, referred to hereafter as intentions information and policy information, and thus states have incentives to rely on them when this information is important.

At the domestic level, where institutional theories are most developed, political actors delegate to institutions for a variety of reasons. They may do so to solve collective decision-making problems, to forge credible commitments, to reduce their workload, or to generate information (Martin 2000; Epstein and O'Halloran 1999; Kiewiet and McCubbins 1991; North and Weingast 1989). Information-based theories of delegation to domestic institutions fall into two main categories based on the type of information that is hidden: those that focus on reducing uncertainty surrounding the principal's preferences and those that focus on the production of policy-relevant information by specialized agents. Typical of the former category, delegation to independent central banks is sometimes understood as a costly sign of a government's devotion to sound monetary policy, which can serve as evidence of creditworthiness to investors (Keefer and Stasavage 2002; Hall and Franzese 1998; Maxfield 1997).[11] Government reliance on central banks and independent judiciaries may also signal to third parties a preference for stability or reform. Generally speaking, the more costly it is for an actor to delegate to such institutions—that is, the more control the actor relinquishes—the more effective they are as signaling devices.

Political actors also delegate to institutions in order to extract policy information. This is generally causal information on the relationship between policy alternatives and the outcomes—their probability and desirability—they can be expected to produce. Policy information is valuable any time a political actor affected by a policy is uncertain about its consequences. For example, because they are politically neutral and have superior expertise, central banks can provide credible information to legislators and political parties regarding the government's

11. Note that these information arguments are distinct from the classic time-inconsistency rationale for central bank independence, where the goal is to tie the government's hands so that it cannot manipulate policy for short-term gain in the future. See Rogoff (1985) and Kydland and Prescott (1977).

policy choices and their economic consequences (Bernhard 1998). Bureaucrats also possess "knowledge and expertise that politicians lack" (Huber and Shipan 2002, 2), and this creates incentives for legislators and executive branch officials to rely on them, especially when uncertainty or technical complexity is high. Institutional agents are most informative when they are autonomous; thus the price of increased policy information is some loss of control over outcomes (Carpenter 2001; Bawn 1995). The search for reliable policy information is constant and ubiquitous.[12]

The question remains, however, of how relevant these domestic delegation arguments are to the issue of state delegation to *international* institutions.[13] In particular, the nature and context of institutional agents are quite different in the two settings: international institutions are on average far less autonomous, less bureaucratic, and less powerful than their domestic counterparts, which typically have more resources and often have statutory or even constitutional foundations. With important exceptions,[14] most international institutions are dominated by their member states, resulting in principal-agent relationships that are often different in kind and degree from those found in domestic polities.

I argue that the phenomenon of delegation to congressional committees, composed of a subset of the legislature, more closely matches circumstances at the international level than does delegation to large, autonomous bureaucracies, which have fewer analogues in international politics. Like these committees, IOs are composed of a subset of states in the international system. IR scholars have tended to overlook this rich body of theory. Driven mainly by the works of Thomas Gilligan and Keith Krehbiel (1990, 1989), informational theories of legislative organization propose that committees serve as sources of policy-relevant information for the legislature as a whole (Krehbiel 1991; see also Krishna and Morgan 2001). The most important design feature of committees is their composition in terms of member preferences, which largely determines how informative the signals sent by them are. Specifically, a committee that is heterogeneous—that is, whose membership is diverse and "bookends" the median preference of the chamber on a given policy dimension—sends

---

12. Information on policy consequences is perhaps most valuable to voters, who must assess candidates' proposals to determine which ones are most likely to produce the benefits they desire.

13. For a general discussion of the problems associated with "scaling up" domestic-level theories of institutions to explain international behavior, see Thompson (2002).

14. Some IOs have autonomous bureaucracies with authority to set agendas and challenge state control in certain circumstances, including the European Union, the dispute settlement aspects of the World Trade Organization (WTO), and the World Bank and IMF, but these are exceptional. For treatments of IO bureaucracies as a source of autonomy, see Barnett and Finnemore (2004) and Reinalda and Verbeek (1998).

more information than a homogeneous committee; and a committee composed of "preference outliers"—that is, whose membership has extreme preferences relative to the chamber median—is less informative than one with a more moderate composition. While all committees have an information advantage insofar as they specialize in a given substantive area, only some—those that are diverse and representative—are able to transmit information that is seen as credible and therefore informative to the legislature as a whole.

These principles of information transmission by institutional agents can be usefully applied to the realm of international institutions. I highlight the distinct role played by formal IOs, as uniquely informative among international institutions, and also explore the implications of variation among institutions in terms of composition and other design variables.

Coercion through IOs

Formal organizations play a distinct political role in international affairs because of their independence, which derives from their ability to act with a degree of autonomy and neutrality that is unique among institutional forms at the international level (Abbott and Snidal 1998).[15] This autonomy and neutrality result from formal institutional features, such as those associated with centralization and decision making, as well as from the representative nature of their membership. It is the independence of IOs, I argue, that allows them to serve as informative agents of the international community. Because they have standing memberships with diverse interests and cannot be controlled by individual states, they have two advantages as information generators: first, they are willing and able to impose constraints on a coercer, allowing them to screen out those with aggressive intentions, and second, they act as representatives of the international community, allowing them to generate information on policy consequences that is regarded as disinterested and thus credible.[16] Information on intentions and policies is important to third-party leaders and their publics as they consider how to respond to coercive action.

This concern with information transmission and the role of both IOs and third parties offers a complex and more true-to-life view of the politics of coercion. Figure 2.1 illustrates the basic framework of the book, including the relevant

15. For an effort to conceptualize and measure IO independence and to explain its variation, see Haftel and Thompson (2006).

16. Of course, IOs vary on these dimensions and thus in their ability to serve as informative agents, an issue addressed below. See also Chapman (2007).

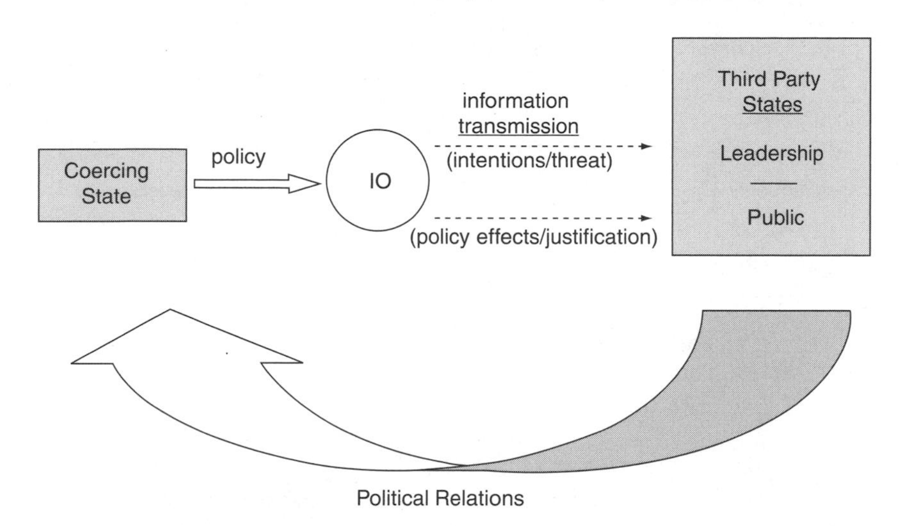

FIGURE 2.1. Coercion, IOs, and information transmission

actors and information transmission pathways. The choice to work through an IO transmits politically important information to leaders and publics in third-party states, thereby producing a more favorable political reaction to the coercive policy. Thus the primary independent variable is IO approval, and the primary dependent variable is international political costs—the degree of support or opposition to the policy. These dynamics are captured in hypotheses 1 to 3, presented below. Consistent with my rationalist assumptions, however, I assume that the anticipated effects of working through an IO drive the choice to do so and the choice among institutional alternatives. Political strategy is thus endogenized as well and treated as a secondary dependent variable, reflected most directly in hypotheses 4 to 6.

Military interventions are always accompanied by some justification for taking action that goes beyond the narrow interests of the intervener. When such claims are made unilaterally by a coercing state, they clearly lack neutrality in the eyes of the international community, and the actions taken are more likely to be viewed as aggressive or threatening. When endorsed by an independent IO, however, the justifications and goals for intervention are rendered believable and defensible.

We should not expect simple multilateralism through coalitions, as a sort of intermediate strategy between unilateralism and IO-based statecraft, to function as a substitute for formal IO approval. Ad hoc coalitions are by definition composed of like-minded states, as the popular phrase "coalition of the willing" reflects. In the language of the legislative signaling literature, they are homogeneous and possibly composed of preference outliers. Because the ideal point

x_i = ideal point of median member of international community
x_m = ideal point of median member of multilateral coalition
x_c = ideal point of coercing state

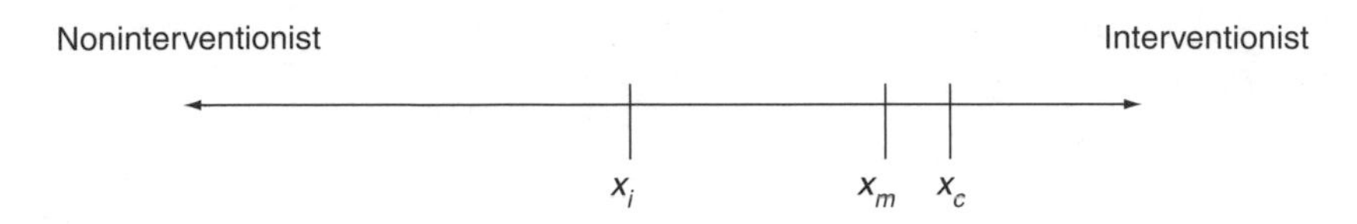

FIGURE 2.2. Preferences with a multilateral coalition

of the median member of such a coalition is close to the ideal point of the coercer on the question of intervention, the coalition is not likely to impose substantial constraints, and approval from the coalition is not informative to the median third-party state (i.e., the median member of the international community). Figure 2.2 maps these preferences. Among the most robust findings in formal theories of strategic information transmission is that actors with more similar preferences can send more informative signals to one another (Krehbiel 1991; Crawford and Sobel 1982). It follows that, by itself, multilateral support of a coercer conveys little information to third parties. Moreover, because formal decision procedures are lacking, members of an ad hoc coalition cannot block or force change in a policy; if they disagree, they simply drop out of the coalition or avoid joining in the first place. These properties explain why most observers "suspect such coalitions of serving parochial national or regional interests rather than common objectives involving international peace and security" (Smith 2003, 97). The involvement of an IO thus offers unique political benefits beyond those conferred by multilateralism alone.

I explain coercion through IOs as a calculated choice by the coercer to generate international support or, at least, to minimize political opposition to its policy. This can be stated in the form of a general hypothesis that captures the coercer's motivation:

> Hypothesis 1 (Coercer's Motivation): *When powerful coercers work through IOs, they do so strategically to lower the international political costs of coercion.*

This proposition goes against the logic that states act through IOs because of an internalized desire to behave in a legitimate or appropriate way, such that they have redefined their interests in terms of a multilateralist norm.[17] By focusing

17. This possibility is discussed in Hurd (2007) and Ruggie (1993).

on political costs and benefits, the hypothesis also rules out material needs and logistical support—that is, burden sharing of various sorts—as the primary motivation. Finally, the argument implies that this behavior cannot be explained solely in terms of domestic politics within the coercing state. (To be clear, various motivations might operate simultaneously in the real world, but they can nevertheless be distinguished analytically.)

The following sections go beyond this general proposition to outline specific causal mechanisms by which information transmission occurs.

Two Pathways of Information Transmission

I have so far discussed the informative properties of IOs in general terms. In this section I address the two specific pathways by which information is transmitted to the international community when states channel coercion through formal organizations. I distinguish between leaders and publics as audiences for this information transmission and argue that leaders are most concerned with receiving information on the coercer's intentions, whereas publics primarily seek information on policy consequences.

I do not mean to imply a strict separation between these two pathways: leaders also seek policy information and publics may be concerned with intentions. However, I assume that leaders are more focused than their publics on the intentions of other states since they are more attuned to the exigencies of international politics and are professionally responsible for anticipating threats to the national interest. With respect to policy information, there is no a priori reason to believe that leaders of third-party states are less well-informed about policy issues than their counterparts in the relevant IO, and thus there is little advantage to be gained by relying on the IO for such information. Publics, however, lack information on policy alternatives and consequences and seek neutral sources to provide it.

Signaling Intentions to Leaders

I assume that state leaders, by comparison with their publics, are relatively well informed about policy alternatives and consequences. They do, however, lack information regarding the intentions of the coercing state's leadership. Coercion involves influence and even domination when pursued by the powerful. While this is clearly the case with respect to the target of coercion, other states may have reason for concern as well. The precise intentions of the coercer determine how threatening its actions will be and how they affect the interests of relevant third-party states.[18] Among coercers, we can usefully distinguish between threatening types, who seek more ambitious and aggressive goals that endanger third parties, and unthreatening types, who seek more defensive and limited aims that pose no risk beyond the target.

As Robert Jervis (1976, 68–70) so forcefully argued, intentions are always difficult to ascertain and convey in international politics; leaders constantly seek objective indicators. Since they usually have the ability to impose forcible solutions, it is especially difficult for powerful states to reassure others that their intentions are limited and unthreatening. The decision to work through an independent IO serves as a meaningful signal of intentions because it imposes costs on a coercer that a more aggressive state (one with goals that threaten third-party states) would be unwilling to pay. In general terms, IOs supply two well-known technologies for self-imposing costs: tying one's hands and ceding power to others (Morrow 1999, 92–93; Fearon 1997).[19] The IR literature has long recognized that institutions impose costly constraints on states and serve to "circumscribe national behavior" (Stein 1982, 299), but conceptualization and identification of these precise costs in practice are not well developed. At least four overlapping costs may be imposed when statecraft is channeled through an IO: freedom-of-action costs, organization costs, costs of delay, and scrutiny costs.

First, a state's freedom of action is almost always limited with IO involvement. The organization defines the limits of acceptable measures, and a coercer accepts these limits when it chooses to work through that organization. History shows that IOs impose real constraints that restrict the set of policy options available to even the strongest states. Even NATO, an IO comprised of relatively like-minded states, imposed profound constraints on its superpower leader's decision making during the Cold War (Gaddis 1997; Risse-Kappen 1995) and during the Bosnia crisis (Papayoanou 1997).[20] Some, perhaps most, policy restrictions occur before the process of seeking IO approval. Once a state chooses to act through an IO, especially a neutral one with distinct and diverse preferences, it must bring to the table a limited and defensible set of goals, accompanied by well-reasoned arguments, in order to gain support. Thus the most ambitious and aggressive policies are ruled out ex ante. Even in ways that are sometimes difficult to detect,

18. The substance of these threats and interests, as well as the set of politically relevant third-party states, varies and must be specified on a case-by-case basis.

19. Morrow is making this point in the context of commitment rather than signaling strategies. Though these are distinct strategic problems, in many cases the same techniques used to credibly commit can also be used to send a costly signal.

20. Gaddis (1997, 201–2) argues that American leaders allowed NATO's concerns to influence their policies even outside Europe and cites several examples.

then, a powerful state that chooses to work through an IO demonstrates that it is willing to have limits placed on its maneuverability and the ability to impose its interests unilaterally.

Second, coercers face organization costs—including the costs of communicating, bargaining, and reaching common positions (Olson 1965, 47)—when they work through an IO. These are a form of transaction costs. Any multilateral approach to foreign policy increases the costs of decision making and of implementing policy—the problems of collective action in coalition warfare in particular are well known. In Somalia, the need to coordinate with the UN and with coalition partners on the ground proved cumbersome and costly for the United States (Haass 1994, 31). Logistical complications are compounded by political factors, or what Paul Milgrom and John Roberts (1990, 58) label more generically "influence costs": "the losses that arise from individuals within an organization seeking to influence its decisions for their private benefit." In Kosovo, for example, the details and intensity of the bombing campaign were modified to keep NATO members on board,[21] and for years in Bosnia the Europeans and Americans struggled to implement a coherent plan as each government sought to shape the policy in its own interest. Another source of organization costs is sidepayments, which are often exchanged for votes. In the context of an IO (in contrast to a temporary coalition), the leverage of other states—whether used to influence the policy or to extract side payments—is formalized in the voting process.[22] Reaching sufficient consensus among states, a requisite for IO approval, requires compromise and leads to outcomes that may differ from the coercer's preferences, often in unanticipated ways.

The third type of cost, delay, is largely a product of the first two. Involving an IO implies a willingness to engage in diplomacy and to wait for approval of the policy and of subsequent decisions as the policy is carried out. In Korea, the United States did not cross the thirty-eighth parallel until it achieved General Assembly authorization in October of 1950, thus exchanging some control over timing for IO support (Chayes and Chayes 1995, 41). Early in the crisis in the former Yugoslavia, European governments balked at any decisive action,

21. As one observer characterizes the process, the use of air power "was subject to constant bickering among NATO members who demanded a say in the choice of targets" (Freedman, *Independent*, March 29, 2003).

22. Even weak states are afforded bargaining leverage over powerful states if their votes are required in an IO context. This can be used to extract side payments or policy compromises. David Baldwin (1985, 115–16) offers the example of U.S. side payments in the context of UN and OAS votes. David Malone's (1998) analysis of the U.S. intervention in Haiti provides an exhaustive account of the many side payments that accompanied the relevant Chapter VII resolution.

delaying intervention by NATO and the United States while the situation worsened. More recently, in confronting Iran over its nuclear program, the United States and Europe have undertaken a protracted and multifaceted diplomatic strategy, one necessitated by the desire to keep Russia and China on board in the context of the International Atomic Energy Agency and the Security Council. The exigencies of maintaining support within an IO—and especially of keeping the most reluctant members on board—encourage incremental over expeditious policymaking and implementation.

Finally, working through an IO increases the level of scrutiny to which a coercer is subject. Since IOs increase transparency and require a more public accounting of actions, the international community is able to track the behavior of a state that chooses to work under their auspices, allowing other governments to determine whether the policy ultimately pursued is proportionate and defensible. A benign coercer might welcome this scrutiny since suspicion is the likely default in its absence.[23] Moreover, the exchange of information and discourse that takes place within an IO tends to reveal information about states' preferences and intended actions (Lindley 2007; Boehmer, Gartzke, and Nordstrom 2004; Wallander 1999), leading to more effective monitoring and higher-quality signaling at the international level. The diversity of IO members is again key. Unlike a unilateral effort or an ad hoc coalition, most IOs include states with disparate interests who will watch one another with a critical eye. This scrutiny almost axiomatically leads to more sincere signaling: "If an information provider believes that the truth of his statement is likely to be verified, dissembling is less likely to get the information provider the outcome he desires. As a result, the more likely verification becomes, the more likely the information provider is to provide truthful information" (Lupia and McCubbins 1994, 368). Under these circumstances a state with unthreatening intentions is more willing to send a public signal by working through an IO.

These various costs, which I refer to generally as the "costs of constraint," are summarized in table 2.1. While not all are manifested in a given case, individually and in combination they allow the coercer to send meaningful information regarding its intentions. Showing restraint and a willingness to cede some control reassures nontarget states, which are less likely to retaliate politically and to oppose the intervention. Under certain conditions, IO participation is mutually beneficial: the coercer benefits from support (or at least reduced political costs) while other states benefit from limiting the power of the coercing state. This logic forms the basis of a second hypothesis:

23. Revealing precisely this logic, Downs, Rocke, and Siverson (1985) have shown how lack of information can lead to unnecessary arms races.

Table 2.1. Costs of IO constraint

1. Freedom-of-action costs
– reduced options
– modifications of policy
2. Organization costs
– diplomacy and logistics
– political influence costs
– side payments for votes
3. Delay
– diplomatic activity
– incremental policymaking
4. Scrutiny
– monitoring by skeptical states

Hypothesis 2 (Intentions Information): *Channeling coercion through an IO sends a signal of benign intentions to leaders of third-party states, thereby increasing the likelihood of international support.*

Sending Policy Information to Publics

Even if other state leaders determine that supporting the coercive policy is in their national interest, they may face domestic barriers to doing so. They must convince their own publics that supporting another state's exercise of power is justified. IO approval helps overcome this additional obstacle by sending policy-relevant information to domestic publics abroad.

While IR scholars have paid increasing attention to how domestic publics influence state interests and policy, the role of domestic publics *abroad* is not well understood. Members of publics are poorly informed relative to leaders; they lack knowledge regarding the reasons for a given policy and the relationship between the policy and potential consequences. In the context of coercive intervention on the part of another state, they do not know if the policy is justified and serving collective interests or whether it reflects only selfish goals with undesirable international consequences.[24]

Public ignorance of policy issues is most acute in the area of foreign policy. International issues are less salient than domestic ones and, unlike foreign policymakers, publics are exposed to little debate and information without significant effort. And since each individual has negligible influence on foreign policy,

24. Martha Finnemore (2003, 73–74) provides an example of this uncertainty: publics are often unsure whether a purported "humanitarian" intervention is truly designed to meet humanitarian objectives.

members of the public have little incentive to gather information and carefully analyze foreign affairs. It is therefore perfectly rational for individuals to remain largely ignorant of international policy matters.

Ignorance, however, does not imply indifference. Publics are looking for "information shortcuts" to assess international issues,[25] and IO endorsements can perform this function (Chapman 2007; Thompson 2006a). Since the claims of IOs are more neutral than claims of individual governments, or of ad hoc coalitions, the signals they convey regarding a policy are more credible and thus more informative. In the context of a military intervention, as law scholar Ruth Wedgwood (2002, 173) observes, IO authorization "can be seen as an impartial certification that an adversary does indeed pose a threat to international peace and security, and that the use of force is not intended to serve the narrow interests of a single country."[26] Publics can infer that the policy's consequences will be broadly favorable for the international community.

This political effect motivates policymakers. In explaining why the United States seeks to work through regional organizations such as NATO and the Organization for Security and Cooperation in Europe, one State Department official referred to the cost-sharing advantages but also to the importance of "political cover": "People in other countries see U.S. policy and say 'okay, the U.S. has already convinced the Russians and other members,' and this changes their view of the policy."[27] This logic is captured in the most fundamental principle behind the informational rationale for committee heterogeneity in Congress. "In the presence of uncertainty," write Gilligan and Krehbiel (1989, 463), "diversity of interests on the committee promotes informational efficiency."[28] Individual members of the public, like legislators, do respond to new information they receive about the reasonableness and effects of policies, and they update their beliefs in sensible ways (Shapiro and Jacobs 2000, 224).

The framing strategies of elites act as an important intervening mechanism for the transmission of information to domestic publics. When it comes to international affairs, publics are largely dependent on their leaders for information and tend to follow their lead.[29] This is especially true since the news media tend

25. Empirical evidence shows that most citizens have little substantive knowledge of policy issues and therefore seek shortcuts to engage in "low-information reasoning." See Popkin (1991).

26. See also Chapman and Reiter (2004), who argue that publics are more likely to support the use of force if they perceive the policy to be a prudent response to a real threat.

27. Author's personal communication with Douglas Wake, OSCE Coordinator, U.S. Department of State, February 6, 2004.

28. Similarly, Daniel Carpenter (2001) argues that bureaucracies are most autonomous and thus credible when they have diverse interests that are distinct from those of political actors.

29. Jonathan Hurwitz (1989, 225–26) shows that public "followership" of presidents is more pronounced in foreign policy matters than in domestic ones.

to "index" their coverage of foreign policy issues to debates among political leaders (Zaller and Chiu 2000; Bennett 1990). Thus most of the international policy information that individual citizens acquire is presented by leaders through the media (Hayward 1994, 224). In the case of military intervention, public ignorance and dependence on leaders are highest in the lead-up to conflict and during its early stages, before other sources of information and independent media access are available (Western 2005). This provides an opportunity for pro-coercion leaders to enhance the signal sent to publics by stressing the IO imprimatur and describing the action in multilateral terms.

Through this process of policy information transmission to domestic publics abroad, a coercer that achieves IO approval makes it easier for foreign leaders to offer support—or at least to refrain from imposing costs. In the language of the two-level-games literature, the information transmitted to domestic publics increases the size of the domestic win-set for leaders in third-party states by minimizing domestic opposition (Putnam 1988). This information logic provides an alternative—though not a mutually exclusive one—to conventional norm-based explanations for why publics tend to favor multilateralism over unilateralism.

This second path of information transmission is captured in a third hypothesis:

> Hypothesis 3 (Policy Information): *IO approval informs domestic publics abroad that the coercive policy has desirable consequences, thereby increasing the likelihood of international support by minimizing domestic opposition.*

Institutional Variation and the Security Council

So far we have focused on the question of why powerful states sometimes turn to IOs in the conduct of military coercion by explicating the political advantages of gaining approval. But we know that states bypass IOs in some cases, opting instead for ad hoc coalitions or pure unilateralism. In this section I extend the argument's logic to explain such choices and to illuminate the unique role played by the Security Council.

To explain the benefits of channeling coercion through IOs, I have described formal organizations as uniquely independent among international institutions. However, we can more accurately think of independence as varying across all institutions—including among IOs themselves. In general, as the independence of institutions increases, so do the constraints and the variance in outcomes associated with working through them. In the event of IO approval, these costs are mirrored commensurately by political benefits: the greater the independence, the greater the information that is sent and thus the lower the political costs of coercion. Considering variation in independence across institutions helps us to identify the conditions under which coercers work through IOs and, more generally, to explain how states choose among institutional alternatives in the conduct of statecraft.

Elsewhere I have described IO independence as a function of structural features such as voting rules, which determine how much influence individual member states have; the presence and discretion of an autonomous bureaucracy; and the presence and legalization of dispute resolution procedures (Haftel and Thompson 2006). Thinking about IO independence in this way, as a matter of institutional design, is useful for a range of interesting questions in IR. However, we can also conceptualize IO independence in relational terms, that is, relative to a given state or states. The same IO may be very *independent* with respect to state A while at the same time *dependent* on state B. The International Monetary Fund (IMF) is a classic example of an organization in which powerful donor countries and larger recipients have more influence and thus a different relationship with the organization than smaller countries (Dreher and Jensen 2007; Stone 2002; Thacker 1999; Swedberg 1986).

There are two key questions for measuring institutional independence relative to a coercing state. First, can the state in question be rejected by the IO? And second, *how likely* is the state to be rejected by the IO?[30] The former is a function of formal decision-making rules, which determine the degree of control exercised by individual states (Cortell and Peterson 2006; Koremenos, Lipson, and Snidal 2001, 772; Voeten 2001; O'Neill 1997). For a state seeking political cover, the higher the threshold required for a declaration of approval (e.g., a supermajority versus a simple majority voting rule), the more difficult its achievement. If the IO operates on a consensus basis or with a veto, any state, even a powerful one, can be blocked or have its policy modified by a single member of the organization.

The answer to the second question—on the likelihood of being blocked by the IO—is largely a function of the composition of the IO's membership in terms of the distribution of interests. A very heterogeneous institution is more likely to have states willing to reject the policy of a given member, whereas an institution composed of like-minded states is more apt to be supportive—in the extreme, it merely supplies rubber stamps.[31] IOs with more neutral member interests have the potential to render meaningful decisions. This follows the informational

30. To be clear, the action itself may not be blocked even if the policy is not approved. A powerful state may choose to proceed regardless of rejection.

31. This is consistent with a wide-ranging literature arguing that agent independence—in institutions ranging from central banks to the European Commission—is greatest when preferences in the institution are distinct from those of powerful political actors (Majone 2001, 109–12; Rogoff 1985).

logic of legislative committees: diverse and representative committees are the most informative to the chamber as a whole.

Because the question of composition and preference distributions has received far less attention than voting rules in the study of IOs, I elaborate more on the former in my theoretical discussion. This focus is also warranted since a crucial audience of information transmission, domestic publics, is more likely to know the nature of an IO's membership—most notably, whether it has a regional or global membership—than the details of its decision-making procedures. With respect to publics (though not necessarily to leaders), variation in membership composition is a more salient variable than variation in voting rules. Nevertheless, since both variables are important ingredients of relational independence and since they interact in practice, neither can be overlooked.

To consider the implications of variation in independence, I treat it as a dimension along which all international institutions are located. Figure 2.3 portrays the trade-offs associated with turning to institutions that are more or less independent, with unilateralism representing a complete absence of independent authorization. Unilateralism allows a coercer to retain full autonomy but does not help reduce international political costs. Thus, we expect to see unilateralism when one or both of two conditions are present: when coercing states require maximum flexibility or when they anticipate the international political costs of coercion to be low. Flexibility is most coveted when vital national security interests are at stake and/or when the mission requires a rapid response, either for military or political reasons. Anticipated international political costs are lowest when the coercive goals are widely viewed a priori as legitimate (as in cases of self-defense or humanitarian intervention) or when action is confined to a great power's recognized sphere of influence.[32]

Multilateral action is a middling strategy: like-minded states do not constrain the coercer as much and are not viewed as impartial representatives of the international community; thus ad hoc coalitions produce only modest political benefits.[33] Formal IOs, with a standing membership and formal decision-making

---

32. Great powers often generate less political backlash when they intervene in their own sphere of influence. U.S. policymakers, for example, base decisions on the assumption that intervention in the Western Hemisphere is less politically costly than it is elsewhere. Author's interview with two State Department officials in the Office of the Special Adviser to the Secretary and the Bureau of Near Eastern Affairs, respectively, Washington, January 11, 2000. Similarly, Soviet interventions in eastern Europe prompted rhetorical outrage from the West but little else (McWilliams and Piotrowski 1997, 495). While the French have traditionally embraced the Security Council as the uniquely legitimate authorizer of military interventions, a historical exception has been made when it comes to UN involvement in former African colonies (Boyer, Sur, and Fleurence 2003, 285).

33. To be clear, here I refer to "simple" multilateralism, defined quantitatively as involving multiple states but lacking the qualitative dimension of more institutionalized multilateralism (Ruggie 1993).

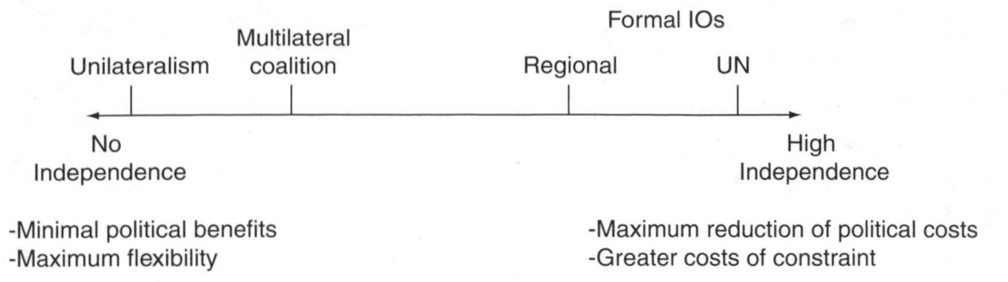

FIGURE 2.3. Variation in institutional independence: Political implications

requirements, are the most independent and therefore the most informative institutions. Involving them reduces international political costs, but (and largely because) they also impose constraints and may produce less desirable and even unanticipated outcomes.

These trade-offs are captured in two ceteris paribus hypotheses that establish the more general conditions under which IO-based action will be chosen.

> Hypothesis 4 (Flexibility): *When coercers place a low value on flexibility (i.e., are less sensitive to the costs of constraint), they are more likely to turn to IOs.*
> Hypothesis 5 (Anticipated Costs): *When coercers anticipate high international political costs for taking action, they are more likely to turn to IOs.*

As figure 2.3 illustrates, choices among IOs themselves, at the right end of the continuum, represent a microcosm of the trade-offs confronted across the continuum. Building again on theories of committee signaling in legislatures, figures 2.4–2.6 represent three variations in IO composition and thus neutrality, a key determinant of independence. Assuming that the coercing state is more prointervention than the median member of the international community (whose preferences are shown distributed normally), the coercer's choice among IOs will determine how much information is sent to foreign leaders and publics. Figure 2.4 portrays a situation where the IO membership is both heterogeneous, reflected in a wide preference distribution, and representative, reflected in a median preference that matches the median preference of the international community. The distance between the IO's median preference and the coercer's ideal point suggests the IO is independent with respect to the coercer; the proximity of x_{IO} and x_i and the heterogeneity of membership interests imply that information transmission to third parties is efficient, that is, that the IO serves as an informative agent of the international community. Channeling coercion through this IO will likely entail costly constraints—including the possibility of having the policy blocked altogether—but will also produce high-quality information regarding

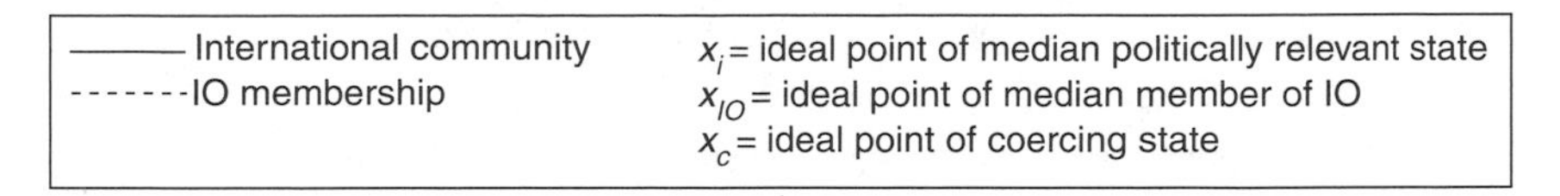

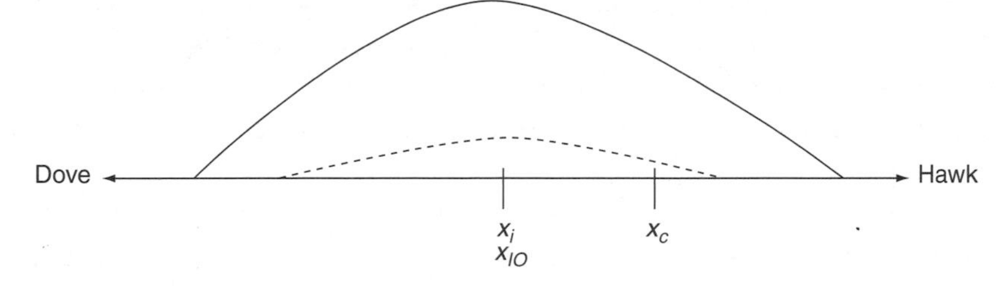

FIGURE 2.4. Heterogeneous IO with representative (moderate) preferences

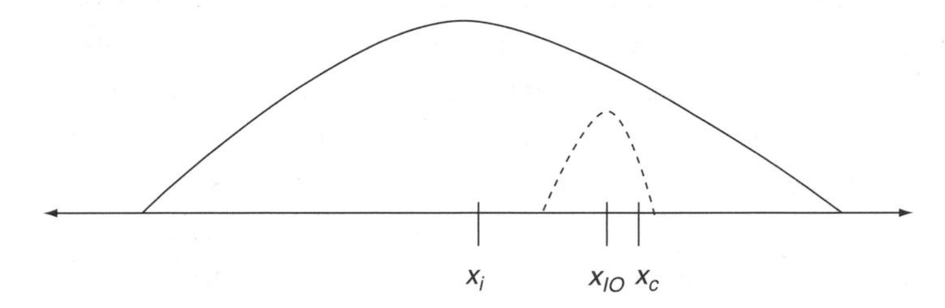

FIGURE 2.5. Homogeneous IO with outlier (hawkish) preferences

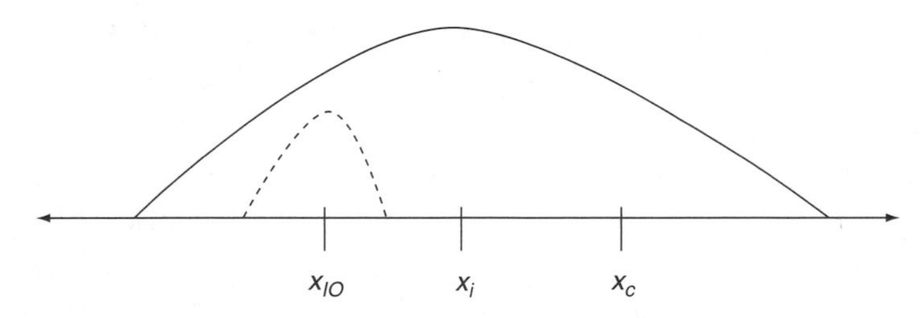

FIGURE 2.6. Homogeneous IO with outlier (dovish) preferences

intentions and the policy. In short, the coercer is relinquishing the most control in return for the greatest political benefits.

In security matters, the Security Council—with its fifteen members, representing various geographical regions and levels of development[34]—best matches these characteristics in terms of composition. It comes closest to operating as a neutral representative of the international community in a case of military intervention (Abbott and Snidal 1998, 28; Diehl, Reifschneider, and Hensel 1996,

34. The ten rotating members are elected to two-year terms by the General Assembly. By agreement, they are distributed according to the following geographic formula: three for Africa, two for Asia, two for Latin America, one for eastern Europe, and two for western Europe and other states.

687–68). The diverse membership combines with a decision-making procedure that makes it difficult for individual states to control outcomes. On all substantive issues, approval from the UNSC requires not only nine members to vote affirmatively but also the absence of any permanent member vetoes. Thus, given its composition and voting rules, it is a relatively conservative institution when it comes to authorizing force (Chapman 2007), and even the United States is likely to have its policies modified and even blocked in the Council (Voeten 2001), as recent experiences with Kosovo and Iraq attest.

Figure 2.5 represents another typical case. The IO members are relatively homogeneous, and though they are less hawkish on average than the coercer, their median preference is much closer to the coercer's than to the median state's.[35] Examples in relation to the United States include NATO and the OAS in their respective regions. They are less neutral than the IO in figure 2.4, and therefore the coercer is able to retain more flexibility and is more likely to achieve an outcome closer to its ideal. While some information will be transmitted to third parties if coercion is channeled through them, this choice of forum is less effective as a mechanism for lowering international political costs.

This logic helps explain why regional organizations, comprised of a less diverse set of states, do not produce a legitimation effect equivalent to that of the Security Council. For example, the OAS is limited in its ability to provide political cover for U.S. interventions (Slater 1969), and authorization of the 1989 Grenada invasion by the obscure Organization of Eastern Caribbean States was even less meaningful and did not prevent widespread condemnation of the action (Luck 2002, 62–63). The United States and Europeans tried repeatedly to gain UNSC approval for interventions in the former Yugoslavia, rather than approaching the more parochial NATO and Organization for Security and Cooperation in Europe. Nevertheless, regional IOs or ad hoc coalitions are chosen when Security Council approval is impossible or too costly to achieve.[36]

Finally, figure 2.6 represents an unusual (but plausible) case and an exception to the rule regarding committee composition. In the context of legislatures, Krehbiel recognizes the possibility that a homogeneous committee composed

35. A graphic representation of an ad hoc multilateral coalition would look most like the IO in figure 2.5, though with less variance in member preferences and an ideal point closer to the coercer's.

36. In some cases, a regional IO strategy may serve as a stepping-stone toward Security Council involvement. This was the case in Kosovo, where NATO action was replaced by a UN "peacebuilding" mission authorized by the UNSC under Chapter VII (Resolution 1244, of June 10, 1999). A more recent example is African Union (AU) efforts in the Sudan, which began before the UNSC could agree to intervene. AU and UN peacekeepers now work together, the latter under the Chapter VII authority of Resolutions 1590 (March 24, 2005) and 1706 (August 31, 2006), which offer a sweeping mandate that includes the right to use "all necessary means" in the areas of deployment.

of preference outliers might make a claim that goes against expectations. In this case, the signal is exceptionally informative. For example, if an agriculture committee proposes to reduce farm subsidies or if a defense committee proposes to cut military spending, this sends clear information to the floor that these policies are reasonable (Krehbiel 1991, 83). This is consistent with game theoretic findings on the value of biased information sources, which have the potential to render unexpected and therefore highly credible recommendations (Kydd 2003; Cukierman and Tommasi 1998; Calvert 1985). An analogy in IR would be a case where the Arab League endorsed intervention against an Arab state.

The information argument presented here thus suggests that institutional variation presents trade-offs that affect the forum-shopping decisions of coercing states. The coercer's choice among institutional alternatives—from unilateralism to ad hoc multilateralism to various IOs—is ultimately determined by its goals and the circumstances of the case, which influence how sensitive the coercer is to the costs and benefits outlined above. In terms of the choice among IOs, when both conditions stipulated in hypotheses 4 and 5 are met, states are most likely to channel coercive policies through the most independent organizations—in security affairs, the Security Council. The following hypothesis captures this logic:

> Hypothesis 6 (IO Forum Shopping): *When coercers place a low value on flexibility (i.e., are not sensitive to the costs of constraint) and anticipate high international political costs, they are most likely to turn to the Security Council. When only one of these conditions is met, they are more likely to turn to regional organizations.*

It is important to note, however, that the coercer may be constrained by the limited availability of appropriate IOs in a given case. Some regions and issues lack relevant organizations to activate, a circumstance that may produce ad hoc multilateralism or unilateralism even when an IO-based strategy is preferred. In general, given the alternatives available, a coercer will seek to work through an institution that is as independent *as necessary*, but no more.

Table 2.2 summarizes the various hypotheses outlined above.

Alternative Arguments

The academic literature and policy discussions on the role of IOs in military statecraft suggest three prominent alternative arguments for why even powerful states channel their actions through formal organizations. They rest, respectively, on the role of legitimacy, the role of domestic politics, and the role of burden

Table 2.2. Hypotheses

Hypothesis 1 (Coercer's Motivation): *When powerful coercers work through IOs, they do so strategically to lower the international political costs of coercion.*

Hypothesis 2 (Intentions Information): *Channeling coercion through an IO sends a signal of benign intentions to leaders of third-party states, thereby increasing the likelihood of international support.*

Hypothesis 3 (Policy Information): *IO approval informs domestic publics abroad that the coercive policy has desirable consequences, thereby increasing the likelihood of international support by minimizing domestic opposition.*

Hypothesis 4 (Flexibility): *When coercers place a low value on flexibility (i.e., are less sensitive to the costs of constraint), they are more likely to turn to IOs.*

Hypothesis 5 (Anticipated Costs): *When coercers anticipate high international political costs for taking action, they are more likely to turn to IOs.*

Hypothesis 6 (IO Forum Shopping): *When coercers place a low value on flexibility (i.e., are not sensitive to the costs of constraint)* and *anticipate high international political costs, they are most likely to turn to the Security Council. When only one of these conditions is met, they are more likely to turn to regional organizations.*

sharing. While each is considered in more detail in the course of the empirical chapters, I briefly introduce them here.

Legitimacy-based arguments, already discussed in chapter 1, rely on a "logic of appropriateness"[37] and are made primarily by social constructivist scholars in IR. There are what we might label strong and weak versions of this argument. The stronger version holds that states contemplating action are motivated by an internalized norm to act multilaterally; they act through IOs because their leaders believe intrinsically that it is appropriate to do so and is therefore in their interest.[38] The weaker version also rests on the normative importance of multilateralism—and especially the UN—in the contemporary world but views action by the intervening or sanctioning state as instrumentally driven. Leaders work though an IO because doing so legitimates their actions in the eyes of the international community, generating increased support for norm-based reasons. States are thus acting strategically to render their actions more acceptable (Hurd 2007, 2002; Finnemore 2003, 75; Claude 1966).

The strong version of the legitimacy argument clashes with the uneven behavior of states—sometimes acting through IOs and other times eschewing

37. This can be distinguished conceptually from a "logic of consequences" (March and Olsen 1989).

38. On this possibility, see Hurd (1999) and Ruggie (1993). On the internalization of norms more generally, see Checkel (2001), Johnston (2001), and Finnemore and Sikkink (1998).

them, sometimes acting multilaterally and other times unilaterally. This resonates with the more general observation that while international norms clearly matter, they do not consistently drive foreign policy choices; material considerations and situational factors often intervene (Herrmann and Shannon 2001). The stated motivations of most decision makers also cast doubt on an unqualified endorsement of the legitimacy logic. Former U.S. national security adviser Anthony Lake, who often favored multilateral policies, plainly states that "only one overriding factor can determine whether the U.S. should act multilaterally or unilaterally, and that is America's interests. We should act multilaterally where doing so advances our interests, and we should act unilaterally when that will serve our purpose. The simple question in each case is this: What works best?" (Lake 1993, 663). After touting his country's penchant for multilateralism, one Canadian foreign policy official conceded that it flowed not from principled motivations but from a "pragmatic recognition" that "we need multilateralism because we can't do it ourselves."[39]

The weaker version potentially explains why states have a baseline incentive to act multilaterally if doing so comports with international norms of legitimate behavior. By themselves, however, legitimation arguments do not account for the strategic behavior of states when it comes to engaging—or bypassing—IOs, partly because they do not emphasize the trade-offs involved in acting multilaterally. Nevertheless, the notion that IOs are valuable because they legitimate state policies is the conventional wisdom and clearly has merit, especially in its weak variant. It must be considered as an important alternative to my information transmission argument.

Other scholars interested in multilateralism focus on the role of domestic politics within the state conducting action (not within third-party states, as I emphasize). One version of this argument holds that leaders seek IO approval in order to appease their domestic public or legislature, who prefer multilateralism over unilateralism either for normative or burden-sharing reasons (Tago 2005; Cortell and Davis 1996). Other versions focus on the self-imposed costs of institutional strategies. Kenneth Schultz (2003) argues that leaders work though IOs in order to tie their hands, thereby credibly committing to a policy and reducing the incentives for legislative resistance. A third view holds that Security Council approval allows leaders to send costly signals to their publics that the policy being pursued is reasonable, thereby enhancing the "rally 'round the flag" effect (Chapman 2007; Chapman and Reiter 2004).

It is certainly true that publics, including Americans, prefer multilateral action (Chicago Council on Foreign Relations and German Marshall Fund 2002;

39. Author's interview with a deputy director in the Department of Foreign Affairs, June 16, 2005.

Kull and Destler 1999; Sobel 1996), and this clearly motivates leaders to work multilaterally in some cases. However, other factors, such as the nature of policy objectives and the probability of success, are more important determinants of public opinion vis-à-vis military interventions (Eichenberg 2005). In addition, recent U.S. cases show that IO endorsements have a mixed effect at best on public opinion during intervention episodes; indeed, presidents are often viewed favorably—as tough and effective—when they proceed unilaterally.[40] If mollifying a reticent legislature motivates leaders to seek IO approval, the incentive should be strongest under divided government, when the opposition seeks to reign in the executive's foreign policy adventures (Howell and Pevehouse 2007; Tago 2005). In the case of the United States and Iraq, at least, there is no evidence that presidents were more likely to seek UN cover when Congress was controlled by a different party. If anything, Clinton's policies became more unilateral after the Republican takeover of 1994, and George W. Bush pursued a UN-based policy for most of 2002 despite an unusually supportive legislature led by his own party. Nevertheless, the influence of domestic politics at home is an important alternative explanation and is explicitly considered in the case studies.

Finally, states may work through IOs simply because that is the best path to burden sharing. Multilateral cooperation can sometimes afford, in David Lake's (1999) terminology, "joint production economies." Help from others is also appealing in terms of domestic politics. As Richard Haass (1994, 31) notes, "Foreign involvement also helps at home, where resentment at the United States' bearing most or all of the burdens of a costly and extended intervention is all but certain to undermine support for that commitment." However, as I show in chapter 3's Gulf War case, and as others have argued in other contexts, working multilaterally is often a drag on efficiency (Zanini and Taw 2000), and cost sharing is rarely a critical motivation for powerful states (Finnemore 1998, 183). Moreover, the burden-sharing logic does not explain why IOs seem to matter so much in coercive episodes, beyond the involvement of allies and coalitions.

While all these explanations have some merit, they do not tell the whole story of statecraft through IOs and lack the potential explanatory breadth of the theoretical framework I present. However, each deserves attention in the empirical chapters that follow. It should be noted that these various logics—legitimacy, domestic politics at home, and burden sharing—are by no means mutually

---

40. Edward Luck reviews public opinion during the Grenada, Panama, and Haiti interventions. Only the third was conducted with UN approval, and yet the incumbent presidents received more of a boost in favorability ratings for the first two. On the basis of this admittedly limited but important set of cases, he concludes that "there is no evidence that that public looks first to international bodies for the legitimation of national decisions to use or not to use force" (2002, 66).

exclusive of each other or of my own argument. We should not be surprised to find more than one at work across cases and simultaneously in a given case. Nevertheless, I hope to show that important cases cannot be understood without applying my theory of information transmission.

Observable Implications and Research Design

The most definitive evidence of the information transmission argument would uncover the motivations of the coercing state's leadership and would show that third parties—both leaders and publics—receive the information hypothesized and react to it accordingly. It is impossible to directly observe intentions or whether particular information has been received, though there are reasonable indicators that shed light on the processes hypothesized here, and consideration of different types of evidence can increase our confidence.

The framework rests on the proposition, embodied in hypothesis 1, that powerful states channel coercion through IOs in a calculated attempt to reduce the international political costs of coercion. Two types of evidence shed light on this argument. First, we should see leaders, in public statements or memoirs, express that their motivation for channeling coercion through an IO was indeed a desire to reduce international political fallout, and this should be confirmed by contemporaneous observations (either by others involved or in press accounts). Alternative motivations, such as a sense that turning to an IO is the appropriate thing to do or a desire for material support from the IO, would have to be ruled out as the chief motivators. Second, we can demonstrate that the political costs of coercion would have been higher absent IO involvement. This can be done counterfactually, by carefully tracing international reactions within the case, and through comparisons with similar cases that vary in terms of IO involvement.

For the second hypothesis, on intentions information, we should observe the imposition of costly constraints on a coercer as a result of IO involvement. We should also adduce evidence that foreign leaders were concerned about the threat posed by the coercer and that the costs of constraint served to minimize concerns over the coercer's intentions. This is best done through historical research and examination of contemporaneous accounts and through the use of counterfactual arguments to demonstrate that the reactions of other leaders would have been different in the absence of IO approval.

The third hypothesis—that IO approval sends policy information to domestic publics abroad—is the most empirically challenging. It is impossible to know precisely how and why individuals have updated their beliefs about a given policy. Within cases, we can establish that third-party leaders are constrained by domestic opposition from supporting the coercer and that they view IO involvement as a palliative against this problem. We should also be able to demonstrate that a pro-coercion shift in opinion occurred following IO approval. In cases involving no IO approval, polling data on whether the coercer's justifications are viewed as credible by foreign publics can help establish that favorable policy information was not conveyed. Across cases, we can compare international public opinion in episodes that vary in terms of IO involvement but are otherwise similar.

Analyzing the framing strategies of leaders can also help us assess hypothesis 3. Observing framing strategies helps us capture both the concerns of publics and the information they receive during coercive episodes. If leaders (of the coercing state and of third-party states) are concerned about domestic publics and understand that IOs can transmit politically useful information to them, we should see them frame their actions in specific ways. In statements designed for public consumption, they should stress not only involvement by the IO but also its informative properties—namely, its neutrality as a function of a diverse and representative membership and its independence from individual national interests. Since the news media base their coverage of foreign policy largely on the statements of high-level government officials, how events are framed by these officials profoundly shapes the information received by publics. Indeed, strategic communication by leaders can even stretch across borders to reach foreign audiences directly (Manheim and Albritton 1984). To the extent that leaders are well informed about their constituents, their framing strategies should further reveal what information is important to publics as they assess policies.

Hypotheses 4, 5, and 6 require both within- and across-case observations to assess whether sensitivity to constraints and anticipation of international political costs are linked as hypothesized with the strategies—unilateralism versus multilateralism, regional IOs versus the Security Council—chosen by coercing states. Comparison across cases is useful in this regard to assess whether the relevant independent and dependent variables are correlated (though such evidence can only be suggestive with such a small number of cases). Process tracing within cases is valuable for demonstrating whether coercing leaders make forum-shopping decisions based on the logic underlying the hypotheses and with consideration of the trade-offs summarized in figure 2.3.

This discussion of indicators is designed to be general enough to guide future research beyond the empirical analysis presented here. For example, in addition to other cases of military coercion, the concepts and indicators can easily be applied to the realms of diplomatic and economic statecraft.

Given the various observable implications, the book requires a research design that combines the virtues of in-depth case studies with the distinct benefits of comparative analysis. Both approaches are necessary to assess the theoretical arguments, which have implications at the macrolevel of outcomes and at the microlevel of decision making and causal mechanisms. I thus seek to combine the congruence method with process-tracing techniques.[41]

Only by looking closely within a case is it possible to uncover "evidence of the causal processes through which the independent variable has an impact" (Collier, Mahoney, and Seawright 2004, 97). The information transmission dynamics hypothesized are impossible to directly observe, and the empirical demands for uncovering evidence of them are fairly high. Tracing processes within a case allows the analyst to at least approximate the motivations behind decisions, to uncover the precise temporal sequence of events, and to link causes to their effects. By going beyond a single outcome for each case, this technique also increases the number of theoretically relevant observations (King, Keohane, and Verba 1994, 227–28; George and McKeown 1985). Finally, detailed case studies are helpful for making convincing counterfactual claims, one of the inferential strategies used here.

The use of individual case studies is combined with comparison across them. The inclusion of multiple cases that vary on the key dimension of IO approval allows me to test a different set of implications focused on outcomes. The two wars at the heart of this study are especially useful in this regard. While they do not offer a perfectly controlled comparison, the two events do share a number of similarities insofar as the same states are involved (and even many of the same individuals), the distribution of power is roughly constant, the relevant IOs are the same, and they take place during the same, post–Cold War era (though the terrorist attacks of September 11, 2001, arguably ushered in a new era, a point discussed in chapters 5 and 6). They thus approximate a "most similar" case design.[42] When we add the variation in UN approval and involvement during the interwar years, outlined in chapter 4, the result is substantial variation in the role and effects of the Security Council across several episodes—a natural laboratory from which to draw conclusions for theory and policy.

41. For an elaboration of both approaches and their role in qualitative research design, see George and Bennett (2005).

42. See Collier (1991, 16–17). My research design shares many characteristics of a before-and-after longitudinal study, where one variable is manipulated to create multiple, similar cases and the effects then analyzed. However, this is not a clean comparison since other variables are clearly shifting as well.

3

THE SECURITY COUNCIL IN THE GULF WAR, 1990–1991

With the conclusion of the Cold War, a new set of opportunities presented themselves to U.S. foreign policymakers. The Soviet counterbalance had disappeared, and the world's lone superpower possessed a newfound ability to wield influence in virtually every corner of the globe—though precisely how it would seize this opportunity was not clear. The international community watched carefully as the United States reassessed its interests and the diplomatic and military strategies that would follow. At the same time, the UN Security Council (UNSC) was at least potentially liberated from its Cold War straightjacket; whether the diminishment of East-West conflict would make a difference in practice remained to be seen, however. In this political context, the Gulf War became the first litmus test. It would help define the role of the world's most influential state and of its most important security institution.

Following the Iraqi invasion of Kuwait in August of 1990, the United States went to great lengths to work through the UN in order to apply diplomatic and economic pressure and ultimately to expel Iraq from Kuwait, seeking UNSC resolutions at every stage of the conflict. The resort to force came only after several resolutions condemning Iraq's behavior and imposing various sanctions, culminating in the passage of Resolution 678, which authorized UN member states "to use all necessary means to . . . restore international peace and security in the area."[1] For arguably the first time in its history, the Security Council functioned

1. See the appendix, which contains the text of 678 and several other key resolutions.

as the collective security institution envisioned in the charter.[2] Most observers of Gulf War diplomacy agree that by turning to the Security Council the United States was able to achieve greater legitimacy and support for its use of coercion. The comments of Richard Haass (1994, 32), a participant in Gulf War diplomacy as a member of the U.S. National Security Council, are typical: "The Gulf War model is important...in that the U.S.-led coalition acted pursuant to various Security Council resolutions, something that cast the UN in the role of legitimizer." Similarly, international law scholar Christine Gray (2002, 8) argues that the Gulf War experience "made clear the advantages of legitimacy which only the Security Council could confer."

But few analysts take the next step by exploring the causal mechanisms underlying this phenomenon. Why and how was the Security Council able to perform this function? Since it was still an overwhelmingly U.S.-led effort, why did the UN role change how the international community reacted to events? The theoretical logic of information transmission presented in the previous chapter helps us address these questions and explain both why the United States chose to channel its actions through an IO and how this choice mattered.

The 1990–91 Gulf War episode is an ideal case for assessing the arguments presented in this book. Because the episode involves an extremely powerful state using military coercion against a much weaker one, it represents a "hard" case for showing the importance of international institutional involvement. The opportunity costs of using institutions are higher for powerful states: they have more to lose by ceding control. As a recent study on delegation to IOs notes, powerful states are less likely to rely on multilateral institutions because they "are able to obtain their goals through their own influence and capabilities. As a result, they have a more attractive 'outside option' and, if they choose to do so, can more effectively realize their preferences" (Hawkins et al. 2006b, 24–25). Moreover, we generally expect states to rely less on multilateral approaches in security matters (Lipson 1984).

The puzzle is especially stark since the Security Council falls on the far end of the institutional independence continuum. U.S. efforts to gain UNSC support have indeed been rebuffed on multiple occasions, a reflection of the body's diversity and the veto power of the permanent members, who frequently have divergent preferences (Voeten 2001). Especially from a Realist standpoint, we should

2. The Security Council did authorize military assistance to South Korea in 1950, though only in the absence of a boycotting Soviet Union. The intervention was further endorsed by a General Assembly resolution (the so-called Uniting for Peace Resolution), a tactic that provided political cover but violated the charter's provisions in the area of peace and security. The Security Council also authorized limited force in the Congo in the early 1960s and imposed sanctions against Southern Rhodesia in 1966 and South Africa in 1977.

not expect a powerful state to willingly place itself in a situation of increased dependence on other states.[3] Looking at a case where the most powerful state turns to the most independent IO should illustrate most clearly the trade-offs and causes identified in my argument.

This chapter proceeds by briefly summarizing the background to the crisis and its key events.[4] The next section explains why the United States chose to intervene against Iraq and what motivated its leaders to channel their coercive response through the Security Council. I then outline the widespread international support for intervention and argue that it was attributable in large measure to the UN imprimatur. These sources of evidence are most relevant to hypothesis 1—that states work through IOs in order to lower the international political costs of coercion—and to hypotheses 4 to 6, on the conditions under which states turn to IOs and to the UNSC in particular. In two subsequent sections, I address hypotheses 2 and 3 at more length by exploring the concerns of other state leaders regarding U.S. intentions and the costly constraints entailed in working through the Security Council, as well as the reactions of foreign publics to the intervention and to UN involvement.

Background and Events

Following its protracted and costly war with Iran from 1980 to 1988, Iraq owed tens of billions of dollars in foreign debt, the servicing of which was increasingly costly to the national economy. Saddam Hussein harbored resentment toward the wealthy oil regimes of the Persian Gulf, especially Saudi Arabia, the United Arab Emirates, and Kuwait, who he felt were ungrateful for his sacrifice and should further compensate Iraq for standing up to Iran. By the summer of 1990, his ire was concentrated on Kuwait. He outlined several grievances against his neighbor: Kuwait's refusal to write off Iran war loans, its suppression of oil prices through overproduction beyond OPEC quotas, and its alleged theft of oil from the Rumaila Field, shared by Iraq and Kuwait. Kuwait was also a convenient target because of its geographic contiguity and its vast wealth, which tended to make it a less sympathetic victim in the eyes of the Arab world (Dannreuther 1991–92, 16). For Iraqis, Kuwait was also a natural target since they had always claimed the territory as part of historic Iraq (Schofield 1993). For its part, the United States

---

3. Kenneth Waltz (1979, 107) makes precisely this argument.

4. A detailed history of the conflict is not warranted here. For good general histories of the crisis, see Malone (2006, chap. 3); Freedman and Karsh (1993); Hiro (1992); U.S. News & World Report (1992); Heikal (1992); and Dannreuther (1991–92).

did not take the threat seriously enough and failed to mount an effective deterrent policy.[5]

On August 2, 1990, two days after delivering an impossible ultimatum to Kuwait, the Iraqi military invaded and later formally annexed its neighbor. Iraq, with the world's fourth largest military, now had control over 25 percent of OPEC's proven oil reserves. Thus, not only did Saddam's move alter the regional balance of power, but it concerned states around the globe that relied on Persian Gulf oil. For U.S. policymakers, the invasion also posed an immediate risk to Saudi Arabia, a strong ally and its most important supplier of oil.

Within a week the United States sent forces to Saudi Arabia as part of a defensive effort—labeled Operation Desert Shield—to prevent further aggression. What followed was months of diplomacy and economic sanctions, including exhaustive attempts at an "Arab solution"[6] and multiple diplomatic interventions by French, Soviet, and American delegations, and by UN Secretary-General Javier Perez de Cuellar. No fewer than twelve Security Council resolutions were passed, designed to isolate Iraq diplomatically and to coerce its leadership through economic sanctions and threats of force (see table 3.1). Sanctions imposed by the UN achieved widespread cooperation and were very effective at curtailing Iraq's trade. These measures culminated in Resolution 678, adopted on November 29, threatening force unless Iraq withdrew from Kuwait by January 15 of the following year. In the end, these efforts short of the use of force failed to reverse the invasion.[7]

On January 16, 1991, a coalition led by the United States launched an air campaign that marked the beginning of Operation Desert Storm. After five weeks of bombing and a brief ground war, President George H. W. Bush brought the war

5. The most emblematic episode was the now-famous meeting between April Glaspie, the U.S. ambassador to Iraq, and Saddam Hussein on July 15, 1990. In response to Saddam's queries, Glaspie simply echoed long-standing U.S. policy by stating that her administration had "no opinion" regarding the Iraq-Kuwait dispute. For more discussion of the failure of U.S. diplomacy in the run-up to the war, see Brands (2004, 113–15); Yetiv (2004, 22–23); Freedman and Karsh (1993, 50–54); and Dannreuther (1991–92, 20–21).

6. The Arab states failed to resolve the crisis because they were simply too divided among themselves. Activities in the Gulf Cooperation Council (GCC) and Arab League illustrate the nature of these cleavages. While the GCC was able to issue a condemnation of Iraq on August 7, when the Arab League met in emergency session in Cairo on August 10, only twelve of the twenty members present (Tunisia did not attend) agreed on a resolution condemning Iraq's invasion and endorsing UN resolutions—namely, 660, 661, and 662—imposing sanctions on Iraq and demanding withdrawal from Kuwait. Iraq, Libya, and the Palestinians voted against the resolution; Algeria and Yemen abstained; and Jordan, Mauritania, and the Sudan expressed support but with "reservations."

7. On the diplomacy leading up to the war, see Baker (1995, chaps. 15–20); Cooley (1991); and Woodward (1991).

Table 3.1. Security Council resolutions prior to Desert Storm

660 (August 2): Condemns invasion of Kuwait; demands immediate and unconditional withdrawal of Iraqi forces; calls for immediate negotiations between Iraq and Kuwait. *Vote: 14–1, with Yemen not participating.*

661 (August 6): Imposes an arms embargo and strict trade sanctions, with exceptions for medical supplies and, in humanitarian circumstances, foodstuffs. *Vote: 13–0, Cuba and Yemen abstaining.*

662 (August 9): Declares Iraq's annexations of Kuwait null and void. *Vote: Unanimous.*

664 (August 18): Demands that Baghdad allow foreign nationals to leave Iraq and Kuwait and rescind its order to close diplomatic missions in Kuwait. *Vote: Unanimous.*

665 (August 25): Allows member states to use limited naval force to enforce economic sanctions, including the right to inspect cargoes. *Vote: 13–0, Cuba and Yemen abstaining.*

666 (September 13): Approves shipments of food to Iraq and Kuwait for humanitarian reasons but only if distributed by approved international aid agencies. *Vote: 13–2, Cuba and Yemen opposed.*

667 (September 16): Condemns raids by Iraqi troops on French and other diplomatic missions in occupied Kuwait. *Vote: Unanimous.*

669 (September 24): Adopts procedural measure entrusting the Security Council's sanctions committee to evaluate requests for help from countries affected by the trade embargo. *Vote: Unanimous.*

670 (September 25): Prohibits air traffic with Iraq and Kuwait except in humanitarian circumstances. *Vote: 14–1, Cuba opposed.*

674 (October 29): Demands Iraq cease taking hostages and oppressing Kuwait; requests states to document financial losses and human rights violations incurred by the invasion; urges secretary-general to undertake peace efforts. *Vote: 13–0, Cuba and Yemen abstaining.*

677 (November 28): Asks UN secretary-general to safeguard a smuggled copy of Kuwait's population register to prevent Iraqi repopulation. *Vote: Unanimous.*

678 (November 29): Authorizes states to "use all necessary means" against Iraq unless it withdraws on or before 15 January. *Vote: 12–2, China abstaining, Cuba and Yemen opposed.*

Source: Texts of all resolutions are available at http://www.un.org/Docs/sc/unsc_resolutions.html.

to a close on February 28. In military terms, the Gulf War was remarkably decisive. After only four days of ground fighting, Kuwait City had been liberated and the Iraqi military was decimated with little resistance—indeed, with mass surrenders and desertion. This was accomplished at an astoundingly lopsided casualty rate: a few hundred allied dead versus tens of thousands of Iraqi soldiers.[8]

8. For a vivid description of the overwhelming nature of the victory, see Sterner (1997, 15–16). Exact figures on Iraqi casualties do not exist. Estimates range from a few thousand to as many as one hundred thousand.

In the end, the United States suffered no serious diplomatic setbacks as a result of the war. The political success of U.S. efforts was reflected in the widespread support it achieved, summarized in table 3.2. Almost forty countries contributed personnel to the coalition, and more than twenty provided military hardware. Financial contributions of $54 billion were also made, substantially offsetting the total costs—about $60 billion—for the war. The largest contributors were Saudi Arabia, Kuwait, the United Arab Emirates, Japan, and Germany.[9] By any historical standard, the extent of participation and support was remarkable. As David Lake (1999, 230) points out, the United States "successfully induced others to contribute to an extent seldom witnessed in international relations."

Even those who did not support the coalition tended not to actively oppose it. Politically important states such as Iran and Jordan grumbled about U.S. intervention but for the most part stood on the sidelines and did not get directly involved. Reflecting on the acquiescence of key Muslim states in the region, Steve Yetiv (2004, 41) notes that their "generally nonhostile position further decreased the potential costs to the United States of taking a strong, and ultimately, military stand against Iraq." While this widespread support—and lack of costly opposition—confirms one observable implication of hypothesis 1, further evidence is clearly needed to establish a causal link between UNSC involvement and the low international political costs incurred by the United States.

Choosing (How) to Intervene

If hypothesis 1 is correct, we should find evidence that U.S. decision makers turned to the UN as an intentional strategy to minimize international political fallout. Other rationales, such as burden sharing and an internalized desire to act legitimately, must be ruled out as the primary motivators.[10] We should also see greater international support as a result of the decision to channel action through an IO, which requires us to rule out the counterfactual that support would have been just as high absent UNSC approval.

The balance of evidence reveals that U.S. decision makers were not motivated by burden sharing or military resource aggregation. The dominance of American forces indicates that they did not need a large coalition in order to restore

9. For summaries of the military contributions, see Lake (1999, 208–10); and Matthews (1993, 313–15). On financial contributions, see Terasawa and Gates (1993); and Freedman and Karsh (1993, 358–61). See also the various appendixes in Watson et al. (1991).

10. I consider a third alternative, domestic politics within the United States, later in this chapter. I also devote an entire section below to the legitimation argument, arguably the most important alternative.

Table 3.2. International support of intervention against Iraq

	COUNTRY	MILITARY AND/ OR MEDICAL PERSONNEL	MILITARY EQUIPMENT	CONTRIBUTIONS TO U.S. AND U.K. (IN MILLIONS OF DOLLARS OR POUNDS)
1.	Argentina	X	X	
2.	Australia	X	X	
3.	Bahrain	X		
4.	Bangladesh	X		
5.	Belguim	X	X	£15
6.	Bulgaria	X[a]		
7.	Canada	X	X	
8.	Czechoslovakia	X	X	
9.	Denmark	X	X	£8
10.	Egypt	X	X	
11.	France	X	X	
12.	Germany	X	X	$6,455 / £275
13.	Greece	X	X	
14.	Honduras	X[a]		
15.	Hungary	X		
16.	Israel		X	
17.	Italy	X	X	
18.	Japan			$10, 012 / £183
19.	Korea (Republic of)	X		$251 / £16
20.	Kuwait	X	X	$16,058 / £660
21.	Morocco	X		
22.	Netherlands	X	X	
23.	New Zealand	X		
24.	Niger	X		
25.	Norway	X	X	
26.	Oman	X		
27.	Pakistan	X		
28.	Philippines	X		
29.	Poland	X	X	
30.	Portugal	X	X	
31.	Qatar	X	X	
32.	Romania	X		
33.	Saudi Arabia	X	X	$16,839 / £580
34.	Senegal	X		
35.	Sierra Leone	X		
36.	Spain	X		
37.	Syria	X	X	
38.	Turkey	X		
39.	UAE	X		$4,088 / £275
40.	United Kingdom	X	X	

Sources: Freedman and Karsh (1993, 361); Lake (1999, 209–10); Matthews (1993, 314–15); and Terasawa and Gates (1993).

[a]Offered troops but turned away for logistical reasons.

the preinvasion status quo. Indeed, the vast majority of the forces and equipment were American—for example, the United States supplied more than twice as many troops as the rest of the coalition states combined—and in the end the United States "took the lead and much of the burden itself" (Bennett, Lepgold, and Unger 1994, 41).[11] In fact, the coalition proved to be a significant *burden* on U.S. plans and actually degraded military effectiveness in some cases. President Bush and National Security Adviser Brent Scowcroft (1998, 342) complain that logistics were complicated by the multinational approach, and others have outlined the incompatibilities—among soldiers, equipment, and doctrine—that plagued battlefield tactics.[12] In turning to the UN, policymakers were seeking political advantages, not military or logistical ones. As Bush himself comments, "I believed it was better politically to work through the UN rather than act on our own" (Bush and Scowcroft 1998, 385). His chief Middle East adviser concurs that the advantage of UN involvement was political, not military (Haass 1994, 33).

The behavior of the United States was clearly driven by an instrumental desire to reduce the international political costs of coercion, not from a preference for acting appropriately by adhering to multilateralist norms. As one Bush administration official conceded, efforts to gain UN support "did not flow from lofty principles of international unity" (Sciolino and Pace, *NYT*, August 30, 1990).[13] Initially, most members of the foreign policy team felt that the United States had sufficient legal grounds to act under Article 51 of the UN Charter, which affirms the right of individual and collective self-defense, without receiving any additional authority from the UN (Bush and Scowcroft 1998, 345, 355–56; Baker 1995, 278; Freedman and Karsh 1993, 144).[14] That they took the issue to the Security Council was the result of a calculation that it would soften American power and minimize political retaliation. "There might be serious political problems," Bush and Scowcroft (1998, 356) reflect, "if we were perceived as launching an attack on Iraq without explicit UN endorsement."

---

11. To be sure, some multilateral assistance was valuable. Forward bases in the Gulf area were necessary for the United States to pursue its preferred strategy, and some hardware contributions were highly valued, if not essential. However, this material assistance could have been achieved with a handful of bilateral arrangements and does not explain why the policy was channeled through the UN.

12. On the problems of coalition warfare in the Gulf, see Lake (1999, 225–26); and Dunnigan and Bay (1992).

13. Newspaper articles throughout the book are cited parenthetically in the text using the author's last name (or, if there is no author, a shortened form of the headline), the newspaper title, and the date. Some long titles are abbreviated, as follows: *Christian Science Monitor* (*CSM*), *Financial Times* (*FT*), *International Herald Tribune* (*IHT*), *New York Times* (*NYT*), *Wall Street Journal* (*WSJ*), and *Washington Post* (*WashPo*).

14. Prime Minister Thatcher was the most insistent in this regard. See Thatcher (1993, 821).

The UN's consent was perceived in Washington as critical for avoiding some very specific and potentially high costs that unilateral coercion might generate, such as increased anti-American terrorism.[15] Relations with other influential states, such as the Soviet Union, were perceived to be at stake.[16] Also important were smaller, developing nations that had come to abhor U.S. intervention in the Third World. "With them," writes then secretary of state James Baker (1995, 281), "our strategy beyond the merits was to point out that we had taken our case to the United Nations, traditionally a haven for the world's have-nots, instead of striking out alone." In sum, the evidence is consonant not only with hypothesis 1 but also with hypothesis 5: U.S. decision makers viewed UN approval as pivotal for minimizing the political costs of using force and predicted that unilateralism would trigger much higher costs.

The previous section outlined the widespread support that was eventually granted to the Gulf War intervention. By itself, however, this evidence is subject to the counterargument that support—and low international political costs more generally—would have existed regardless of any IO involvement. This points to a potential endogeneity problem: UN approval may have been a *result* rather than a *cause* of widespread international support. This possibility must be confronted if we are to draw inferences regarding the positive relationship between IO approval and lower international political costs, one of the key observable implications of hypothesis 1.

The argument that international support preceded UN approval can be rejected for two reasons. First, most states that ultimately supported the intervention were deeply torn initially and through much of the prewar period. Arabs loathed the idea of Western troops entering the region, and many viewed Saddam as a hero of Arab nationalism (Heikal 1992, 225–26; Lesch 1991). Even King Fahd of Saudi Arabia, facing the most immediate threat of continued Iraqi aggression—U.S. satellite photos shared with the king showed Iraqi tanks and supplies moving south into a potentially offensive position (Woodward 1991, 266–69)—was highly reluctant to allow American troops and aircraft to use his country as a base of operations. As Mohamed Heikal (1992, 213) recounts, "Never in his eight years on the throne had King Fahd faced a decision as difficult.... Saudi instincts rebelled against pressure to accept American

15. The specter of terrorism as a risk of the war was mentioned specifically by one National Security Council (NSC) official. Author's interview with a senior staff member of the NSC, Washington, D.C., May 17, 1999. On terrorism as a risk of the war, see also Yetiv (2004, 220) (quoting the U.S. ambassador to Saudi Arabia, Chas Freeman, expressing this concern).

16. Author's interview with a bureau director at the NSC, Washington, D.C., May 17, 1999. Baker convinced Bush that unilateral action would alienate the Soviets (Bush and Scowcroft 1998, 352).

help."[17] For those in the region with close economic ties to Iraq, especially Egypt, Turkey, and Syria, the disruptions of war would cost them dearly (Brumberg 1997, 97; Sayari 1997, 202).

Non-Arab leaders were no more eager. It was difficult to generate any enthusiasm in the Soviet Union, where political and economic turmoil at home forced foreign policy into the back seat and where memories of Afghanistan rendered military intervention unappealing.[18] Soviet president Mikhail Gorbachev faced strong domestic opposition to supporting the United States and insisted through the end of October that the use of force was unacceptable (Curtius, *Boston Globe,* October 30, 1990). France was Iraq's foremost Western ally and faced substantial losses due to the cessation of trade and the arms embargo (France was Iraq's largest defense supplier) (Grunberg 1997, 119; Terasawa and Gates 1993, 182–83). Germany and Japan faced cultural and constitutional barriers to supporting military action, and the former was preoccupied with the East-West unification. Turkey, a strategically important U.S. ally in the region, hoped at the outset to remain neutral (Hale 1992, 683). Finally, though all agreed that Saddam's actions were extreme, many leaders saw merit in his accusations against the Kuwaiti royal family (Khalidi 1991).

Second, by November, with the exception of the U.K., every European and Arab member of the emerging coalition, as well as Canada and the Soviet Union, had made UNSC approval a condition of their support for offensive action.[19] Without such a resolution, continued sanctions and diplomacy were almost universally preferred. In sum, support of U.S. action in the Gulf was by no means a foregone conclusion, and Security Council endorsement was a key variable in determining reactions to the policy. Washington had good reason to believe that intervention without such an endorsement would have been unwelcome throughout much of the international community. I sharpen this conclusion in the remaining chapters by illustrating the much lower support exhibited for interventions that lacked Council approval.

It should be noted that the same Bush administration was indeed willing to act unilaterally in a case of low anticipated political costs. The Panama invasion of 1989 followed a failed effort by the United States to secure support from the

17. Moreover, Saudi Arabia had historically dealt with potential threats through appeasement and bribery, preferring to avoid conflict. U.S. policymakers worried that this would be the Saudis' preferred approach in response to the Iraq crisis.

18. As Eduard Shevardnadze characterized prevailing attitudes at the time, "At home, war still meant Afghanistan" (quoted in Woodward 1991, 334).

19. For reports to this effect, see Apple, *NYT,* November 16, 1990; "Canada Wants UN to Sanction Force," *Toronto Star,* September 13, 1990; Hoffman, *WashPo,* November 9, 1990; and Brumberg (1997, 93).

Organization of American States to take concrete action against Manuel Noriega. Bush nevertheless proceeded for two reasons (Thompson 2006c, 249–50). First, his military planners concluded that continued diplomacy and delay could threaten their principal objectives, to arrest Noriega and retrieve an imprisoned CIA operative. Second, he had reason to believe that the political fallout from the invasion would be manageable. Most governments outside the Western Hemisphere were content to let the United States operate with a free hand in its traditional sphere of influence. Latin American leaders reacted with indignation but were ultimately too dependent on the United States to retaliate effectively. As one observer notes, "the Bush administration was prepared to weather the inevitable protests since the complainants were either unable or unwilling to make Washington pay any tangible price" (LeoGrande 1990, 619). Just as hypothesis 5 predicts, anticipation of fairly limited international political costs allowed the Bush administration to proceed without IO approval.

Hypotheses 2 and 3 go beyond these more general arguments to identify the specific causal mechanisms underlying the salutary political effects of IO approval. The next two sections speak, respectively, to the transmission of intentions information to other state leaders (hypothesis 1) and the transmission of policy information to domestic publics abroad (hypothesis 2) that resulted from Security Council involvement.

Signaling Intentions to State Leaders

According to hypothesis 2, channeling coercion through an IO sends a signal of unthreatening intentions to leaders of third-party states, thereby assuaging their fears and increasing the chances that they will offer support (or at least refrain from imposing costs). If this proposition is correct, we should find that other leaders were indeed concerned about U.S. goals in the Persian Gulf and viewed UN involvement as a way to allay these concerns. Since the proposition rests on the logic of costly signaling, it should also be the case that working through the UN imposed meaningful constraints on the United States that would have been absent with a unilateral or ad hoc multilateral strategy. In this section I adduce evidence in support of these various observable implications.

Concerns over U.S. Aims

As the United States contemplated the use of military coercion, it had to take into account likely reactions to the introduction of its tremendous military might into a politically sensitive region of the world. The international community was clearly concerned with American intentions. Goals that included overthrowing Saddam, occupying Iraq, or establishing an indefinite, large-scale military presence were viewed as threats to third-party interests. Goals limited to restoring the preinvasion status quo, by contrast, were viewed by most leaders as benign.

Gulf states had a genuine concern for their sovereignty and the encroachment of American military influence.[20] Arab leaders reacted with fear and suspicion of ulterior motives, including a desire to exploit local resources and establish political dominance in the region (Khalidi 1991, 167; Azzam 1991, 481). Local governments were disturbed by Baker's repeated references, as he mobilized support behind Washington's policies, to the establishment of a "new security order" in the Middle East, fearing that this implied a new era of U.S. domination. Syria's defense minister, Mustafa Tlass, worried that "America has its intentions and Syria has hers. Our basic objective is the liberation of Kuwait. . . . But America certainly wants to remain in the region and wants to exploit Arab oil" (quoted in Hinnebusch 1997, 222). Similarly, Saudi Arabia's King Fahd suspected the United States of wanting to establish additional permanent military bases (Heikel 1992, 212), and others believed that weakening Israel's neighbors was an important goal of intervention. War aims that included toppling Saddam were entirely unacceptable to Arab regimes.

Those outside the region were worried about the precedent being set and with their own political influence in the Gulf. European governments viewed initial U.S. reactions to Iraq's invasion as hasty and aggressive (Frankel, *WashPo*, August 26, 1990). For example, the French hoped that Iraq would not be unduly weakened so that their trading relationship could be preserved, and France's defense minister warned that U.S. "hegemonic temptations" in the Gulf would threaten France's "freedom of choice" in the Middle East (Lhomeau, *Le Monde*, January 31, 1991). After losing Europe to the West, the Soviets had political and strategic apprehensions over U.S. motivations and long-term goals in the Middle East, a major Cold War battleground (Freedman and Karsh 1993, 162–65; Alexandrova 1991, 233–34).[21] As one Foreign Ministry official complained early in the standoff, "There are no guarantees that the United States will leave Saudi Arabia after the crisis is over" (Keller, *NYT*, August 31, 1990). Gorbachev told Bush during Desert Shield that he "was nearly as eager to get U.S. troops out of Saudi Arabia as he was to get Iraqi troops out of Kuwait" (Beschloss and

20. As Lake (1999, 235–36) points out, those states most immediately affected, such as Kuwait and Saudi Arabia, were effectively being asked to submit to protectorate status for the duration of the American military presence.

21. Indeed, many Soviet commentators saw the conflict as pitting NATO against the Soviet Union, especially since the Iraqi military had been largely trained and supplied by the latter.

Talbott 1993, 262).[22] The Foreign Ministry's Arabists, in particular, were "deeply suspicious of American motives in the Middle East, and dead-set against a U.S.-led military buildup in the region" (247).[23] The broader historical context must be understood: an ambitious and long-term intervention by the United States would have signaled the Soviets' waning influence in the region and its decline as a superpower.

While these concerns over U.S. aims were muted somewhat as it became clear that the policy was being conducted through the UN, the international coalition grew wary once again as U.S. forces in the region reached levels sufficient for offensive action. A turning point came on November 8, 1990, when Bush declared publicly that he would double his forces in Saudi Arabia, to more than four hundred thousand. Doubts among leaders, especially those in the region, were renewed. "The catalyst for this," writes Dannreuther (1991–92, 35), "was uncertainty over U.S. military intentions, as troop levels in Saudi Arabia began to reach their full complement."[24]

For most leaders, American muscle flexing was inherently threatening and undesirable. In September, as the crisis seemed to be moving toward a large-scale military intervention, Bush heralded a "new partnership of nations" and "a world where the strong respect the rights of the weak" (U.S. Congress 1991, 25). But these were costless statements that could not serve to reassure. As Scowcroft asks, "How could we act without it appearing as aggression on the part of the coalition?" (Bush and Scowcroft 1998, 383).

The Costs of Constraint

The leadership of the United States faced the problem of signaling its intentions, and the costs of IO constraint helped to do this. Aside from the operational difficulties that arose from putting together a multinational force, addressed above, American political and military leaders faced a number of very real constraints in

---

22. During a meeting with Bush on September 9, Gorbachev sought assurances that the U.S. intended to withdraw its forces from the region as soon as possible following the conflict (News Conference 1990, 1345).

23. In his memoirs James Baker (1995, 282) recalls, "Despite my assurances to Shevardnadze in Moscow three days earlier, his Arabists seemed convinced that the President was plotting a unilateral strike against Iraq."

24. By contrast, the Bush administration was apparently not worried about how the U.S. public would react to this dramatically augmented commitment. As one national security official reports, "We weren't thinking about domestic support when we decided to send more troops.... [W]e always assumed that we'd have the support to do what needed to be done" (quoted in Zaller 1994, 258). This reflects confidence in the rally effect and casts doubt on whether domestic politics more generally were driving U.S. statecraft during the crisis.

the form of policy changes and delays, as well as the extent of the coercive goals pursued. The Bush administration was constrained by the methodical decision-making process and influence costs that resulted from seeking approval during each phase. As one senior administration official lamented, "When you try to bring people on board, you have to listen to them" (quoted in Watson 1990, 20).

At two stages in particular U.S. policies were delayed and modified in order to mollify the Security Council: the decision to enforce the initial embargo on Iraq and the decision to launch Desert Storm. Resolution 661, passed on August 6 (see appendix), imposed a trade and arms embargo on Iraq, but the first enforcement measures (an Iraqi merchant vessel was boarded and discovered to be empty) did not take place until August 31. Though the United States—and Britain, whose navy was also patrolling the Gulf—was willing and able from the start to enforce the embargo, ships were allowed to pass through the blockade for several weeks. Scowcroft describes the dilemma faced by decision makers:

> The question was, do we move unilaterally to stop them, or do we wait and try to get additional authority from the UN? We had lengthy discussions with the British about it and of course Thatcher said go after the ships.... The French, on the other hand, while they saw the need to interdict, preferred explicit UN authorization to provide a basis in international law.... Baker was insistent that we wait. He convinced the President we would lose the Soviets (who were still adamantly opposed to using force) and perhaps the chance for a positive vote in the Security Council on enforcement if we went ahead unilaterally. (Bush and Scowcroft 1998, 351 52)

Colin Powell, the chairman of the Joint Chiefs of Staff, and Defense Secretary Richard Cheney agreed that, for political reasons, they should wait for UN approval (Woodward 1991, 284).

The French and Soviets worried that enforcement action would provoke retaliation by Iraq and thereby trigger war, and they argued that 661 alone could not be used as authorization. "For both countries there was the worry that the U.S. and U.K. were being too impatient.... Both the Soviet Union and France felt that more time should be allowed to explore the prospects of a political solution" (Dannreuther 1991–92, 29). The Soviets in particular were a major obstacle, delaying by at least ten days a new resolution approving force ("Soviets Back U.N. Blockade," *Toronto Star*, August 25, 1990). Beyond the P5, a majority of the Security Council argued that enforcement of the embargo required further legal justification, and Perez de Cuellar personally stated his objection to any military action at that point: "Any interventions," he proclaimed, "whatever the country, would not be in accordance with either the letter or the spirit of the United Nations Charter" (quoted in Connaughton 1992, 161). Ultimately, approval for enforcement came on August 25 in the form of Resolution 665, which authorized the use of force to disable ships destined for Iraq that refused to stop for inspection.

Waiting for UN endorsement to enforce the embargo was costly—to begin with, military and other supplies were getting through to Iraq in the meantime. More important, perhaps, there was a credibility issue, as Lawrence Freedman and Efraim Karsh (1993, 147) point out: "Here was the first potential use of force and the United States dare not back down lest it appear a 'paper tiger.' If it hesitated, inevitable questions would be raised about its readiness to stay the course." Moreover, waiting for another resolution raised the prospect of lost flexibility. Seeking further approval, Thatcher (1993, 821) complained to her U.S. counterparts, would "tie our hands unacceptably."[25] This fear proved well founded. China, the Soviet Union, and France insisted on strict wording for the resolution that did not simply state that "minimum use of force" could be used—the Americans' preferred syntax, which had almost unlimited interpretations—but rather spelled out that only measures "commensurate to the specific circumstances as may be necessary" could be employed. Moreover, there is some evidence that France and China explicitly sought Resolution 665 as a way to stall and impose limits on the use of force.[26] As one British journalist noted at the time, "the Soviet Union wanted to get as many constraints as possible on U.S. military action in the Gulf" (Doyle, *Independent,* August 27, 1990).

For U.S. decision makers, the next great debate—and delay—was over the launching of Desert Storm. Once again, Thatcher argued to Bush that going back to the UN was too risky; she worried that it would constrain the United States and Britain unduly. In seeking a further resolution, she argued, "We risk amendments"; therefore it was preferable to "go to war on our own terms" (Bush and Scowcroft 1998, 384). Cheney and Scowcroft similarly "worried that we would not be able to garner a consensus on actually going to war without some crippling amendments" (Ross 2007, 87). Of course, it was precisely the prospect of constraint and even outright rejection, a function of the Security Council's neutrality and voting rules, that made going to the UN so politically important. Bush chose to stay the UN course.

In the end, the United States waited four months from the date of the invasion until Resolution 678 authorized the use of force on November 29. Considerable diplomacy and consultations took place before the Bush administration could even propose language for a resolution, and UNSC voting rules (the dual

25. For more on Thatcher's wariness of Security Council-imposed constraints in the context of the Falklands War and Gulf War experiences, see Lepgold (1997, 76–80).

26. For more on the passage of Resolution 665, see Freedman and Karsh (1993, 143–50).

obstacles of supermajority and the veto) gave other governments considerable leverage. Washington was compelled to involve other Security Council governments in the drafting of 678 from an early stage (Ross 2007, 88). A senior Bush administration official described the difficult process of garnering the necessary votes: "We have an idea of the kind of resolution we'd like. But that's very different than presenting countries with draft language of a proposal that you are going to consider tabling in the council.... Each country is one vote; you need nine votes to pass a resolution, and some are in different places on this" (Goshko, *WashPo,* November 16, 1990). Indeed, the intended strategy of other Security Council members was to insist on a resolution authorizing force so they would have influence over the timing and scope of any potential combat (Friedman, *NYT,* November 11, 1990).

In addition to these influence costs, designed to shape the policy itself, favors and side payments were handed out by the United States to many countries, including at least Egypt, Poland, Syria, and Turkey, and Security Council members Colombia, the Ivory Coast, Ethiopia, Malaysia, the Soviet Union, and Zaire. Economic inducements included extending credit, forgiving loans, and making trade concessions. Egypt provides a striking example. Almost immediately following the war, Egypt received an IMF loan of $372 million at the urging of the United States (and despite a history of flouting IMF-imposed conditions). Shortly thereafter, in May of 1991, the United States and other members of the Paris Club, an informal group of the world's richest creditor nations, agreed to forgive half of Egypt's $20 billion in foreign debt to them. The U.S. Treasury also forgave 70 percent of Poland's $3.8 billion in debt to the United States in return for its participation in the coalition.

The Bush administration made political concessions as well, effectively pardoning China for the violent suppression of dissident students in Tiananmen Square the year before and relieving diplomatic pressure and sanctions on Syria for its support of terrorism.[27] While regional allies and great powers were needed for logistical and political reasons, some governments received attention simply because they were members of the Security Council whose votes were needed. Even small IO members are able to extract benefits this way. As one scholar (Weston 1991, 523) notes regarding the case at hand, "To ensure the votes of the Latin American and African delegations (Colombia, the Cote d'Ivoire, Ethiopia, Zaire), the United States is said to have promised long-sought financial help and attention." Yemen, by contrast, was punished for its lack of cooperation: the

27. For more detailed lists of the various gifts and political compromises used to curry support, see Lake (1999, 245–46); U.S. News & World Report (1992, 94–95); and Weston (1991, 523–24). A range of examples are discussed at more length throughout Bennett, Lepgold, and Unger (1997).

United States withdrew $70 million in annual aid following its "no" vote on Resolution 678.[28]

Side payments such as these are part of the "organization costs" of working through a formal IO. As one account summarizes Washington's efforts, "Bush would offer billions in aid and forgiven loans to help construct the coalition of nations against Saddam Hussein. The final accounting would be staggeringly high—in terms of both actual dollars and compromised principles" (U.S. News & World Report 1992, 94). Baker spent much of the month of November communicating with leaders and traveling to capitals, painstakingly organizing support by soliciting input, making concessions, and offering both carrots and sticks.[29]

The Soviets took the hardest line on Resolution 678. They pushed for more moderate language and more time throughout the month of November. Though Soviet foreign minister Eduard Shevardnadze and Baker had agreed on basic wording for the resolution as early as November 8, the Soviets insisted on more time for diplomacy (Freedman and Karsh 1993, 230–32). It was not until a visit by Iraq's foreign minister, Tariq Aziz, to Moscow on November 26, during which the Iraqi regime showed no signs of pliancy, that Gorbachev finally agreed to support 678. Even when a date for a Security Council vote was settled, while the United States hoped to set a relatively prompt deadline for Iraqi withdrawal, the Soviet Union and France insisted on a "pause for peace" as a condition of the resolution's passage. The Soviets asked for a January 31 deadline; the French compromise of January 15 was selected. The very idea of an "announced" war, it should be noted, represented a constraint, as U.S. planners had preferred a more flexible approach (Apple, *NYT*, November 14, 1990).

Delay was costly to U.S. military planners and policymakers for three reasons. First, it allowed Saddam to prepare for hostilities and consolidate his defenses, requiring the size of the allied force to be revised upward (Connaughton 1992, 114). The president expressed his concern in early January that, "Each day that passes, Saddam's forces also fortify and dig in deeper into Kuwait. We risk paying a higher price in the most precious currency of all—human life—if we give Saddam more time to prepare for war" (Bush 1991). Part of this waiting period was needed to move troops and equipment into position, but its duration exceeded by weeks the optimal length of time.[30] Another potential cost of delay came in the

28. After the vote on 678 in the Security Council, a senior U.S. diplomat reportedly informed the Yemeni delegate: "That was the most expensive no vote you ever cast" (Friedman, *NYT*, December 2, 1990).

29. On Baker's diplomatic tour, see Ross (2007, 87–92); Brands (2004, 125–27); and U.S. News & World Report (1992, chap. 11).

30. On November 22, during a visit to Saudi Arabia, Bush told the Kuwaiti emir that the United States was ready and pledged imminent action: "Rest assured, Your Majesty, we are going to fight,

domestic political realm. The antiwar movement rapidly developed momentum in January, including among Democrats in Congress. Delay was thus risky for Bush from a political standpoint, and it almost cost him dearly by jeopardizing the successful passage of an authorizing resolution (Mueller 1994, 59–60; U.S. News & World Report 1992, 206–7). When the vote was finally taken on Capitol Hill, coming only three days before the January 15 deadline, the margin in the Senate was dangerously narrow: fifty-two in favor and forty-seven opposed. Finally, delay had a potential international cost: some feared it would be hard to maintain a coalition over time as diplomacy and the fading memory of Iraq's transgression rendered the military option less appealing.[31]

Indeed, parallel diplomatic initiatives by the French and Soviets sometimes threatened the policy being carefully built by the Bush administration. France in particular repeatedly frustrated the United States by second-guessing its choices and slowing down the process with diplomatic maneuvering. For example, President Mitterrand made a speech before the General Assembly in which "he appeared to recognize the legitimacy of some of Iraq's territorial claims on Kuwait, and, no less importantly, suggested that the resolution of the Kuwaiti crisis would be followed up by a comprehensive peace conference on the Middle East" (Freedman and Karsh 1993, 167). This was exactly the sort of linkage that U.S. policymakers had tried so hard to avoid, especially following Saddam's August 12 peace initiative designed to link the Kuwait and Palestinian questions. The Soviets caused similar headaches when Gorbachev sent Yevgeni Primakov, his top Arab specialist and a conservative, to meet with Saddam Hussein in October. Primakov proposed a conference on Palestine as well and also explored the possibility of a mere partial withdrawal by Iraq, an equally unacceptable political solution from Washington's standpoint (Dannreuther 1991–92, 37). Beyond the delay created by such parallel initiatives, these are clear examples of influence costs and scrutiny costs, as other members of the Security Council sought to contribute to ongoing policy in self-serving ways and to question the Bush administration's methods. These episodes also demonstrate the heterogeneity of interests on the Council.

In the end, the wait endured by Washington was valuable politically: it satisfied European countries that hoped to further explore diplomatic solutions, and it allowed Arab leaders to investigate Arab solutions. It also showed that the U.S. leadership was willing to be constrained and to accommodate the interests of others in its approach to the conflict. Reflecting the success of this benign signal,

---

and we are going to fight quite soon" (Heikel 1992, 275). He does not seem to have anticipated that Resolution 678, passed a week later, would require an additional six-week wait.

31. This argument was made most prominently in a November 11, 1990, *Washington Post* editorial by Henry Kissinger.

Gorbachev told Baker in early November, "[We] have noticed that in this situation you are not losing your cool" (quoted in Aldrich-Moodie 1998, 18).

Status Quo Objectives

When the United States declared a cease-fire on February 28, 1991, after a mere hundred-hour ground war, reactions were mixed. Saddam was still in power, and another day of fighting would have led to the destruction of far more Iraqi equipment and the capture or killing of thousands more Iraqi troops. This abrupt end and what some perceived as signs of failure sparked postwar accusations that the coalition had not truly succeeded. Americans were especially disappointed that the demonized Saddam was still in charge, and within months of the war's conclusion Bush's popularity had plummeted. Early in the episode, various options, including invasion and the removal of Saddam, were on the table.[32] The IO-based strategy required that these more ambitious goals be removed in order to generate consensus in the UNSC. Saddam's gains would be reversed, restoring the status quo, but no more would be done. To be sure, there were other reasons to avoid a march to Baghdad and regime change,[33] but acquiring and maintaining the Security Council's support was a critical factor—it simply removed more ambitious goals from the panoply of options.

Bush knew it would be costly to accept and adhere to a limited UN mandate, as prewar polls showed a strong public desire to remove Saddam (Mueller 1994, 41–42, 54.). Yet U.S. leaders remained committed to limited goals and were willing to suffer the domestic costs because they felt constrained by the mandate and did not want to risk forfeiting the political benefits that came with it. According to Bush, "I firmly believed we should not march into Baghdad. Our stated mission, as codified in UN resolutions, was a simple one—end the aggression, knock Iraq's forces out of Kuwait, and restore Kuwait's leaders. To occupy Iraq...would have taken us way beyond the imprimatur of international law bestowed by the resolutions" (Bush and Scowcroft 1998, 464). George W. Bush confirms that his father felt constrained by the resolutions to do no more than force Saddam from

32. According to Bob Woodward (1991, 237), as early as August 3 (a day after the invasion of Kuwait) a meeting of the National Security Council included discussion of a covert CIA operation to overthrow Saddam. In the end, this took the form of stimulating resistance within Iraq, not direct intervention.

33. Bush and Scowcroft were wary of getting bogged down in Iraq, which they believed—presciently, given the post-2003 experience—would leave them in the uncomfortable position of being "an occupying power in a bitterly hostile land" (Bush and Scowcroft 1998, 489). Powell was concerned over who would replace Saddam if he were deposed; there was no guarantee that his successor would be more palatable. Others were concerned that weakening Iraq too much would alter the regional balance of power in favor of Iran (see Yetiv 2004, 219).

Kuwait (Woodward 2002, 329). On the decision to stop short of Baghdad, Powell (1995, 521) explains: "Our forces had a specific objective, authorized by the UN, to liberate Kuwait, and we had achieved it. The President had never expressed any desire to exceed that mandate, in spite of his verbal lambasting of Saddam." While General Norman Schwarzkopf, the United States' top commander in Iraq, had second thoughts about reining in the U.S. war machine after only four days of the ground war, he seems to appreciate the political rationale behind the decision:

> In the Gulf War [as opposed to Vietnam], we had great international legitimacy in the form of eight [sic] United Nations resolutions, every one of which said, "Kick Iraq out of Kuwait." Did not say one word about going into Iraq, taking Baghdad, conquering the whole country and hanging Saddam Hussein. That's point number one. Point number two—had we gone on to Baghdad, I don't believe the French would have gone and I'm quite sure that the Arab coalition would not have gone. The coalition would have ruptured and the only people that would have gone would have been the United Kingdom and the United States of America. (Quoted in PBS 1997)

While some consequences of pursuing more ambitious aims would have materialized even with an ad hoc multilateral coalition, the costs were ensured and exacerbated in the context of action channeled through a formal IO. To shed the aegis of the UN by pursuing more ambitious goals would have risked alienating states around the world, and more expansive goals would have been interpreted as unilateral and aggressive. U.S. leaders repeatedly asserted that their intervention goals were limited. Ambassador to the UN Thomas Pickering, for example, assured his colleagues that the "purpose of these actions is the liberation of Kuwait, not the destruction, occupation or dismemberment of Iraq" (UN Doc. S/22090, 2). Such statements might have been interpreted as so much cheap talk. Relinquishing some decision making to the Security Council, a costly diplomatic endeavor and a meaningful constraint on American freedom of action, allowed the United States to credibly signal that it preferred a limited operation (restoration of the preinvasion status quo) and was not motivated by hidden ambitions. U.S. assertions that it had limited goals consistent with the UN mandate were more credible than Iraqi arguments that the intervention policy represented an effort "to impose domination on the fate of a region" (quoted in "Mideast Tensions," *NYT*, November 30, 1990). A day after the war began, the Egyptian foreign minister expressed his confidence that it "does not have the purpose of destroying Iraq but of liberating Kuwait" (UN Doc. S/22113, 4). Consistent with hypothesis 2, UNSC involvement increased confidence regarding U.S. intentions and made leaders more willing to offer international support.

Transmitting Policy Information to Foreign Publics

From the time American troops began arriving to defend Saudi Arabia, leaders throughout the international community faced tough domestic political questions in deciding whether to support a U.S.-led intervention. Potential coalition governments knew that IO approval would help them sell support of the war to their own domestic audiences, and this helps explain their push for a UNSC-based approach to the crisis. For their part, U.S. policymakers clearly had foreign publics in mind when they chose to work through the Security Council. Scowcroft believed that the UN "could provide a cloak of acceptability to our efforts and mobilize public opinion behind the principles we wished to project" (Bush and Scowcroft 1998, 491). Hypothesis 3 captures this as a process of information transmission: IO approval serves as an information shortcut for publics as they assess the likely consequences of intervention. A policy that offers the prospect of collective international benefits will be more worthy of their government's support. Such information therefore allows third-party governments to back a coercive policy without suffering politically at home.

When they address domestic politics, scholars studying the role of IOs in U.S. military intervention typically focus on the domestic audience at home. With respect to the Gulf War, for example, Andrew Cortell and James Davis (1996) argue that the primary advantage of Security Council approval was to mollify opposition in Congress (see also Schultz 2003), and others focus on the role of American public opinion (Tago 2005; Chapman and Reiter 2004). This raises one of the alternative explanations offered in chapter 2: perhaps the decision to work through the UN was driven by domestic political calculations.

By focusing instead on the role of publics *abroad,* I am not arguing that politics in the United States were unimportant during the Gulf conflict—Baker (1995, 278) confirms that multilateralism benefited the Bush administration in terms of public opinion and especially in swaying the debate in Congress. Nevertheless, the evidence suggests that decision makers were not primarily motivated by political concerns at home when they channeled policy through the UN. Bush was clearly willing to proceed to war without majority approval and without a favorable vote in Congress. According to Powell (1995, 499), Bush had resigned himself to war in December, before Congress voted on the issue, and would have proceeded regardless of the vote's outcome.[34] In fact, it was not until after the UN had set a deadline and authorized force at the end of November (with Resolution 678) that Bush made a concerted effort to court Congress, which was a secondary

---

34. For a related discussion, see Bush and Scowcroft (1998, 446). Defense Secretary Dick Cheney opposed even seeking congressional approval.

concern (Yetiv 2004, 99). Moreover, as John Mueller (1994, 70) notes, "It was readily predictable...that the war would trigger a very substantial rally-round-the-flag effect," and, indeed, the percentage of the U.S. public favoring war shot up by about 20 percent at the onset of Desert Storm. By the end of the war Bush's approval rating had climbed to 89 percent.[35] The prospect of a rally may explain why the president was not especially concerned with domestic opinion. Robert Gates, Bush's deputy national security adviser at the time, recalls: "The president privately, with the most inner circle, made absolutely clear he was going to go forward with this action even if he were impeached. The truth of the matter is that while public opinion and the voice of Congress was important to Bush, I believe it had no impact on his decision about what he would do. He was going to throw that son of a bitch out of Kuwait, regardless of whether the Congress or the public supported him" (quoted in PBS 1997).

We can reasonably conclude that domestic political considerations, while important, were not a decisive constraint on how statecraft was conducted in the lead-up to the Gulf War.

Skeptical Publics Abroad

In most third-party states, publics were far more skeptical of intervention than they were in the United States. After all, they were being asked to support the coercive policy of another country. As the crisis escalated, many governments, having concluded that it might be in their interest to support American action, initially felt constrained by their publics from doing so. Domestic audiences in the Arab and Muslim world were the most dubious of the emerging policy. Western military involvement in the Middle East was a sensitive issue, stimulating memories of colonialism and drawing attention to the Arab-Israeli conflict. This made it very difficult for leaders to openly support U.S. intervention. Indeed, even before the initial invasion, as Iraq amassed troops on the Kuwaiti border, Arab leaders pleaded with the United States to take a low profile, fearing that the relatively strong U.S. reaction would only inflame the situation and embolden Iraq (Freedman and Karsh 1993, 51). Following the Iraqi invasion, no Arab regime dared to call publicly for U.S. assistance; even Kuwait's desperate call for international help was qualified with an explicit preference for an Arab solution.

For its part, the Bush administration was rightly concerned that support from Arab governments could be disrupted by their publics (Pollock 1992, 29). Dennis Ross, Baker's director of policy planning at the State Department, recalls the

35. For these polling figures, along with a discussion of the Gulf War rally effect, see Mueller (1994, 70–73).

administration's sensitivity to the plight of local regimes, who, in being asked to join with an outside power against a fellow Arab, "would be fearful of domestic reactions as a result" (Ross 2007, 79).

Among the Arab publics, even those who were strongly opposed to Iraq's invasion saw the U.S. role as a separate matter and were strongly opposed (Heikal 1992, 239). "For many Arabs," explains one regional expert, "the prospect of a U.S. military presence shifted the political argument from the issue of Iraqi aggression to the issue of Western neocolonialism" (Lesch 1991, 37). Early in the crisis, there was a clear negative correlation between assertive American involvement and Arab public support for action against Iraq (Heikal 1992, 225).[36] At least eight majority-Muslim countries, including Egypt, Jordan, Malaysia, Morocco, Somalia, Sudan, Yemen, and the Palestinian Territories, witnessed significant anti-American demonstrations (Telhami 1993; Azzam 1991). Equally important for Arab leaders was the mobilization of opposition groups, most of which were Islamist in orientation. Their position was initially strengthened by U.S. involvement (Azzam 1991, 478–79). The opposition parties in Egypt, for example, "threatened to mobilize their constituencies in the event of military alliances with Western forces" (Brumberg 1997, 104). King Fahd faced an influential religious-right opposition that bristled at the notion that their kingdom, the caretaker of Mecca and Medina, might host Western troops on holy Muslim land (Yetiv 2004, 34). Even organized groups that opposed Saddam, such as the Muslim Brotherhood, still objected to the American presence (Lesch 1991, 44; Azzam 1991, 476–77). Naturally, Saddam fanned these sentiments by portraying the struggle as anti-American and anti-Israel.[37]

The situation facing President Ozal of Turkey was representative of the types of constraints facing leaders in the region who were disposed toward helping the United States. Sabri Sayari's (1997, 203–4) assessment is worth quoting at some length:

> [D]omestic opposition to pursuing an activist policy against Iraq during the 1991 Gulf War was potentially the most significant political constraint on Turkey's contribution to the Allied coalition.... [N]ot only was Turkish public opinion unfavorably disposed toward Turkey's involvement in the Gulf War, but the opposition political parties, the military, the press, and even some members of the cabinet and the governing

36. Azzam (1991, 474) concurs, noting that the U.S. decision to send troops to Saudi Arabia "heralded the beginning of a growing opposition to the U.S.-led coalition in almost every Muslim country, though this opposition varied in strength."

37. In another tactic along these lines, Saddam proposed a peace initiative on August 12 that made any discussion of Kuwait contingent on Israel's withdrawal from the Occupied Territories.

> Motherland Party (MP) expressed varying degrees of opposition to Turkey's contributions to the coalition. Traditionally, Turkish governments had little difficulty generating societal support and domestic political consensus on major foreign policy decisions during regional or international crisis. The Gulf War proved to be an exception. President Ozal's strategy of aligning Ankara closely to Washington's policies was a source of criticism and political controversy from the early days of the crisis until the decisive outcome of Operation Desert Storm. In short, Turkey's contributions to the coalition were far from overdetermined, and they could easily have been much lower.

While Ozal was prepared to support the United States and preferred to do so directly with a military contribution to the coalition, his public and parliament "were not prepared to risk direct involvement in the Gulf for the sake of American favours or a higher international profile" (Hale 1992, 684). In the end, Turkey's contribution would have to be indirect, allowing the use of its bases and helping to enforce economic sanctions.

Arab and other regional leaders who were convinced that U.S. intervention did not pose a threat and hoped to offer support were therefore torn between international and domestic politics. A comprehensive study of Arab public opinion during the Gulf War (probably the most extensive in existence) concludes that Arab governments were in fact constrained by domestic attitudes and calibrated their policies accordingly (Pollock 1992).

The domestic political challenges facing leaders outside the region were qualitatively different but also important. As one newspaper characterized the situation in Europe in late August of 1990, while condemnation of Iraq was unanimous, "domestic political difficulties and wariness about jumping aboard a U.S. bandwagon are still causing division on the issue of military action outside a UN umbrella" (Helm, *Independent*, August 25, 1990). The French were initially skeptical about a military solution and the government distanced itself from the strong Anglo-American response. It was only after the passage of resolution 665 that a slim majority came to view their country's participation in the eventual use of force favorably (Evans, *Times*, August 31, 1990). In the British parliament, the opposition called for a Security Council mandate to enforce the blockade and to authorize military force to evict Iraq from Kuwait. While initially resisting, the government "came around to the view that politically, if not legally, a UN resolution was necessary to sanction the use of force against Iraq" (White 2003, 312). Opinion polls of Germans, already grappling with unification and the state of their economy, showed "little enthusiasm for any extensive involvement in the gulf crisis" (Friedman, *NYT*, September 16, 1990). Many Germans initially viewed the conflict as one over oil and held large demonstrations against intervention; the public was certainly opposed to any direct military involvement (Nolte 2003, 235; Hellman 1997, 170). For Germany's leadership, the Iraq crisis could not have come at a worse time in terms of domestic politics. With campaigns under way for the 1991 elections, the Green Party and the Social Democrats both vowed to block any move by Chancellor Helmut Kohl to support the Gulf coalition. Two-thirds of Italians polled in August were against military involvement (Binyon, *Times,* August 22, 1990). Spain dispatched ships to the region to help enforce the embargo but did so amid significant domestic opposition to any aggressive approach (Helm, *Independent,* August 25, 1990). With the UN's role still unclear, most Europeans were skeptical of a military solution and opposed toeing the American line, posing an obstacle to governments contemplating support.

Domestic constraints affected governments outside Europe as well. Public opposition and "deepseated pacifist commitments" in Japan divided the main political parties on how to respond (Unger 1997, 152). In both Australia and Canada, the governments were widely criticized at the domestic level for appearing too eager to support U.S. policy early in the crisis (Cooper and Nossal 1997, 282). The Soviet Union, in particular, was a key partner—indeed, its consent was virtually required for the United States to proceed. But Gorbachev and Shevardnadze faced myriad domestic challenges, leading them to insist that any decisions on military action be taken by the Security Council (Hoffman, *WashPo,* November 9, 1990). In the wake of Afghanistan, it was difficult to generate public enthusiasm for any overseas intervention, and Gorbachev was under immense pressure from the right to dissociate Soviet policy from the appearance of excessive U.S. influence (Fuller 1991, 58). From the perspective of the military and nationalist groups, Soviet involvement simply could not be in the form of a pro-United States policy.[38] The prospect of supporting action against Iraq, a traditional ally, triggered fierce attacks by hard-liners and Arabists in the Soviet foreign policy establishment against Shevardnadze, whom they publicly portrayed as pro-American (Alexandrova 1991, 232–33; Shevardnadze 1991, 202). Because Iraq and the Soviet Union had had close ties through the Cold War, the pro-Iraq position garnered much sympathy, and the prime minister, defense minister, and KGB head all preferred to "preserve the warm Soviet relationship with Iraq" (Beschloss and Talbott 1993, 247). Speaking to Baker, Gorbachev put a fine point on the problem: "You are asking the Soviet Union to approve the use of *American* force against a long-time ally of

38. As Alexandrova (1991, 233) points out, the "very idea of closer cooperation with the USA was and is alien and suspect to the Soviet military."

the Soviet Union" (BBC Television, January 17, 1992, quoted in Freedman and Karsh 1993, 231; emphasis added). The bottom line was that no group in Soviet politics could envision supporting an explicitly "American" military campaign, and diplomatic efforts by the United States to get the Soviet Union on board were frustrated as much by domestic opposition as by any international factor (Baker 1995, 282; Beschloss and Talbott 1993, 247).

These obstacles illustrate clearly that domestic publics abroad play a key role in episodes of military coercion, the central premise of hypothesis 3. In the Gulf War case, these domestic political barriers were largely removed as a result of the UN's involvement. Demonstrating directly what information was sent by UNSC approval and what information was received by publics is impossible. As outlined in the final section of chapter 2, however, various observable implications can help us assess whether IO approval influenced publics—and thereby third-party governments—by transmitting policy information.

Appeasing Publics through the UN

As U.S. policy toward Iraq became increasingly enmeshed in the UNSC, and certainly by the time Desert Storm was launched with authorization from Resolution 678, domestic opposition around the world had diminished to the point where few governments felt constrained. Despite significant lingering opposition, "predictions that the presence of Western forces in the Gulf would set the 'Arab street' ablaze largely fizzled" (Lake 1999, 243 n. 173). Governments with Arab and Muslim populations saw a UN-based approach to Iraq as key to overcoming domestic political opposition to the intervention. Egypt and Turkey, for example, strongly urged Baker to seek UNSC resolutions "to protect themselves against domestic political opposition" (Friedman, *NYT*, December 2, 1990). It is interesting to note that even those governments that supported Saddam throughout most of the crisis still endorsed UN sanctions and welcomed UN involvement (Lesch 1991, 36; see also Khalidi 1991, 162–63).

Once a few key Arab states, such as Egypt, Syria, and Saudi Arabia, decided that the risks of a more powerful Iraq were too great to countenance, and that Western intervention was sufficiently unthreatening, these leaders targeted their publics with a "coordinated information campaign [that] portrayed a uniform picture of events" centered around the multilateral nature of the intervention (Telhami 1993, 194). In this way, the pro-coercion governments were able to prevent Saddam from imposing his own interpretation of events—as an Iraqi-American conflict—by "controlling some of the variables that help shape Arab public opinion" (183). For example, UN cover allowed Egyptian president Hosni Mubarak to argue to his citizens that Saddam "is one man against the world" (quoted in Miller, *NYT,* November 8, 1990) and his pro-intervention stance was ultimately supported by 84 percent of the population.[39]

In the end, Gorbachev and Shevardnadze were also able to maintain enough domestic support—albeit barely—by pointing to Security Council approval and by framing the operation to the public as a collective mission. The UN became the rhetorical focal point of Soviet policy. For example, almost as soon as Desert Shield was announced, the Foreign Ministry spokesman justified his country's involvement by declaring, "The experience of many years shows that the most correct and sensible way of acting in conflict situations is through collective efforts and the utmost use of UN mechanisms.... We are for the Security Council to tackle this most urgent issue now" (quoted in Freedman and Karsh 1993, 125). The U.S. willingness to stick with the UN and its ability to achieve endorsements for action, especially through the embargo enforcement debate in August, lent credibility to the notion that collective interests were at stake, and this appealed to the Soviet domestic audience. In a sixteen-sentence joint statement released by Gorbachev and Bush, following a meeting in Helsinki on September 9, there were seven references to the UN or the Security Council. Calling upon "the entire world community," the two leaders insisted, "Nothing short of the complete implementation of the United Nations Security Council Resolutions is acceptable" (Bush and Gorbachev 1990). Gorbachev understood that his domestic audience would be influenced by knowledge of the UN's role. As one observer notes, the UN umbrella "made it possible for the Soviet Union to support the anti-Iraq coalition without any explicit connection to the United States" (Friedman 1991, 50).

Various Western leaders also relied on the UN to make support politically possible. Most observers agree that "France would not have been drawn into the Gulf except under the aegis of the UN" (Connaughton 1992, 106–7). Though Mitterrand felt that Article 51 was sufficient from a legal perspective, he did not believe it could justify military coercion to his domestic audience. "Article 51 doesn't mind public opinion," he explained to Baker. "Fifty-five million French people are not international lawyers. We need that resolution [to authorize the use of force] to ensure the consequences it will entail" (Baker 1995, 315).

In order to justify their financial and political support, in terms of both law and public opinion, the German and Japanese governments framed the intervention as a collective effort under the UN's umbrella (Kaufman, *Boston Globe,* September 14, 1990; *Daily Telegraph,* September 10, 1990; Purrington and A.K. 1991,

---

39. This figure is reported in "Poll Shows Majority Egyptians Back Government Policy," Xinhua Overseas News Service, January 20, 1991 (accessed via Lexis-Nexis), citing a poll conducted by the American Chamber of Commerce in Cairo.

318–19). Helmut Kohl was careful to point out that any German assistance was in support of a *UN* mission: "As a member of the United Nations, we cannot stand aside when the United Nations calls on us to take responsibility" (Schmemann, *NYT,* September 9, 1990). Though Japanese public opinion during the crisis was diverse and sometimes contradictory, it is interesting to note that those who supported a UN-centered role for Japan were generally opposed to cooperation with the United States and its forces (Purrington and A.K. 1991, 319–20). Prime Minister Kaifu was able to justify his country's financial assistance by arguing that support of UN-sanctioned "collective security" missions was desirable and constitutional. For the Conservative government in Canada, UNSC approval also served as a prophylactic against domestic opposition. "During the Gulf War, whenever it was challenged by domestic opponents to the war," writes Fen Osler Hampson (2003, 152), the Canadian government "justified its participation in the US-led coalition on the grounds that the enforcement action was taking place under UN auspices."

For publics in these politically important countries, Resolution 678 in particular "converted the *United States* policy of military coercion against Iraq…into a *United Nations* policy of military coercion" (Matthews 1993, 76; emphasis added). While support of—and subordination to—the United States was distasteful, support of the UN was politically acceptable and indicated to publics that collective interests were at stake. These processes are precisely what is predicted by hypothesis 3.

Framing the Intervention

The Gulf War was truly one of mass communications. The media, especially television, were "crucial in determining public perceptions" (Hayward 1994, 232), and both sides attempted to take advantage of this publicity. U.S. leaders in particular avowedly used the media as a diplomatic tool of warfare, and by almost all accounts the media were fairly cooperative, acting as a relatively passive mouthpiece (Parasiliti 1994; Hayward 1994; Bennett and Paletz 1994; Badsey 1992, 220). With their unique influence over the global media, they were able to communicate directly to other societies and geared their framing strategies to sending favorable policy information, justifying the intervention, to publics abroad. These framing strategies were perpetuated by foreign leaders in their own countries.

While I have already noted the prevalence of general references to the UN mandate in public statements by pro-coercion leaders, more specific framing strategies were used to emphasize the policy's benefits. In particular, U.S. and allied leaders framed their coercion of Iraq in two important ways: (1) the conflict was portrayed as an issue of Iraq versus the *world community,* and (2) the coalition was said to be *enforcing compliance* with international rules. Explicit Security Council approval was obviously necessary to facilitate both of these framing strategies. The details of leaders' framing strategies are further consistent with the information rationale for IO influence. Beyond references to UN involvement, in statements designed for public consumption U.S. and third-party leaders stressed certain characteristics of the Security Council to emphasize its neutrality—namely, that its membership was heterogeneous and representative of the international community. This evidence corresponds to the observable implications derived from hypothesis 3.

James Baker (1995, 278) understood the political importance of framing the fight against Saddam as a collective effort in the collective interest: "We believed it was imperative to keep the debate from turning into an Iraq-versus-the-United States confrontation, which would have made it more difficult to build and maintain a coalition." Accordingly, Bush presented a remarkably consistent message. In an August 22, 1990, news conference, he stated: "[A]s the votes of the United Nations show, this is not a matter between Iraq and the United States of America. It is between Iraq and the entire world community" (Bush 1990a, 57). He repeated this position before Congress on September 11: "This is not, as Saddam Hussein would have it, the United States against Iraq. It is Iraq against the world" (U.S. Congress 1991, 25).

As evidence that the collective international will was consistent with U.S. behavior and that broad interests were at stake, American leaders pointed to the votes of the UN Security Council. "These goals are not our own," Bush proclaimed before Congress. "They have been endorsed by the United Nations Security Council" (U.S. Congress 1991, 25). From the very beginning of the crisis, with the passage of Resolutions 660 (August 2) and 661 (August 6), which condemned Iraq and imposed economic sanctions, the discourse surrounding the standoff changed completely. After an August 6 White House dinner with Thatcher and NATO Secretary General Manfred Wörner, Bush offered to the press his view that "the will of the nations around the world... will be to enforce these sanctions" (quoted in Stanfield 1990, 1959). This language was designed to make it clear to publics that the intervention was more than a policy that reflected U.S. interests; rather, it would have broadly favorable consequences. Resolution 678 was particularly important for framing the coercion strategically. By the end of November, on the day after the passage of 678, Bush was taking full advantage of the Security Council's role in a statement before the press:

> We are not alone in these goals and objectives. The United Nations, invigorated with a new sense of purpose, is in full agreement. The

> United Nations Security Council has endorsed 12 resolutions to condemn Iraq's unprovoked invasion and occupation of Kuwait, implement tough economic sanctions to stop all trade in and out of Iraq, and authorize the use of force to compel Saddam to comply. Saddam Hussein has tried every way he knows how to make this a fight between Iraq and the United States, and clearly, he has failed. Forces of 26 other nations are standing shoulder to shoulder with our troops in the Gulf. The fact is that it is not the United States against Iraq; it is Iraq against the world. And there's never been a clearer demonstration of a world united against appeasement and aggression. Yesterday's United Nations Security Council resolution was historic. (Bush 1990b)

The passage of various UN resolutions allowed U.S. leaders to portray it to publics as a justified response to violations of international rules.

In the days leading up to the air war, the framing strategy intensified, producing two statements that stripped the United States almost entirely of any role. Following an unsuccessful meeting with Iraqi foreign minister Tariq Aziz, Baker spoke to the press. In a brief, one-page statement he referred four times to the UN in general and three times to the resolutions. While the words "Iraq" and "Iraqi" are used fourteen times, the United States is mentioned only once, left out in favor of the terms "international community" (used twice), "the twenty-eight nations which have deployed forces to the Gulf in support of the United Nations," and "our coalition partners." The following sentence is typical: "The message that I conveyed from President Bush and our coalition partners [to Aziz] was that Iraq must either comply with the will of the international community and withdraw peacefully from Kuwait or be expelled by force."[40] In Washington on the same day, Bush met with the press. In a somewhat shorter statement, the United States was once again mentioned only a single time, whereas Iraq was referred to ten times and Saddam three times. The UN and its resolutions, the international community, and the coalition partners were stressed repeatedly. Iraq could "rejoin the international community," Bush urged, "by its full compliance with all twelve relevant United Nations Security Council resolutions."[41]

U.S. leaders specifically stressed the independent character of the UN, especially the Security Council. The diverse composition of the Security Council at the time gave it considerable credibility. In addition to the P5 (the Soviet Union, France, the United Kingdom, China, and the United States), the ten rotating members were Canada, Colombia, the Ivory Coast, Cuba, Ethiopia, Finland,

---

40. Baker's January 9 statement is reprinted in Sifry and Cerf (1991, 172–73).
41. Statement reprinted in Sifry and Cerf (1991, 176).

Malaysia, Romania, Yemen, and Zaire. If a coalition of allies had sided with the United States, this would have conveyed little information; the consent of the Security Council membership, on the other hand, suggested that the United States was justified in its policy of coercion and was not pursuing narrow interests. The heterogeneity of the Security Council allowed Bush to credibly point out during his January 29, 1991, State of the Union address that "diverse nations are drawn together in common cause."

Before long, third-party governments began to play on many of the same themes evident in the American discourse. Thatcher was quick to frame the issue as inherently multilateral: "The fundamental question is this: whether the nations of the world have the collective will effectively to see the Security Council resolution upheld" (Office of the President 1990, 1182). Announcing that more British troops and equipment would be sent to Saudi Arabia, the U.K. defense minister, Tom King, stated that he sought "the implementation of the UN resolutions" (quoted in Freedman and Karsh 1993, 114). In a clear indication of the type of political information that was valuable to the British public, the House of Commons used the following language in a motion to justify its support of the war: "This House expresses its full support for British forces in the Gulf and their contribution to the implementation of United Nations resolutions by their multinational force, as authorized by United Nations Security Council Resolution 678."[42]

In a sixteen-sentence joint statement released by Bush and Gorbachev (1990), following a meeting in Helsinki on September 9, there were seven references to the UN or the Security Council. Calling upon "the entire world community," the two leaders insisted that "[n]othing short of the complete implementation of the United Nations Security Council Resolutions is acceptable." At a press conference following the Helsinki meeting, Gorbachev referred to "efforts being taken by the international community working together within the Security Council" (News Conference 1990, 1345). The Canadian government, a key ally for the Bush administration, repeated these themes. In a speech before the House of Commons following the passage of 678, Canadian external affairs minister Joe Clark summarized the situation facing Iraq: "It is now up to Saddam Hussein to determine whether the international community will have to use the authority of the UN to achieve our collective goal through the use of force" (*Toronto Star*, November 29, 1990, p. A1). Referring more directly to the informative properties of the Security Council, French foreign minister Roland Dumas described

42. House of Commons Debates, vol. 184, col. 24, January 21, 1991, http://www.publications.parliament.uk/pa/cm/cmse9091.htm. On favorable attitudes of Britons toward the UN, see Lepgold (1997, 81).

the body as "an expression of the community of nations as a whole and also of all that community's diversity" (UN Doc. S/PV.2943, 33). Speeches by Kohl and German foreign minister Genscher both portrayed the crisis as a confrontation between the "international community" and Iraq.[43] During Security Council meetings throughout the episode, representatives repeatedly referred to the UNSC and its resolutions as representing the "voice" and "will" of the international community.[44]

In other words, leaders were careful to stress the institutional characteristics that render institutional agents—ranging from legislative committees to IOs—most informative: a heterogeneous and representative membership. In the end, framing the intervention in terms of the UN was crucial in generating public support. References to the UN appealed to publics who were looking for shortcuts to make their assessments of the likely consequences of a coercive intervention. While public statements often tell us little about what motivates speakers themselves, they are potentially revealing with respect to their intended audience. Following from the two assumptions identified in chapter 2—that the information received by publics about foreign affairs derives largely from their leaders, and that leaders have some understanding of what information is persuasive to their publics—this evidence on public framing strategies lends further support to the policy information argument captured in hypothesis 3.

Finally, while a more expansive discussion is offered in chapter 6, a brief comparison with public opinion in the Second Iraq War, conducted with no Security Council mandate, is enlightening. While roughly 70 percent of western Europeans supported intervention going into the 1991 war, only 19 percent of Europeans polled by Gallup in January 2003 supported the later one (which began that March).[45] UN authorization seems to have been a key variable. When asked if the United States should intervene militarily in Iraq without UN approval, a plurality in only one European country (Slovakia) out of thirty agreed. When asked if their country should participate in a military intervention *with* Security Council approval, the number of pluralities jumped to fifteen. A Gallup International poll also conducted in January 2003 showed that few populations were in favor

43. See passages from two speeches quoted in Hellmann (1997, 172).

44. For examples of such statements by representatives of Canada, Ethiopia, Finland, France, the U.K., Malaysia, Romania, the Soviet Union, and Zaire at key junctures of the Iraq episode, see the following UN documents: 2/PV.2934, 13–15, 16, 21; S/PV.2938, 33, 38, 48; S/PV.2943, 33, 46, 66, 74; S/PV.2963, 79. It should be noted that statements made before the Security Council are carefully crafted and intended for public consumption rather than for debating purposes within the Council.

45. The first figure is from a Gallup poll conducted in October 1990, summarized in Hoagland, *WashPo*, October 25, 1990. The second figure is reported in Gallup's International Crisis Survey. See EOS Gallup Europe (2003).

of war. When asked if their country should support a war, majorities in only the United States and Australia responded positively; in the remaining thirty-seven countries there was no majority support. The prospect of UN authorization, however, raised favorable attitudes toward the war by 30–50 percent in most EU countries, and by 46 percent in Canada, 56 percent in Australia, and 29 percent in India (Gallup International 2003a). Absent UN approval, publics were highly skeptical of whether war was justified. The problem was most acute in the Middle East. Among Turks, 60 percent believed in the week preceding hostilities that the United States was fighting a war "against Muslim nations," while only 22 percent believed the motivation was the threat posed by Saddam (Pew Research Center 2003a). Publics had substantially more negative views of the policy than in the first Iraq war and generally did not find the stated coalition rationale to be credible.

In both wars, even when government leaders had decided that supporting the intervention was in their country's interest, they often faced domestic opposition. The Security Council's imprimatur was the most powerful tool for convincing these publics that the coercive policy was justified and worthy of support.

In this section I have offered indirect but suggestive evidence that channeling coercion through the UN during the 1990–91 episode served to transmit policy-relevant information to publics around the world, thus removing a domestic political barrier to third-party support. Many leaders were constrained by domestic politics from supporting the United States initially, but these constraints largely disappeared as the policy became firmly entrenched in the Security Council.

Assessing the Role of Legitimacy

This chapter has so far focused on providing confirming evidence of the informational role of the Security Council, while considering various alternative explanations for why the United States channeled its Gulf War policy through the Council—namely domestic politics in the United States, the burden sharing motivation, and endogeneity (i.e., that UNSC approval was a product rather than a cause of widespread international support). I have not directly addressed the most prominent theoretical alternative: that the observed effect of IO approval on international support rests on the importance of *legitimacy.* It is possible that foreign leaders and members of their publics view IO approval as conferring legitimacy on state actions, appealing to a norm that legitimate behavior is more appropriate and thus worthy of support. Indeed, the legitimacy logic is arguably the conventional wisdom for understanding the political effects of IO approval, and the notion of legitimation is often invoked to explain the role of the UN in the Gulf War. This argument thus merits additional scrutiny as an alternative to mine.

It is difficult to disentangle these distinct logics—rational information transmission versus normative legitimacy—since their broad effects are observationally equivalent: in both cases IO approval leads to more international support. And we should expect them to work alongside each other in the real world. However, there are distinct observable implications for both mechanisms that can help us assess their relative role in a given case. I consider three sources of evidence in this section: the design features of the Security Council, the behavior of foreign leaders, and the attitudes of publics.

Security Council Design

The legitimacy and information rationales make different predictions about what sorts of institutional design features generate the greatest legitimation effect. I have noted the consensus among scholars and practitioners that the UN, especially the Security Council, is a uniquely powerful legitimizer of state policies. Some argue that the UNSC stands as the *only* international institution that can legitimize the use of force (Boyer, Sur, and Fleurence 2003; Ku and Jacobson 2003, 352). Leaders covet its approval over regional endorsements, and publics are more likely to support the use of force if it is endorsed by the Security Council rather than by regional IOs or allied coalitions.[46] So we might usefully ask whether the Security Council's design is more consistent with an *informative* institution or with a *legitimate* institution.

I have already adduced evidence that the heterogeneity and representative nature of its membership make it a neutral and thus credible information provider to the international community. By contrast, the Security Council has few features of a legitimate institution or of an institution that creates legitimate rules. For example, it lacks the requirements of procedural legitimacy, such as transparency, democracy, and accountability,[47] and its decisions are inconsistent and based on ambiguous law (Schachter 1989).[48] We would not therefore expect it to be effective at conferring legitimacy through its resolutions. Indeed,

46. For evidence that this is true of publics, see Asmus, Everts, and Isernia (2004, 83–87) (analyzing data from the Transatlantic Trends 2003 survey); and Chapman and Reiter (2004).

47. Voeten (2005) offers a useful discussion of the Security Council's lack of procedural legitimacy. For a related discussion of the UN's questionable "input legitimacy," see Keohane (2006). On the procedural legitimacy of institutions more generally, see Barnett (1997); and Franck (1990). On accountability as a characteristic of legitimate institutions, see Keohane and Nye (2004); and Hurd (1999, 383).

48. Linking these concerns, Ku and Jacboson (2003, 358–61) argue that the Council fails the test of democratic accountability and that the lack of transparency in its proceedings means that the reasoning behind its decisions is often murky.

with specific reference to the case at hand, one law scholar (Weston 1991, 518) argues that "the Resolution 678 decision process was not legitimate in any rigorous or thoroughgoing sense" because it was highly politicized and was not firmly grounded in the principles of international law.

Moreover, if legitimacy is operating, we might expect smaller IOs with more homogeneous memberships to be more influential in generating support. Constructivist scholars show that norms and socialization processes matter most in more intimate, "in-group" settings (Checkel 2001; Johnston 2001). Ian Hurd (1999) and Thomas Franck (1990) both argue that legitimacy can operate only in the context of a coherent social community. We would thus expect common standards of legitimacy to be strongest among countries that share values and norms, such as within NATO or the OAS.[49] The Security Council, by contrast, has a diverse, worldwide membership—and one with no shared culture or values (Johnstone 2003, 456)—and yet its endorsements matter more in practice. In short, UNSC features are more consistent with an information function than with a legitimacy function, and the legitimacy argument cannot readily account for the Security Council's unique ability to generate international community support.

Leader Behavior

Turning to the behavior of leaders, I have already shown that U.S. policymakers, in seeking UNSC approval, were motivated instrumentally and not by an internalized desire to act appropriately. But perhaps foreign leaders were motivated differently. As Ian Hurd (1999, 387–88) notes, if legitimacy is operating, we should see leaders supporting the policy from a sense that it is the right thing to do rather than from a cost-benefit assessment of self-interest. What we see in fact is that leaders such as Gorbachev, Mitterrand, and Fahd were calculating the effects of intervention on their own domestic and international positions, as a function of U.S. intentions and their own publics' reactions. Broader security concerns were also in play. Egypt's Mubarak was motivated by a desire to maintain a regional balance of power (Brumberg 1997). Leaders in the U.K., Turkey, France, Germany, and Japan were partly motivated by fears of U.S. abandonment in the wake of the Cold War (Lepgold 1997, 74–76; Sayari 1997, 205–68; Grunberg 1997, 124; Hellman 1997; Unger 1997). France and Turkey were further motivated by a desire to share in the spoils of victory and to enhance their influence in the Persian Gulf (Bennett, Lepgold, and Unger 1994, 72–73; Sayari 1997, 207). These

49. Schimmelfennig (1998) makes precisely this argument.

material and security rationales overwhelmed any sense that confronting Iraq was simply the right thing to do.

Moreover, as I have already noted in discussing the costs of IO constraint, many leaders sought to extract side payments in return for their support. The examples of Egypt, Turkey, Syria, and the Soviet Union illustrate the types of incentives that helped bring and keep key countries on board. After Mubarak initially said he would not send troops to Saudi Arabia and did not approve of Western forces entering the region, the United States hinted that it would be willing to forgive Egypt's debt. Two days later Cairo shifted its position toward support of intervention and later sent troops to Saudi Arabia (Brumberg 1997, 105). Washington also pressured other governments to forgive Egyptian debt, and by the end of the war tens of billions of dollars in Egyptian obligations had been erased (Meital 1993, 197).

The United States offered Turkey—which provided diplomatic support for U.S. policy, mobilized tens of thousands of troops to its border with Iraq, allowed use of the Incirlik airbase, and was a crucial player in the economic embargo—assistance to modernize its military and promised improved access for Turkish goods to U.S. markets. As Turkey's fears mounted over the economic burden from its loss of trade with Iraq, the United States took the lead in convincing other coalition members and international financial institutions to compensate Turkey (Sayari 1997, 207–8). Finally, Turkey was allowed to resell a number of American F-16 fighter jets for a handsome profit (U.S. News & World Report 1992, 94–95).

Syria reaped diplomatic and economic benefits from supporting the coalition politically and with a symbolically important troop deployment. In October of 1990 the United States gave its blessing to a military intervention against a Lebanese general who sought Syria's expulsion from Lebanon and even convinced Israel to tolerate Syrian aircraft over Lebanese airspace. Washington also convinced the Saudis and others to extend about $2 billion in compensation to Syria. Finally, the United States and the European Community lifted economic sanctions against Syria tied to its sponsorship of terrorism, and Britain restored diplomatic relations (Hinnebusch 1997, 222).

After the September Helsinki summit with Gorbachev, Bush told the press, "There are many ways that we can endeavor to be of assistance to the emerging economy in the Soviet Union" (Hoffman, *WashPo,* September 10, 1990). In December, as an apparent reward for supporting Resolution 678, the White House announced a multifaceted aid package that included increased access to U.S. commercial credits, $1 billion in credits for grain purchases, and donations for medical supplies. The United States also brokered a deal whereby Saudi Arabia, the United Arab Emirates, and Kuwait provided $3 billion in low-interest loans to help prop up the ailing Soviet economy. These economic carrots were joined by political ones: various Gulf monarchies agreed to normalize their diplomatic relations with the Soviet Union, and the United States for the first time "agreed to welcome the Soviets as partners in any future Arab-Israeli peace process" (Hannah 1997, 255). The United States also turned a blind eye toward the Soviet crackdown in the Baltics (Atkinson 1993, 54).

As Iain Johnston (2001, 510) notes, such material motivations are inconsistent with behavior driven by social norms. Legitimacy-based support would have been automatic rather than calculated and derived from normative rather than material concerns (though, to be sure, these concerns were likely combined in many cases).

Public Attitudes

One might expect that foreign publics were more likely than leaders to have reacted to UNSC approval through legitimacy rather than information mechanisms. However, two sources of evidence suggest that the legitimacy mechanism was not operating in a decisive way for publics in this case. First, while UNSC approval led to more international public support for the U.S.-led intervention, opinion polls show that this support did not equally translate into a desire to actively participate in the intervention. Arguably, a normative motivation would be associated with a willingness to participate in what is perceived as a legitimate enforcement action, just as legitimate rules inspire a felt obligation to comply (Franck 1990).

Several European examples illustrate the point. In October of 1990, while 73 percent of French approved of Bush sending troops to Saudi Arabia and 75 percent approved the use of force, only 42 percent of those polled in early November approved of French participation. On the eve of war, while support for the use of force was high, 57 percent were opposed to French military involvement. Similarly, while most Spaniards supported Bush and favored the use of force, 60 percent were against their government's move to send troops and warships. Three-fifths of Italians favored the use of force and approved of Bush's actions, but only a third favored sending Italian combat troops.[50] Thus although there was support for the policy and the consequences it would entail, there was much less desire to participate. I argue that these attitudes are more consistent with a rationalist-materialist logic than with a normative one. Publics should

50. See various polls conducted by Gallup and Sofres-Le Figaro, cited in "UK Leads Europe," *Times*, October 19, 1990; "Europeans and the Gulf Crisis," *WSJ*, October 19, 1990; Canal Ipsos, February 11, 2003, http://www.ipsos.fr/CanalIpsos/articles/1067.asp; and Hastings and Hastings (1992, 579–80).

want and even feel obligated to participate in an action they view as legitimate. What we see instead is support coupled with a desire to free ride.

The second source of evidence again involves the public statements and framing strategies of leaders. If the legitimacy conferred by IO approval is important to publics, we should see leaders framing UNSC involvement in legitimacy terms. I analyze the content of the four Security Council resolution debates most closely associated with the question of coercion during the Gulf War conflict: the August 6 discussion of Resolution 661, imposing an economic embargo; the August 25 discussion of Resolution 665, authorizing enforcement of the embargo; the September 25 discussion of Resolution 670, extending and strengthening the blockade; and the November 29 discussion of Resolution 678, authorizing force.[51] All four resolutions invoke Chapter VII.

While there is considerable discussion of the informative properties of the Security Council, as discussed above, there is virtually no mention of its institutional legitimacy or the legitimacy of its resolutions. In 325 pages of transcribed speeches, the terms *legitimacy* and *legitimate* are used approvingly to describe the Security Council or its resolutions only once (by Russia on September 25). Ironically, the only representatives who address the issue of UNSC legitimacy are from Cuba and Iraq—and they do so to condemn its actions as *il*legitimate. The question of legitimacy was certainly on the minds of Security Council representatives, as they referred at least twenty-eight times to the legitimacy of the Kuwaiti government in exile and its authority. But despite their preoccupation with the concept as applied to political institutions, in these lengthy and carefully crafted public speeches there was seemingly no concern with stressing the legitimacy of the Security Council. This is suggestive evidence that they and their respective publics were not motivated primarily by legitimacy concerns and were not swayed by UNSC approval through legitimacy-based mechanisms.

This section by no means provides a test between these two theoretical perspectives, information versus legitimacy, and is not intended to do so. I have offered several observable implications of the legitimacy argument involving institutional design, the behavior of leaders, and the attitudes of publics, and in each case there are reasons to question whether conventional arguments regarding the legitimacy conferred on state action by IO approval tell the whole story. Especially with respect to publics, it is quite likely that the relevant actors are motivated by both a logic of consequences and a logic of appropriateness, and any complete theoretical account of the legitimation effect should include both components.[52] More generally, we are likely to learn far more about the role of

---

51. The relevant UN documents are S/PV.2933, S/PV.2938, S/PV.2943, and S/PV.2963.

52. For further discussion, see Thompson (2005).

international organizations in international politics by keeping an open mind to different theoretical perspectives, and by integrating the concerns of rationalist and constructivist scholars, than by insisting on rigid, simple theoretical explanations.

Channeling its actions through the UN was a key component of the American political strategy during the Gulf crisis. Security Council approval helped to lower the political costs of taking coercive action and, indeed, contributed to the widespread support by states in the region and beyond. Moreover, there is ample evidence to support the mechanisms theorized in this book. Confirmation of hypothesis 1—that when states work through IOs, this serves to lower the international political costs of coercion—can be seen in the evidence that Bush administration policymakers were motivated by an instrumental desire to seek political cover when they chose the IO option. I have also established that international support was causally connected to the UN stamp of approval. Put differently, it is very unlikely that support would have been high without this crucial variable.

Separate sections were devoted to hypothesis 2—that working through an IO sends a signal of benign intentions to third-party leaders—and hypothesis 3—that IO approval sends favorable policy information to foreign publics. Regarding the former, I outlined the concerns of other leaders over U.S. intentions and demonstrated that these concerns were largely abated as a result of the UN role. In support of the signaling logic, evidence was presented regarding the various costs of constraint paid by the United States, especially in the form of delays, influence costs that modified the policy, side payments required to generate support, and limits on U.S. freedom of action. Regarding hypothesis 3, the chapter first demonstrated that publics around the world were highly skeptical of U.S. intervention and that leaders in key states initially felt constrained by domestic opposition from supporting the policy. Public skepticism largely dissipated as the policy was channeled through the UN. For further evidence of the hypothesized mechanism, I analyzed the framing strategies of leaders (in the United States and in third-party states) to show that they stressed UN involvement and, more specifically, that they emphasized the features of the Security Council that render it neutral and informative. Relying on reasonable assumptions, we can conclude that leaders provide their publics with information that is politically meaningful to them—in this case, information that is more likely to result in support of the intervention policy.

The evidence presented in this chapter sheds somewhat less light on hypotheses 4, 5, and 6, on the conditions under which states turn to IOs and to the Security Council in particular. However, hypothesis 5—the higher the anticipated political costs of coercion, the greater the likelihood that coercers will turn to IOs—does receive considerable support. U.S. policymakers were clearly concerned about a political backlash and were not eager to deploy forces to such a politically sensitive region, one where governments and publics reacted with skepticism in the face of the United States' swift political response to Iraq's invasion. This stands in contrast to the Bush administration's unilateral intervention in Panama just a year earlier, where fears of international political costs were much lower for a smaller-scale action taken within the traditional U.S. sphere of influence. In general, the last three hypotheses are better assessed through more careful comparison with other cases, and they are thus addressed at more length in subsequent chapters.

With respect to questions of institutional forum shopping, it is important to note that the United States had few other viable institutional options since it was not a member of any regional IOs in the Middle East. Some NATO governments considered a more direct role by the alliance. At an emergency meeting of NATO foreign ministers on August 12, the organization supported Bush's strong stance and endorsed the Security Council's resolutions condemning Iraq but did not go so far as authorizing coordinated military action by the alliance. According to NATO Secretary-General Wörner, since the conflict was outside NATO's area, "there could be no action under NATO integrated command structures" (MacLeod, *Christian Science Monitor*, August 13, 1990).

In effect, then, the choice facing U.S. decision makers was a highly constrained one between the Security Council or no IO at all—either an ad hoc coalition or pure unilateralism. This affects what we can infer relative to hypotheses 4 and 6. While the Bush administration may indeed have valued flexibility and viewed UNSC-based action as costly in this regard, it did not have a less constraining regional option.

4

COERCIVE DISARMAMENT

The Interwar Years

Following the sound defeat of Iraq by a military coalition led by the United States and backed by the United Nations, the Security Council imposed a comprehensive peace settlement with Resolution 687, passed on April 3, 1991. The postwar resolution proclaimed the inviolability of the Iraq-Kuwait border, established a UN-monitored demilitarized zone between the countries, and declared Iraq liable for any damages caused by its invasion and occupation. Invoking Chapter VII, it also applied continued pressure on Iraq by renewing the economic sanctions and arms embargo laid out in Resolution 661 (with more humanitarian and civilian exceptions) and by requiring Iraq to declare and submit to the destruction of its weapons of mass destruction (WMD) and long-range missile capabilities. To this end, 687 imposed an inspections process to be carried out by the UN Special Commission (UNSCOM), in cooperation with the International Atomic Energy Agency (IAEA), to verify the destruction of proscribed weapons and to establish ongoing monitoring of related programs.

It was not obvious in the aftermath of Desert Storm that the United States would continue to channel its Iraq policies through the UNSC. Settlement terms and subsequent disarmament and containment strategies could have been established bilaterally or in conjunction with allies on a more decentralized basis. Indeed, David Hannay, the British ambassador to the UN at the time, was surprised to learn in late March of 1991 that postwar policy would be international organization-based. As he recalls,

> Up to that point, there had been no indication from either Washington or London that the post-war procedures would be handled through the UN, rather than from capitals.... I seem to remember [U.S. ambassador Thomas Pickering] appearing one day from Washington and simply saying, "Washington has decided to throw the whole thing to us." And that was what they did. Basically, the U.S. administration decided that the best way to handle the post-war continuation of this episode was to do it through the instruments of multilateral international law, and therefore to do it through a Security Council resolution.[1]

This approach, centered on the UN, represented a continuation of the political strategy that had marked U.S. statecraft since Iraq's invasion of Kuwait in August of 1990.

In fact, in some ways the UN would be relied upon to an even greater extent from this point. Its postwar role in Iraq was extensive and multifaceted. The Iraq-Kuwait Observer Mission (UNIKOM) played the traditional peacekeeping role of monitoring the postconflict border; humanitarian relief was coordinated by the UN, including the deployment of UN "guards" in northern Iraq to protect Kurdish refugees; and the sanctions regime was managed by the Secretariat and overseen and enforced by the Sanctions Committee, comprised of UNSC member states.[2] UNSCOM's role was the most dramatic, as it would be performing a vital operational role and dealing with the Iraqi government directly. Moreover, since Resolution 687 made the lifting of sanctions contingent on successful disarmament, the entire multilateral apparatus rested on the work of UN inspectors in the field and their leadership in New York. Inspections were the linchpin of the postwar regime.

From the U.S. perspective, Resolution 687 constituted a broad mandate to coerce and neutralize Iraq. In testimony in July of 1991, Pickering (1991) explained to Congress that "687 represents a comprehensive program designed to assure Iraq's fulfillment of all resolutions occasioned by its invasion of Kuwait and to strengthen the basis for peace and security in the northern Persian Gulf." Most of the United States' Iraq policies during the postwar years were linked to the mandate supplied by 687 and previous resolutions, though these links became more varied and tenuous over time.

---

1. Yale-UN Oral History Project interview with Sir David Hannay, September 21, 2000, pp. 2–3 (hereafter "Hannay interview").

2. For an overview of the UN's role in Iraq after the Gulf War, see Malone (2006, chaps. 4–6); and United Nations (1996).

This chapter traces U.S. statecraft and its relationship to the UNSC—both its resolutions and its member states—during the interwar period, with an emphasis on disarmament and the role of UNSCOM. Its most general function is to supply an empirical bridge between the two wars. Without analyzing the intervening years, it is difficult to appreciate the full consequences of the Gulf War and impossible to understand the origins of the Second Iraq War. This chapter is thus essential for understanding the twenty years' crisis to which I referred in chapter 1.

More important for our purposes, the interwar years provide an additional set of observations against which to assess the book's theoretical arguments. An intriguing aspect of this period is that the role of the Security Council—the extent and nature of its approval—shifts over time, sometimes in ambiguous ways. This fluctuation is an analytical inconvenience: it requires careful attention to identify the value of the main independent variable at a given point in time. International organization approval can be a matter of degree rather than a simple dichotomous variable. To capture this nuance, the chapter traces positions on the Council and perceptions of the prevailing mandate over time and links these trends to international reactions to the coercive tactics employed by the United States across the episode. This evidence is used to further assess hypotheses 1 to 3, on how IOs lower the political costs of coercion.

The interwar years also provide variation on the choices made by the United States as it decided how to channel its power. By exploring the evolution of U.S. policy and its relationship to the UN over time, we can shed additional light on the hypothesized conditions under which IO options are chosen by powerful states (captured in hypotheses 4 to 6). As predicted, these choices were largely a function of the anticipated political costs of acting unilaterally and of the perceived need for flexibility. As these variables changed, so did the role of the UN in U.S. statecraft.

The next section offers a broad overview of U.S. coercive policies during the interwar years, explains the focus on the inspections and disarmament regime, and offers an explanation—based on the hypothesized variables of anticipated political costs and sensitivity to IO constraints—for why coercion was initially channeled through the Security Council. Three sections then trace the history of the coercive disarmament regime, with an emphasis on growing disunity in the Council and how this affected both UNSCOM's ability to achieve its goals and the United States' incentives to maintain a UN-based approach. I then turn to the dissolution of inspections and outline the post-inspections coercive policies of the United States, beginning with the Operation Desert Fox bombing campaign of December 1998. I explain the diminishing role of the Security Council in these actions and its impact on international reactions to U.S. policy toward Iraq. A final section summarizes and returns to the book's main themes.

Channeling Power between the Wars

The Tools of U.S. Statecraft

The American coercive strategy in the interwar period aimed primarily at containing Iraq and was comprised of five related components (Byman and Waxman 2000, 25–29). First, the imposition of a weapons inspections regime—implemented through UNSCOM—served the purpose of disarming Iraq and also allowed the international community access to the country, thus providing an ongoing window onto its weapons programs. Second, sanctions, particularly in the form of an oil and arms embargo, were used to weaken Iraq's military power and its ability to threaten its neighbors. At the same time, sanctions limited Saddam's internal power by reducing his revenue and therefore his ability to buy off potential challengers and to make Iraqi society dependent on the regime's largesse. Figure 4.1 illustrates the comprehensive impact of the sanctions regime on oil exports during the first half of the 1990s (before the implementation of the Oil-for-Food Program, which allowed exports in return for food and other civilian supplies).[3]

These first two components of the coercive strategy were the most important and were intrinsically connected: only with successful disarmament and the establishment of a monitoring system could the sanctions be lifted. Indeed, paragraph 22 of Resolution 687 linked sanctions specifically and exclusively to arms compliance and not to any of its other requirements. This meant that the politics of sanctions were inextricably tied to the politics of inspections. Both

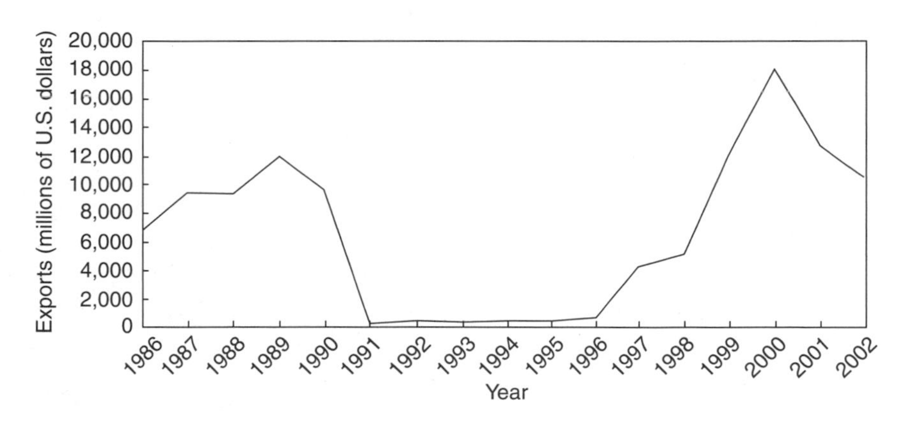

FIGURE 4.1. Iraq's petroleum exports, 1986–2002
Source: OPEC (2005, table 5)

3. The sanctions had a devastating impact on Iraq's economy in the immediate postwar years, reducing the value of Iraq's exports from $12.3 billion in 1989 to $10.3 billion in 1990, and then to $377 million in 1991—a thirtyfold decrease in less than two years. OPEC (2005, table 4).

efforts had multilateral support in the aftermath of the Gulf War and were channeled through the Security Council, with explicit authorization in Resolution 687 and the various prewar resolutions.[4]

These primary coercive tools, sanctions and disarmament, were complemented by three subsidiary components of the containment strategy: diplomatic isolation; the maintenance of tens of thousands of U.S. military forces in the region; and an internal containment strategy, designed to keep Saddam boxed in and to protect Kurdish and Shia civilians, which included the policing of no-fly zones in northern and southern Iraq (Operations Northern Watch and Southern Watch, respectively). While the United States referenced UNSC resolutions to justify these further activities, the link was less direct and became increasingly debatable—and the policies commensurately less popular at the international level—over time. By the late 1990s, a sixth coercive strategy emerged: an explicit—but indirect and largely passive—policy of regime change on the part of the administration of President Bill Clinton. This was entirely outside any UN mandate and epitomized the shift away from IO-based action.

While all these coercive tactics were important and related, disarmament was Washington's "central goal" (Pollack 2002, 33), and thus the weapons inspections emerged as the main focus of U.S. policy (Byman and Waxman 2000, 29). After all, it was because of its military capabilities that Iraq posed a potentially serious threat to its neighbors and to U.S. interests in the region. The effort to rid Iraq of its WMD was also uniquely important since the continuation of the whole range of coercive tactics hinged on the fate of the weapons search and on Iraq's cooperation with UNSCOM. The inspections regime is therefore the primary analytical focus of this chapter.

Choosing a UN Approach

U.S. policymakers believed that maintaining the extensive Gulf War coalition was the best way to contain and weaken Iraq following the war. As the war came to a close, Secretary of State James Baker (1995, 441) recalls, "We needed the coalition as much in the postwar period as we had before the war," and he indicates two reasons for this. First, the United States hoped to implement intrusive weapons inspections, an effort that would have to be conducted under the auspices of the UN. And second, the United States planned to maintain economic

4. Among the prewar resolutions, the most relevant were 661 (imposing sanctions), 665 (authorizing the enforcement of sanctions), and 678 (authorizing "all necessary means"). These are discussed at more length in chapter 3. The texts of these resolutions and of 687 are available in the appendix.

sanctions on Iraq for the foreseeable future. To be effective, sanctions required widespread participation, and the best way to assure such participation was through a continued UN mandate.[5] Thus, as Baker (441) further explains, "To put Saddam Hussein in that cage, so to speak, we needed implementation of existing U.N. resolutions (and an additional U.N. resolution enacted), and we needed all our coalition partners to be with us to achieve this."

Post-Gulf War policy was therefore channeled through the UN for pragmatic political reasons. Consistent with hypothesis 1, the primary motivation was to reduce the political costs of neutralizing Iraq; the UN would supply a cover for the allies' coercive tactics. All the factors that led the Bush administration, leading up to the Gulf War, to fear the international political costs of acting alone in the Middle East were still relevant—indeed, these potential costs rose as the duration of American involvement grew. This provided an incentive for the United States to work through the UN (following the logic of hypothesis 5). In addition, there were purely practical considerations: multilateral cooperation was needed in order to implement effective sanctions and to isolate Saddam diplomatically. In sum, the best—and probably the *only*—way to maintain the anti-Iraq coalition and widespread political support was to continue to operate through the Security Council.

To further illustrate the importance of anticipated international political costs in driving U.S. statecraft, a comparison with the postwar efforts to provide humanitarian assistance to Kurds and the Shiites in Iraq is instructive. These interventions were for the most part *not* channeled through the UN. This occurred, I argue, because the anticipated political costs of intervening were low given the policy's widely supported humanitarian goals—in contrast to the largely military and geopolitical goals of sanctions and disarmament.

In the aftermath of the Gulf War, a coalition of Western states initiated two actions in response to the plight of the Kurds: they established a no-fly zone over northern Iraq, and they deployed ground forces inside Iraq to establish safe havens that were off-limits to Iraqi forces. The first action was conducted by planes from the United States, France, and Britain. The latter, named Operation Provide Comfort, involved more than thirteen thousand soldiers from Australia, France, Italy, the Netherlands, Spain, Britain, and the United States. The primary aim of these efforts, begun in mid-April of 1991, was to provide aid to Kurdish refugees and to facilitate their return home. A similar no-fly zone was established a year later in southern Iraq to help protect the persecuted Shiites.

---

5. Studies of economic sanctions show that effectiveness is best achieved with multilateral participation in conjunction with the involvement of a multilateral organization. Without an IO role, sanctions coalitions tend to be leaky and to dissipate over time. Miers and Morgan (2002); Drezner (2000).

These partly coercive actions represented a substantial intervention into the domestic affairs of Iraq and were not explicitly endorsed by the Security Council. The United States, France, and the U.K. justified intervention in terms of Resolution 688, passed on April 5, 1991, which demanded that Iraq immediately end repression, especially of the Kurds, and insisted "that Iraq allow immediate access by international humanitarian organizations to all those in need of assistance in all parts of Iraq" (see appendix). However, 688 did not invoke Chapter VII, was not intended by most UNSC governments to authorize additional military intervention (Wheeler 2000, 141–46), and even contained language reaffirming "the sovereignty, territorial integrity and political independence of Iraq." Thus the U.S.-led humanitarian intervention was of questionable legality and was not approved by the UN in a meaningful sense (Gray 2002, 9–11; Franck 1995, 235–36; Malanczuk 1991).

Despite this lack of authorization, there was "little difficulty in welcoming the allied military intervention in Iraq" to protect civilians (Malanczuk 1991, 123). Because the actions were taken against severe repression and human rights violations, they enjoyed a sort of built-in legitimacy across the international community. The Americans, British, and French were careful to justify the interventions on humanitarian grounds and used the forum of the Security Council to describe in great detail the Iraqi regime's transgressions in the north and south (see UN Doc. S/PV.3105). The Bush administration took advantage of an emerging international norm that increasingly recognized that sovereignty could be compromised to uphold human rights. In October of 1991, the deputy assistant secretary of state for international organization affairs, John S. Wolf, reported to Congress that "Saddam Hussein's continued brutality against his own people has driven many hitherto reluctant countries to concede that there may indeed arise circumstances in which extraordinary humanitarian needs compel the international community's intervention in the internal affairs of a sovereign state" (U.S. House of Representatives 1991, 192). The media also played an important role in swaying public opinion around the world. As Nicholas Wheeler (2000, 140) notes, "publics were bombarded with images of the human suffering of the Kurds" and this allowed—even encouraged—governments to support U.S. actions. Consistent with hypothesis 5, anticipation of relatively low international political costs gave Washington the flexibility to channel its humanitarian policies outside the UN, though there was certainly an effort to maintain as broad a coalition as possible.

While sensitivity to international political costs was an important motivation for the United States, hypothesis 4 points us to the additional consideration of policy flexibility: a powerful state is most willing to entangle its policy in an IO when concerns over flexibility are sufficiently low. Hypothesis 6 presents this as a likely condition for UNSC-based action in particular.

The United States was willing to accept the constraints of working through the UN for two reasons. First, the postwar efforts to contain Saddam were not especially urgent. Saddam no longer represented an immediate threat, and the twin policies of disarmament and sanctions were to be imposed for an indefinite duration. Second, and most important, the Security Council was seen as a friendly and like-minded forum in the wake of the Gulf War. To be sure, there were concerns by some in Washington about maintaining a UN-based approach. Testifying before Congress in April of 1991, Assistant Secretary of State John R. Bolton referred to the postwar period as "an important testing time for the United Nations." He continued: "Each day that goes by brings new questions on the appropriate role for the United Nations in this era, and new questions on whether the United Nations can perform these new roles" (U.S. House of Representatives 1991, 24).

These fears were assuaged largely because there was a sense that working through the Security Council, at least for the foreseeable future, would not impose costly constraints on U.S. policy. As Bolton noted, referring to Resolution 687, "The fact that a sweeping majority of the Security Council's members could agree to such a complex and far-reaching resolution bodes very well." This gave Bolton confidence that the United States was facing "a new and more responsible UN, a UN capable of meeting the challenges of the 21st century." When pressed by a congressman concerned that the UN did not have the collective will to implement 687, Bolton responded: "I think...that one of the things that has been most impressive has been the unity of purpose of the international community as reflected in the Security Council. And I think that it is that continued unity of purpose that gives us confidence that we can continue to support the United Nations in the actions that it has taken" (U.S. House of Representatives 1991, 24, 26, 106). Testifying in October of 1991, Assistant Secretary of State Wolf estimated (quite presciently), "For the next few years to come, it looks like there is a group in the Security Council who will hold similar views" (U.S. House of Representatives 1991, 205). A year later, the new U.S. ambassador to the UN, Edward J. Perkins, reported to Congress that, despite resistance by Iraq to the inspections and sanctions, these policies "continue to have the solid support of the members of the Council" (U.S. House of Representatives 1992, 91).

U.S. policymakers did not anticipate that the inspections process would take many years. Indeed, there was a sense among most governments and UN Secretariat staff that it would take only a matter of months (Trevan 1999, 86), and Saddam was apparently equally optimistic (Cockburn and Cockburn 1999, 96).[6] The

6. Formally, the Security Council established a 120-day timetable for the inspections and destruction of weapons, after which the situation was to be reviewed. The initial report by the

leadership in Washington also misjudged Saddam's ability to hold on to power domestically; many anticipated that he would be overthrown shortly after the war. Given that the Security Council appeared to be united in the foreseeable future behind the goal of keeping pressure on Saddam and removing his WMD threat, channeling policy through the UN was not viewed as risking excessive costs of IO constraint. At the very least, these potential constraints were not outweighed by the substantial political benefits of maintaining the UN's stamp of approval. Thus the two conditions for channeling coercion through the UN, as outlined in chapter 2 and captured in hypothesis 6, were met in the post-Gulf War setting: the potential international political costs were still high while the anticipated costs of being constrained by the UN were relatively low.

Fading Council Approval

For the first few years after the Gulf War, the UNSC mandate allowed the United States to pursue a coercive sanctions and disarmament policy that was both efficacious and politically cost-effective. Over the course of the 1990s, however, the UNSC imprimatur on U.S. actions became progressively weaker for two reasons. First, the passage of time itself made the link between the relevant resolutions, especially 678 and 687, and coercive activities of the United States more tenuous. Just as repeated affirmations of law over time can reify its importance and normative sway on states,[7] the *failure* of reaffirmation over time can weaken its influence. Second, the United States increasingly chose coercive tools—namely, the use and threat of military force and later regime change—that were at best implicitly justified by the relevant resolutions. While sanctions and inspections were very clearly mandated by the UNSC, air strikes to enforce Iraqi compliance with these arrangements and to defend no-fly zones required invocations of implicit approval rather than explicit authorizations. Regime change was a plainly unilateral initiative. By the end of the decade, the passage of time and the shifting mixture of coercive tools rendered ambiguous the UN umbrella over U.S. activities.

The episode illustrates well the trade-offs that come with Security Council independence. The range of interests represented, combined with the operative decision-making rules, made it possible for other Council members to frustrate U.S. goals and to increase the costs of constraint. Chapters 2 and 3 demonstrate the

---

secretary-general on how UNSCOM should be structured referred to its functions as "time-limited" and suggested that "the whole exercise will be carried out in the shortest possible time" (UN Doc. S/22508).

7. This is a central principle of international legal scholarship and is the basis in particular of customary law. See Malanczuk (1997, 39–43).

theoretical and practical importance of Security Council diversity in producing a legitimation effect through the transmission of information to the international community. The inspections episode, however, illustrates the downside of diversity. Even when the UNSC reaffirmed the basis for coercive actions against Iraq, the signals conveyed to the international community weakened over time as unanimous votes were clouded by abstentions and as P5 statements and behavior outside the Council increasingly contradicted their votes inside. As the stamp of approval faded, so did the clarity of the signal regarding the benefits and consequences of the coercive policies. At the same time, the leadership of the United States increasingly demonstrated that it was willing to act parallel to—and sometimes in contradiction of—the UNSC. This produced a diminishing sense that the superpower was meaningfully constrained, and the signal to other leaders of restraint and limited intentions was commensurately weakened.

This result is consistent with the information transmission theory of IO legitimation: diminishing UNSC authorization produces weaker signals to the international community, which in turn increases the political costs of taking coercive actions.

The episode also points to an extension of the argument regarding IO membership diversity. To perform the disarmament task, the Council delegated authority to UNSCOM. Despite considerable achievements in ridding Iraq of its weapons (made fully evident only following the 2003 invasion), the inspections regime ultimately failed: Iraq was never certified as weapons-free by the UN, and war was not averted. As I demonstrate in this chapter, UNSCOM's frustrations were due to both Iraq's obstructionist tactics and growing divisions on the Council, which increasingly served to undermine UNSCOM and its mission. Over time, UNSC disunity had the effect of diminishing UNSCOM's legitimacy, strengthening Iraq's resolve in defying the inspectors, and reducing international community support for the disarmament task. Thus while preference heterogeneity is virtuous when the Security Council acts as an agent of the international community, it is a potential liability when the Council itself delegates and acts as a collective principal.[8] I return to this theme in the concluding section.

In the sections that follow, I do not attempt to provide a comprehensive history of the inspections saga in Iraq.[9] Rather, the case study focuses on the evolution of U.S. policy and its varying relationship to the Security Council. I also examine the relationship between the Council and UNSCOM to assess the

8. On some of the complications arising from collective principals in international settings, see Nielson and Tierney (2003); and Thompson (2006b).

9. The best general histories of the inspections are Krasno and Sutterlin (2003) and Pearson (1999). Insider accounts include Blix (2004); Butler (2000); Trevan (1999); and Ritter (1999, 2005).

influence of the former's uneven support for the latter and for the disarmament task more generally.

The Postwar Honeymoon

In the glow of the coalition's success in the Gulf War, Security Council members were determined to rid Iraq of its weapons and to remove any potential threat posed to the region. The P5 were able to agree on a series of coercive measures, including continued sanctions and a comprehensive and indefinite disarmament regime with UNSCOM at its center. Section C of Resolution 687 identified four types of weapons as proscribed: nuclear, chemical, biological, and ballistic missiles with a range greater than 150 kilometers. It required Iraq to declare the locations and types of the proscribed weapons, to "unconditionally accept the destruction, removal, or rendering harmless, under international supervision" of such weapons, and to accept a system of ongoing monitoring and verification (OMV) to ensure that it remain WMD-free into the future. To implement these requirements, the resolution called for the establishment of a "Special Commission" as the primary inspections, disarmament, and monitoring body and required Iraq to cooperate with UNSCOM—and with the IAEA, which worked alongside but formally subordinate to the Commission, on the nuclear side—by declaring and yielding all prohibited weapons. In May of 1991, Rolf Ekeus, a respected Swedish diplomat, was chosen as the first executive chairman of UNSCOM, with Robert Galluci of the United States as his deputy. The first inspections began in June.

A series of subsequent resolutions throughout 1991 mandated that Iraq should ultimately be responsible for all costs associated with inspections and disarmament (Resolution 699, passed on June 7);[10] required that Iraq grant "immediate, unconditional and unrestricted access," as well as logistical support, to UN inspectors (Resolution 707, passed on August 15); and clarified UNSCOM's right to conduct unannounced inspections (Resolution 715, passed on October 11). By most accounts, UNSCOM was set up as "an efficient and effective executive body" (Pearson 1999, 12) with wide latitude to achieve its goals. It was explicitly subordinated to the Security Council and not to the secretary-general or the UN

10. As a practical matter, however, UNSCOM was dependent on cash contributions from UN member states until the implementation of the Oil-for-Food Program, which set aside a small percentage (0.8) of Iraq's oil revenue to fund inspections. These funds, about $30 million per year, became available beginning in early 1997. UNSCOM also relied on member states for various in-kind contributions, including the provision of aircraft (including German helicopters and an American U-2 spy plane), equipment (such as computers), and intelligence analysis.

membership as a whole; indeed, the Secretariat and the General Assembly were intentionally kept out of the loop, except for some administrative support from the former (Krasno and Sutterlin 2003, 5). The Commission's executive chairman was given substantial discretion to run operations to maximize effectiveness and without seeking constant approval. For example, he could designate for inspections any location he chose, including those not declared by Iraq, and could make organizational decisions and hire personnel—mostly seconded by governments—as needed to achieve UNSCOM's objectives.[11] In sum, UNSCOM was given "far-reaching authority" in ways that were "unprecedented for a multilateral verification organization or a body of the UN" (de Jonge Oudraat 2002, 149).

At the dawn of the UNSCOM era there was considerable agreement in the Council, among permanent and nonpermanent members alike, that Iraq's possession of WMD represented a potential threat to international peace and should be kept in check. This unity was buttressed by a newfound sense of purpose for the Security Council as manifested in the Gulf War experience. UNSCOM and Ekeus thus received strong backing from the Council initially. There was consensus behind the plan developed in 1991, which was truly a multilateral effort. Pickering describes the process of drafting resolution 687: "The effort was to try to work out all problems before introduction to the other members of the Council, and then, as we did with the Iraq resolution [i.e., 678], receive their proposals and ideas for change; try to incorporate as many as we could, and to build a consensus."[12] Hannay recalls that the P5 "met almost constantly for about three weeks to put it together."[13] Following the conclusion of the Gulf War, as Krasno and Sutterlin (2003, 9) characterize the situation, "The Security Council demonstrated that it had the unity, the will, and the capacity—for a while—to act against this threat."

Once the inspections began, this unity was fueled by Iraq's defiance. Figure 4.2 shows instances of Iraqi obstruction of inspectors and the responses by the Security Council in the form of either resolutions or presidential statements. It demonstrates that during the first few years, Iraqi tactics were matched by Council denunciations. In the early 1990s, these denunciations came largely in the form of strongly worded and unanimous resolutions, backed by the threat of force.

UNSCOM quickly discovered that Iraq was hiding documents and materials. Combined with the evasive and belligerent rhetoric of Iraqi officials, this

11. Most UNSCOM staff felt that this hiring system was effective at ensuring specialized expertise appropriate to each mission. Author's interview with a former UNSCOM commissioner and chief inspector, January 12, 2006.

12. Yale-UN Oral History Project interview with Thomas Pickering, April 3, 2000, p. 5.

13. Hannay interview, p. 3

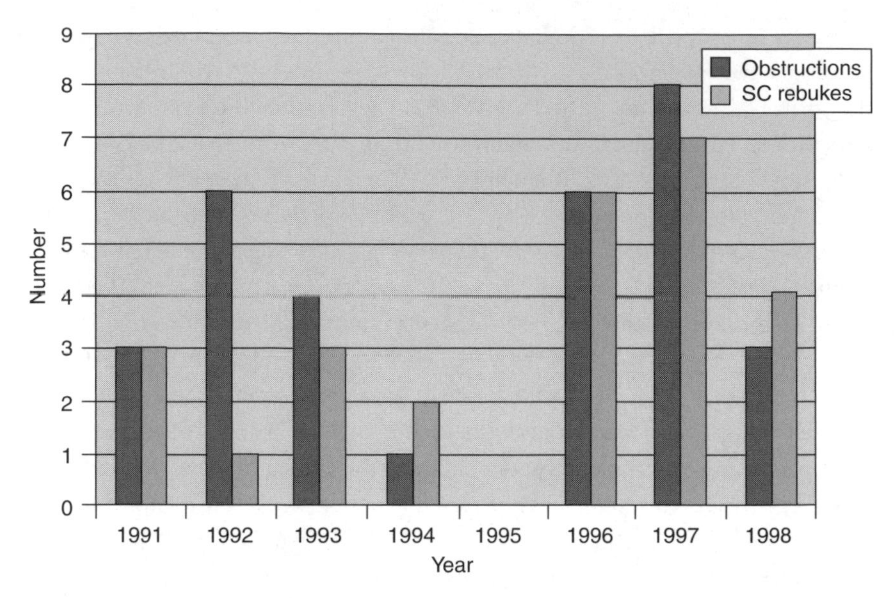

FIGURE 4.2. Iraqi obstructions and Security Council rebukes, 1991–1998
Source: Compiled from Pearson (1999)

served to solidify Security Council resolve, especially through the end of 1992. This resolve was reflected in several early resolutions, including 707 and 715, harshly condemning Iraq and both reiterating and extending the cease-fire conditions. Beyond the resolutions, the United States, the U.K., and France threatened bombing several times during the first two years and received approval from other Council members for doing so.

An episode in September of 1991 is illustrative. When IAEA inspectors found documents revealing undeclared efforts to develop nuclear weapons, Iraqi officials confiscated them. The next day the inspectors found more documents and refused to turn them over, prompting Iraq to prevent them from leaving the site. The standoff came to an end following a forceful statement on September 24 from the president of the Security Council condemning Iraq and stating that "the Council reiterates that the Special Commission, acting under the authority of the Council, is the sole judge of the definition of the documents, sites or material subject to inspection" (United Nations 1996, 319). This was backed by threats of force from the United States, seconded by the U.K. and France.

In February of 1992, the minister of foreign affairs proclaimed that Iraq should be allowed to retool weapons-related material and equipment for civilian purposes, rather than destroy them, as UNSCOM was preparing to do. In March, in response to this and other noncompliant actions, UNSC members issued an additional statement admonishing Iraq with a single voice: "In the view of the Security Council, the Government of Iraq has not yet complied fully and unconditionally with those obligations, must do so and must immediately take the appropriate actions in this regard" (UN Doc. S/23709). A month later the foreign affairs minister demanded a halt to UNSCOM's aerial surveillance flights "in order to avoid any unfortunate incidents" that might "endanger the aircraft itself and its pilot" (United Nations 1996, 84). This thinly veiled threat was met with anger from UNSC members, who issued a statement demanding Iraqi assurances that UNSCOM's rights would be respected and threatening "serious consequences" (UN Doc. S/23803). Two days later Iraq reversed its position and assured the Council that UNSCOM aircraft were safe. Following its refusal to allow access to the archives of the Ministry of Agriculture in July of 1992, Iraq again backed down in the face of enforcement threats from Council members.

Thus, during this early period the members of the Council showed a willingness to act in concert with one another and in support of UNSCOM. Edward J. Perkins, the successor to Pickering as U.S. ambassador to the UN, was able to report to Congress in July of 1992 that, despite "Iraq's uncooperative behavior on most aspects of Resolution 687," the sanctions and inspections regime "continues to have the solid support of members of the Council" (U.S. House of Representatives 1992, 91). Moreover, key regional allies, such as Turkey and Saudi Arabia, were supportive of UNSCOM and of adopting a tough stance against Iraq when it came to inspections (Waxman and Byman 2000, 41). The UN-based approach was key to this support. According to Hannay, the United States and its allies "had not overstepped 678, and therefore there were no reasons to suspect them, as subsequently suspicion has been aroused."[14]

Small fissures began to show in the Council's unity in early 1993, when Iraq threatened to shoot down UNSCOM planes flying from its staging center in Bahrain and suggested instead that they either use Iraqi aircraft or approach by land from Amman. This was unacceptable from UNSCOM's point of view: it would make short-notice inspections impossible and would increase opportunities for eavesdropping by Iraq. When Ekeus turned to the Security Council for support, the French and British ambassadors flinched, initially urging Ekeus to accept Iraq's conditions.

After Washington applied pressure on Paris and London, however, unity was maintained, and the Security Council issued a statement calling Iraq's demands an "unacceptable and material breach" of existing resolutions and warning of "serious consequences" (UN Doc. S/25081). Iraq persisted in denying UNSCOM's unfettered right to fly and, at the same time, conducted incursions on the

14. Ibid., p. 7.

Kuwaiti side of the postwar demilitarized zone (apparently to rescue equipment left behind). The Council issued a further statement on January 11 (UN Doc. S/25091), once again labeling the behavior a "material breach" and threatening "serious consequences." Invoking this statement, the United States, the U.K., and France conducted bombing raids on targets in southern Iraq, including a weapons production facility. Iraq modified its position but still insisted that UN aircraft flying from Bahrain circumnavigate the no-fly zone and approach from Jordan. Thus on January 18 and 19 the United States and U.K. attacked radar sites and a suspected nuclear facility with heavy bombing. The next day Iraq relented and announced that UNSCOM could fly unfettered (Krasno and Sutterlin 2003, 14–15; United Nations 1996, 86–87).

A year-long period of relative success followed, with a series of diplomatic discussions resulting in the establishment of an OMV plan. Significant progress was made in the chemical weapons area, with substantial materials turned over and destroyed. It came as somewhat of a surprise, therefore, when in September of 1994 Iraq threatened to cease its cooperation with UNSCOM and then deployed troops near the Kuwaiti border in early October. The United States quickly sent forces to Kuwait and threatened air strikes, while the British and French both sent warships to the region. The Security Council issued Resolution 949 on October 15, 1994, which, invoking Chapter VII, called on Iraq to cooperate fully with UNSCOM and to withdraw its military forces to their original position. Iraq complied and, despite the political and military posturing, cooperated with inspectors throughout the episode.

Iraq's obstruction of UNSCOM flared up again in 1995 as the inspectors homed in on the biological program and demanded more complete disclosures. Ekeus's June 1995 report recounts the defiance of Tariq Aziz, the deputy prime minister. Aziz declared that "Iraq required statements, on the one hand from the Special Commission that the chemical weapons and missile files were closed and the ongoing monitoring and verification system was operational, and on the other from IAEA that the nuclear file was closed" (UN Doc. S/1995/494). In other words, only once UNSCOM had declared the country disarmed in these areas would Iraq continue cooperation in the remaining area (biological). This was compounded when Saddam declared in a July speech that his government would end its cooperation with UNSCOM unless there was progress in the Security Council toward lifting sanctions. Aziz subsequently set a deadline of August 31 for evidence of such progress (Pearson 1999, 30).

This defiance was temporarily quelled the next week by the defection of Hussein Kamel Hassan to Jordan. Kamel was a general and son-in-law of Saddam who, as head of Iraq's Military Industrialization Commission, had overseen all weapons programs. Anticipating that Kamel would reveal what he knew (which he did, though perhaps not as much as the Iraqis feared), Baghdad suddenly became very cooperative.[15] Aziz claimed that Kamel, acting independently, had hidden information on prohibited weapons from UNSCOM *and* from the Iraqi leadership, and he pledged to cooperate fully in providing the necessary transparency. Kamel's defection contributed directly and indirectly to the uncovering of important weapons programs, especially on the biological weapons front but also in the nuclear area.[16]

The defection also revealed just how much UNSCOM did *not* know despite years of effort. As one experienced inspector notes, after Kamel's defection, "we started to believe that there was a *mechanism,* rather than individual cases or mistakes that were not interconnected."[17] By exposing the extent of Iraq's concealment efforts, the defection set UNSCOM on a collision course with Saddam's regime—and, as it turned out, with some on the Security Council.

Cracks in the Coalition

Over time, there were two issues around which UNSC unity over the inspections process began to fray. First, there was disagreement regarding the legitimacy of Iraq's sovereignty concerns. This led to differences over the extent to which Iraq should be treated as a negotiating partner with reasonable concerns rather than an aggressor to be dictated to, as well as the extent to which the principle of "immediate, unconditional and unrestricted access" should be compromised in response to Iraqi sensitivities. Second, there was disagreement over the proper mixture of carrots and sticks to be employed in the face of Iraqi behavior. Some states preferred a lower bar of disarmament for sanctions to be lifted and, short of this, favored the temporary suspension of sanctions in return for good behavior (i.e., cooperation with UNSCOM) as a useful positive incentive. Others felt that threatening the use of force was more effective in the face of intransigence. They

---

15. In one amusing episode, Iraqi officials led an UNSCOM team to a farm purportedly owned by Kamel, where they claimed to have "discovered" documents hidden by him. In the chicken house were boxes filled with papers, photographs, videotapes, and computer disks containing weapons information. UNSCOM's end-of-the-year report notes an unusually high degree of cooperation during the second half of 1995 (UN Doc. S/1995/1038).

16. Kamel's main direct contribution was to confirm information that was already suspected, though he also provided new information on biological and nuclear programs that had gone undetected (Gellman, *WashPo,* January 7, 2004). Indirectly, his defection caused Iraq to reveal considerable information in an effort to preempt his revelations and to appear cooperative. Author's interview with former senior UNSCOM official #1, November 13, 2003.

17. Yale-UN Oral History Project interview with Nikita Smidovich, February 3, 1999, p. 14 (emphasis added).

interpreted resolution phrases like "serious consequences" as including military force and viewed Resolution 678, authorizing the war, as still active.

Oversimplifying somewhat, the growing disunity on the Security Council pitted the more sympathetic French, Russians, and Chinese against the more hawkish Americans and British. Driving the wedge even deeper was a growing debate—between the same two camps among the P5 but also in the broader international community—over the desirability of maintaining harsh economic sanctions on Iraq. Now with emerging allies on the Council and with waning enthusiasm for sanctions, Iraq began to complain more about the inspections and to actively resist UNSCOM. The United States and Britain found it increasingly difficult to count on unqualified support on the Council for pressuring Saddam to disarm.

P5 Divergence and the Sanctions Debate

Following Kamel's revelations in 1995, UNSCOM's methods became more intrusive. Ministry offices and other nonmilitary sites were increasingly targeted, and Ekeus approved "special collection missions," headed by American Scott Ritter, a former Marine Corps intelligence officer, with the goal of uncovering Iraq's concealment program. As Security Council governments began to appreciate the extent of the arms programs and to realize how much was not known, the size and likely duration of the disarmament task were becoming clearer. A process they had expected to take months was taking years, with no end in sight.

An indefinite inspections process implied indefinite sanctions since, following 687, successful disarmament was a sine qua non for lifting sanctions. Thus the fight over inspections was partly a proxy war in the political struggle over sanctions. Following the Gulf War, there was widespread support for sanctions but also an assumption by most governments that they would be successful in relatively short order given the weakness of postwar Iraq and the perceived precariousness of Saddam's regime. As Megan O'Sullivan (2003, 105) notes, "They anticipated that Iraq would grudgingly, but quickly, comply with United Nations resolutions, paving the way for the lifting of sanctions and the resumption of more normal, if guarded, relations with the international community."

These expectations were not fulfilled, and attitudes among the P5 began to diverge by the mid-1990s. China had always been lukewarm about confronting Iraq—it had, after all, abstained from Resolution 678—and its enthusiasm weakened further with time. France and Russia were more openly skeptical of sanctions. By demonstrating that Iraq was actively concealing proscribed weapons programs, the Kamel defection episode took the wind out of the sails of a French and Russian initiative to move toward the lifting of sanctions (Malone 1999, 397). But this was only temporary, and these governments increasingly exhibited a growing desire to bring the inspections regime to an end.

By all accounts, the UN-imposed sanctions had a devastating impact on the Iraqi population, especially in combination with the effects of war and the economic redistribution policies of a dictatorial regime.[18] While most observers do not view humanitarian concerns as the primary motivation behind French, Russian, and Chinese calls to curb sanctions (Graham-Brown 1999, 60–61, 90; Freedman 2002, 5–8; Hawkins and Lloyd 2003, 448–49), growing concern among public audiences over the plight of Iraq's people certainly made opposition to sanctions more appealing.

The French and Russians in particular were clearly driven by economic and political interests as well. France had traditionally relied on oil from Iraq and coveted oil investments and contracts for its companies, all of which were dependent on the cessation of sanctions in order to be reactivated. Decades of close ties between France and Iraq resulted in a powerful set of domestic actors who pushed for more favorable policies toward Iraq. These groups included government officials in the foreign policy establishment, an influential pro-Iraq lobby and its allied parliamentarians, and the oil industry, especially the large oil companies Elf and Total (Styan 2004, 375–8). After his ascendancy to the presidency in 1995, Jacques Chirac, as part of an effort to enhance France's profile in the Middle East and to carve out a distinct French policy, "spoke publicly in favour of restoring Iraq to its normal place in the international community" (de La Gorce 1997). Under his leadership, a permanent mission was established in Baghdad to represent French commercial interests, and a French cultural center was reopened there in the fall of 1996.

More generally, the French view of Saddam differed fundamentally from the U.S. position. "Unlike the Americans, the French believed that negotiations with Saddam Hussein were possible. They believed that the only exit strategy in Iraq was to allow Iraq to reintegrate into the international community and to offer Iraq a 'light at the end of the tunnel'" (de Jonge Oudraat 2002, 146). Paris was also more "relaxed" than Washington about the threat of Iraqi WMD (Moisi 1999, 133). Thus not only were the costs of sanctions higher for France, but the perceived benefits were lower as well.

For its part, Russia was owed money by Iraq—more than $8 billion—for weapons sales and could recoup its debt only once the sanctions regime was

---

18. Many assessments have been conducted on the humanitarian consequences of the Iraq sanctions. A good overview can be found in Craven (2002, 45); Cortright and Lopez (1999); and Graham-Brown (1999, chap. 5).

terminated. When Yevgeny Primakov took over as foreign minister in January of 1996, he brought to the office a long and warm relationship with Iraq and with Saddam personally. Political and economic cooperation between the two countries expanded, and Aziz paid several visits to Moscow during the 1996–97 period (Ismael and Kreutz 2001, 97–98). A major goal of the Russian government's Iraq policy in the 1990s was to "assist in the pursuit of major Russian business interest in Iraq, especially for Moscow's oil companies and GASPROM, interests that could be developed once the UN sanctions regime against Iraq was lifted" (Freedman 2002, 5). Primakov specifically complained to U.S. Secretary of State Madeleine Albright about the loss of oil trade with Iraq as a result of sanctions (Albright 2003, 275).

Thus, partly because of a desire to return to normal commercial and diplomatic relations and partly out of humanitarian concerns, the French and Russians viewed a partial lifting of sanctions as a legitimate carrot strategy in return for Iraqi cooperation, even absent a clean bill of health, and preferred a lower bar overall for lifting the sanctions entirely. France had floated a proposal in 1993 and again in 1994 to offer Iraq carrots, in the form of easing the sanctions regime, in return for its *partial* fulfillment of disarmament obligations. "France stressed that it was a dangerous disincentive for Iraq not to recognize its progress" (Teixeira da Silva 2004, 209). More generally, the French and Russians wanted the Security Council to "emphasize the advantages of compliance for Iraq" (Wren, *NYT,* February 27, 1998). The United States and the U.K. opposed this approach in favor of maintaining pressure on Iraq and demanding total and verifiable disarmament in return for sanctions relief. This was UNSCOM's view as well (Ruiz Fabri 2002, 158).

Exacerbating the Council's disunity was the reality that Resolution 687 was subject to various interpretations. Paragraph 22 called for an end to sanctions only once Iraq had "completed all actions" related to disarmament and monitoring. Paragraph 21, on the other hand, raised the possibility that the Council could "reduce or lift" trade prohibitions "in light of the policies and practices of the Government of Iraq." This last phrase was vague. Could cooperation by Iraq be rewarded through reduced or suspended sanctions, or was complete disarmament required? In the face of this ambiguity, only the Security Council acting collectively had the authority to provide clarification through further resolutions—and only a *unified* Council would have been able to do so.

As it became clear that disarmament would take years, France and Russia grew increasingly eager to return to the prewar status quo. Along with China, which had been a major supplier to Iraq of military equipment, these countries took the lead in the latter half of the 1990s in "softening the Council's resolve" (Krasno and Sutterlin 2003, 17). As one former UNSCOM official put it, France, Russia, and China "started to get more involved politically" at this point.[19] According to one account, these three governments "created a kind of 'pro-Iraq lobby' in the UN Security Council in order to weaken the sanctions and to constrain U.S. action against [Iraq]" (Ismael and Kreutz 2001, 98).

Council members began to interfere more in UNSCOM's work, especially once Ekeus left his post in May of 1997.[20] It should be noted that Iraq was often aware of disagreements among UNSC members even when they were not publicly aired. In closed sessions of the Council, for example, word of what transpired was often leaked to Iraq by sympathetic member-state delegates and Secretariat officials present at the meetings.[21] Once unity began to unravel, UNSCOM lost its leverage with Iraq and Saddam started to employ divide-and-conquer strategies against the P5. As Charles Duelfer recalls, "I think Iraq sensed that there was a growing division between what they called the Anglo-Saxons and other members of the Council. And they tried to work that wedge, partially successfully."[22]

By 1996 it was clear that the United States and its allies against Iraq were promoting widely divergent paths forward. For Washington, maintaining a UN-based approach to its coercive disarmament policy would entail increasingly high freedom of action and organization costs, as the interests of other UNSC members would have to be accommodated through policy modifications, increased diplomacy, and side payments.

Negotiation over Coercion: The Sensitive Sites

Another spate of inspector obstructions occurred in 1996, justified by Iraq in terms of sovereignty and national security concerns. UNSCOM's more intrusive approach led them to very sensitive areas of Saddam's security forces, including the Special Security Organization (who guarded Iraq's leadership) and the Special Republican Guard (who guarded Baghdad, especially against coups), both headed by Saddam's son Qusay. As investigation revealed that some of Saddam's most trusted personnel were involved in concealment (Trevan 1999, 358; see also Ritter 2005, 128–29), further hostility and obstruction emerged from the Iraqi

19. Author's interview with a former senior staff member of UNSCOM, New York, November 14, 2003.

20. Yale-UN Oral History Project interview with Sergey Lavrov, April 18, 2001, p. 4 (hereafter "Lavrov interview"). Lavrov was the Russian ambassador to the UN.

21. Rolf Ekeus recounts that he learned this from Tariq Aziz, who informed him that "we know every word which is spoken in the closed session of the Security Council." Yale-UN Oral History Project interview with Rolf Ekeus, February 3, 1998, pp. 20–21.

22. Yale-UN Oral History Project interview with Charles Duelfer, October 7, 2000, p. 11 (hereafter "Duelfer interview").

side. This led to a series of standoffs beginning in March of 1996 and repeated in June, August, and November (Pearson 1999, 34–35).

In the June episode, Iraq blocked access to a number of "sensitive sites" closely linked to the regime. In some case these were Special Republican Guard offices, and in other cases they contained palaces. UNSCOM had followed the trail of Iraq's concealment apparatus to these locations, while the Iraqis claimed they were unrelated to any weapons programs and were symbolic of Iraq's right to sovereignty even in the face of intrusive inspections. Rather than categorically back Ekeus, the Security Council instructed him to return to Baghdad to negotiate renewed access. The result was a signed agreement whereby Iraq promised unconditional and immediate access, but it was accompanied by an informal document containing what came to be known as the "sensitive site modalities"—guidelines, agreed to by Ekeus and Aziz, for how UNSCOM was to proceed in such locations. Among other procedures, the modalities called for UNSCOM to be accompanied by a senior official from Baghdad as it conducted its inspections. As a practical matter, this arrangement meant that UNSCOM had to wait once it arrived at a site, sometimes for hours (depending on how far the site was from the capital). In effect, then, visits were announced, and any incriminating materials could be destroyed, hidden, or spirited away.

The Council accepted this arrangement between Ekeus and Aziz, though with reluctance on the part of the United States and the U.K. (Teixeira da Silva 2004, 207). The former, in particular, had favored the threat of military force to break the sensitive sites impasse and tried to forge a consensus on the policy in the Security Council. Charles Duelfer, deputy executive chairman of UNSCOM, recalls this period: "It was a difficult, difficult time.... Washington was spending a lot of time in capitals and in New York, bringing them together in a consensus, [saying] 'Look, if the Iraqis don't agree to this, we're going to thump 'em, and we want your support, or we're going to thump 'em seriously.'"[23] Consensus was lacking on such a stance, however, so Ekeus was compelled to pursue a compromise with Iraq. As Tim Trevan (1999, 190) notes, "Rolf Ekeus would only be able to talk the Iraqis into allowing access if he were bearing a tough message on behalf of the whole UN Security Council." One former UNSCOM official goes further, arguing that the modalities were fundamentally political and designed to please certain Security Council members by weakening UNSCOM's position vis-à-vis Iraq.[24] Without unified backing, UNSCOM's leadership had few cards to play. The upside of the modalities outcome was that a period of relative cooperation on Iraq's part followed.

---

23. Duelfer interview, p. 21.

24. Author's interview with a former UNSCOM commissioner and chief inspector, January 12, 2006.

It was clear by this point that the strong Security Council backing disarmament enjoyed in the early 1990s would not be forthcoming in the face of Iraqi defiance. Duelfer reflects on the significance of the sensitive site modalities: "In my view, that undermined, that was the last time there was going to be a consensus on the use of force against Iraq to enforce this, and I think to me it was an inflection point.... I think the Iraqis then saw that there were definitely going to be limits on what the Council would permit. I think as a matter of practice, the modalities did not allow the full type of inspections we needed, and they didn't work, and I think in practice that was it."[25] The episode illustrates how UNSC disunity increasingly allowed Iraq to politicize and weaken the inspections.

Saddam again reacted strategically to exploit these divisions. As one Iraq expert characterizes his reaction, "Saddam perceived the feckless behavior of France and Russia and the ever-weaker responses of the Security Council to his provocations as a window of opportunity for him to further divide the international community and have sanctions eased or lifted" (Baram 1998, 74). While most of Saddam's strategies for dividing the Council were diplomatic (complaining about the unfairness of the sanctions and inspections), the Oil-for-Food Program, up and running as of late 1996, offered him economic tools as well. Over time, imports from France, Russia, and China were favored over those from the United States. The pattern of oil-marketing contracts awarded by the Iraqi government tells a similar and remarkable story. Saddam's initial strategy was to distribute contracts relatively evenly among the P5 countries in an effort to curry favor across the board. However, beginning in late 1997 priority was granted to "friendly" governments on the Council, such that by 1998 two-thirds of all contracts were awarded to French, Russian, and Chinese companies, with fewer than 7 percent granted to British and American ones (O'Sullivan 2003, 133–34). The former therefore had disproportionate incentives to bring the inspections—and thus the sanctions—to a close.

The Decline of UN Inspections

Another spike in Iraqi interference occurred in the fall of 1997. Iraq pointed weapons at UNSCOM helicopters and in September prevented teams from inspecting three sensitive locations, labeled "presidential sites" by Iraq and ruled off-limits to inspectors. Some cameras and other monitoring equipment were also moved or blacked out. In effect, Iraq was attempting to expand the sensitive sites agreement worked out with Ekeus to include numerous additional

25. Duelfer interview, p. 23.

buildings and storage facilities the inspection of which, they argued, should be subject to the sensitive site modalities. Richard Butler, UNSCOM's new executive chairman, refused to accept this and, in any case, argued that he was not bound by Ekeus's arrangement with Aziz from the previous year since it was not an official agreement between UNSCOM and Iraq (Butler 2000, 88–91).

This episode triggered a series of events that eventually led to the expulsion of inspectors and the downfall of the disarmament regime. In particular, the Security Council proved itself so weak and divided in the face of Iraqi intransigence that UNSCOM was left with no leverage and Saddam with little incentive to cooperate. The United States, sometimes with the U.K., continued to threaten force but searched in vain for backing from the other permanent members and support from the international community. An effective UN-based approach to disarming Iraq proved impossible from this point forward.

The Debate over Resolution 1134

When Butler appealed to the Security Council following the September 1997 obstructions, the United States and U.K. responded by drafting a strongly worded resolution condemning Iraq's noncooperation and threatening further consequences. They immediately faced opposition in the rest of the Council and were compelled to soften the language. The final draft described Iraq's obstruction as a "flagrant violation" of previous resolutions and demanded that Iraq "cooperate fully with the Special Commission in accordance with the relevant resolutions, which constitute the governing standard of Iraqi compliance." In the event of further obstruction, the resolution threatened international travel restrictions on any Iraqi official known to have participated in noncompliance. Finally, the resolution suspended the periodic sanctions reviews pending improved cooperation.

When the resolution (1134) was finally put to a vote on October 23, 1997, it passed with only ten affirmative votes and five abstentions (see appendix for the text). Three of the abstainers were permanent members China, France, and Russia—formally breaking with their counterparts for the first time in the course of the inspections saga.

While the resolution's proponents felt that strong condemnation was appropriate, the dissenters felt the resolution would merely serve to aggravate tensions with Baghdad and that more emphasis should be placed on progress and positive steps taken by Iraq (Teixeira da Silva 2004, 211; Ismael and Kreutz 2001, 98). The contrasting statements made that day in the Security Council provide a window onto the sources of disagreement more generally (UN Doc. S/PV.3826). The U.K. representative praised UNSCOM's efforts, pointed to "repeated Iraqi failures," and argued that "the Council should react robustly to continued Iraqi flouting of Security Council resolutions.... The message that needs to be sent clearly is that if the Government of Iraq chooses to challenge the will and authority of the United Nations Security Council, it can be sure of a firm and principled response." The U.S. ambassador reminded his colleagues that "UNSCOM operates as an arm of the Security Council and gets its mandate solely from Security Council Resolutions. When Baghdad challenges UNSCOM, it challenges the Council." He criticized the notion that they "ought to reward Iraq because it is, in their view, cooperating with UNSCOM to a greater degree now than it has in the past," and he proposed a more absolute metric: "Cooperation is not a matter of degree. Either Iraq is in compliance with its obligations or it is in breach of those obligations."

On the other side of the debate, the Chinese ambassador emphasized progress in the inspections and noted that "in most cases, Iraq has cooperated with UNSCOM." While recognizing the importance of disarmament, he also argued that "the sovereignty, independence and territorial integrity, as well as the reasonable security concerns, of Iraq should also be respected." Similarly, the Russian representative stressed UNSCOM's and the IAEA's progress and characterized Iraqi obstruction as "isolated incidents." He preferred to see the glass as half full rather than half empty: "There is an obvious lack of balance in this draft. Ignored in it are various substantial elements of the fulfillment by Iraq of relevant provisions of resolution 687." The French representative agreed that the resolution lacked "proportionality" by raising the specter of additional sanctions.

These fundamental divisions, which had festered for years, were now fully exposed. Iraq had finally succeeded in publicly splitting the Security Council, securing a long-standing goal (Trevan 1999, 361). According to Butler, with the abstentions on Resolution 1134, "the signal went out to Iraq that the tide had turned, that permanent member unity had broken.... They could bring their war with UNSCOM to its final and concluding stage.... A period unfolded, which we can now recognize as the concluding period of the Iraq-UNSCOM conflict."[26]

Compromising with Saddam: The Secretary-General Intervenes

Iraq was emboldened. In late October 1997, Aziz announced that Iraq would not cooperate with Americans—who, along with the British, were threatening military action—and expelled all U.S. nationals working for UNSCOM in Iraq. Aziz also demanded the cessation of U-2 flights. Out of principle, Butler responded by withdrawing almost all UNSCOM personnel, leaving only a skeleton crew

26. Yale-UN Oral History Project interview with Richard Butler, July 25, 2001, p. 20 (hereafter "Butler interview").

in Baghdad, and effectively suspending UNSCOM's operations (Krasno and Sutterlin 2003, 122; de Jonge Oudraat 2002, 143). The United States responded with a show of force, directing the aircraft carrier *George Washington* to the Gulf from the Mediterranean, placing fighter jets on alert at the Incirlik base in Turkey, and sending F117 and B52 bombers to the region. Secretary Albright (2003, 276) recounts that "President Clinton was firm in his position that UNSCOM should be allowed to conduct its work unfettered and backed up this sentiment by ordering a buildup of U.S. military forces in the Persian Gulf." Such actions met with little support beyond the reliable British. The Arab League expressed its collective disapproval of the use of force, and both Turkey and Kuwait voiced opposition (de la Gorce 1997). The Gulf War coalition had disintegrated.

In November 1997, Russia chose to intervene diplomatically on a unilateral basis. An envoy from Moscow traveled to Baghdad and managed to convince Saddam to once again grant access to the inspectors. Russia was able to achieve this short-term victory by promising to advocate on Iraq's behalf in the Security Council to weaken the inspections and sanctions regimes (Trevan 1999, 362). Primakov and Aziz even issued a joint statement on November 19 professing their shared goals: "On the basis of Iraq's fulfillment of the relevant UN Security Council resolutions, Russia . . . will energetically work for the earliest possible lifting of the sanctions against Iraq. . . . To this end, active steps will be taken to increase the effectiveness of the Special Commission's work while showing respect for the sovereignty and security of Iraq" (quoted in Ismael and Kreutz 2001, 99).

By January of 1998, the situation deteriorated once again when Ritter attempted to inspect a sensitive site suspected of holding clues to Iraq's concealment program. Iraq had declared the location to be "presidential and sovereign"—a new category invented by the Iraqis—and therefore off limits to UNSCOM. After failing to resolve the issue in a meeting with Aziz, Butler reported back to the Security Council on January 22 that UNSCOM was being barred from eight presidential sites identified by Iraq—some of which were very large complexes with hundreds of buildings. Moreover, Butler explained to the Council, the demeanor of Iraq's representatives had changed. While previous discussions had been businesslike, the Iraqis were now verbally abusing UNSCOM personnel and blaming them for the fact that sanctions remained in force (UN Doc. S/1998/58).

The situation was resolved only through the intervention, for the first time, of the UN secretary-general. There was strong support from the French, Russians, and Chinese for Kofi Annan's involvement and, more generally, for the idea that Iraq's concerns should be taken seriously. The United States was not enthusiastic (Teixeira da Silva 2004, 211) and threatened air strikes if the impasse was not broken, but the Clinton administration may have relented because of domestic political considerations—namely, a public unconvinced that air strikes were called for (de Jonge Oudraat 2002, 144; Malone 1999, 397). However, Secretary of State Madeleine Albright did try to impose certain constraints on the negotiations, as Annan recounts:

> Yes, Mrs. Albright and I met before I left, and of course she indicated that they were not enthusiastic, but they had decided to join the consensus since others felt the trip would be useful, but they had "red lines" that one should be aware of—"red lines" meaning issues of importance to them that one should not compromise on. And that we discussed, that sort of issues like free and unfettered access to all areas that they would want to inspect, including the Palaces, and the cooperation of the Iraqi authorities to allow the inspectors to get their work done and nothing that should be done to dilute the resolutions which had already been approved. And of course I had no intention of doing that, so the American "red lines" posed no problems for me.[27]

Annan traveled to Baghdad in February 1998 and negotiated a memorandum of understanding (MOU) with Iraq that reaffirmed the principle of immediate and unconditional access (UN Doc. S/1998/166). With regard to the presidential sites, the understanding laid out some general conditions and provided that UNSCOM be accompanied by a group of diplomatic escorts—named the Special Group—as a way of protecting Iraqi sovereignty against overzealous inspectors. Since this procedure required arrangements in advance, the element of surprise was again lost.

Nevertheless, the Security Council approved the agreement with Resolution 1154 (see appendix) and expressed support for Annan's apparent success. The United States questioned the MOU's value but supported the resolution after inserting a clause threatening "severest consequences" if Iraq reneged as a way of giving it some teeth (Wren, *NYT,* February 27, 1998). Clinton argued that this language gave the United States the authority to use force in the event of Iraqi violations of the MOU, though France, Russia, China, and Annan himself went on record as opposing the notion of any such "automatic" trigger ("U.S. Softens Stance," *Australian,* March 11, 1998). In fact, the U.S. leaders were compelled to go along with the MOU compromise partly because they were worried that the alternative, unilateral air strikes, would inflame Arab public opinion and by extension make support from Arab governments difficult to achieve (Albright 2003, 278).

Most UNSCOM staff viewed the MOU as a victory for Iraq and a serious blow to the inspections regime. Beyond the humiliation of being monitored

---

27. Yale-UN Oral History Project interview with Kofi Annan, May 10, 2000, pp. 4–5.

by diplomats with no technical expertise, the inspectors saw the entire episode as a political victory for Iraq in its ongoing efforts to undermine UNSCOM's authority. As Ritter recalls, "I viewed what Kofi Annan was doing in February as basically the good offices of the Secretary-General working against UNSCOM at the behest of Iraq."[28] Insofar as UNSCOM's executive chairman was not the only recognized interlocutor, the body had lost its leverage with Saddam (Trevan 1999, 360, 366). Thus while Annan's spokesman declared triumphantly that "We have a deal" (United Nations, Department of Public Affairs 1998), UNSCOM staff wondered why "deals" were being struck at all with a flagrantly defiant Iraq. For its part, Iraq "feted the agreement as a victory" (White and Cryer 1999, 280).

In the event, the first expedition of the Special Group—a bevy of twenty senior diplomats from various governments who accompanied UNSCOM and IAEA experts—did not have much success. After a visit to eight presidential sites in March and April of 1998, the head of the inspections team reported, "It was clearly apparent that all sites had undergone extensive evacuation. In all sites outside of Baghdad, for example, there were no documents and no computers. In the Baghdad area,...most buildings were emptied of contents" (UN Doc. S/1998/326). This was not surprising since Iraq had had more than a month to prepare and to sanitize the sites. For this reason Annan's compromise was inherently flawed from a disarmament standpoint. Baghdad, in turn, was "emboldened by this success" (de Jonge Oudraat 2002, 144). The compromise was thus flawed from a political standpoint as well.

The experience of the presidential sites, and the sensitive sites more generally, epitomized the victory of politics over objective, effective inspections. The elaborate process imposed on UNSCOM made surprise—and therefore any real progress in uncovering concealed weapons information—impossible. At the same time, the very idea of negotiated modalities and interventions by third parties (Russian diplomats and the secretary-general) legitimated Iraq's complaints against the inspections regime and weakened UNSCOM's authority.

Unilateral Pressure from Washington

Butler (2000, 2) reports that by early 1998 he felt the French and Russians were working against him in some respects and that their positions "had begun to distinctly favor Iraq." France, Russia, and China began to openly urge Butler to produce a "final report" so that UNSCOM could focus on OMV rather than

28. Yale-UN Oral History Project interview with Scott Ritter, October 27, 1998, p. 41. For a similar sentiment, see Duelfer interview, p. 25.

inspections and so that sanctions could be lifted (*Financial Times,* 15 June 1998, p. 4). By contrast, U.S. ambassador Bill Richardson stressed "the reality that [Iraq] had a way to go before it would resume selling oil, and even further to go before the broader trade embargo would be lifted completely" (Crossette, *NYT,* June 17, 1998). In the summer of 1998, Russia, repeating an Iraqi mantra, pushed for the Council to declare the nuclear file closed and direct the IAEA and UNSCOM to shift their resources to the OMV stage. France and China supported this proposal. The United States and the U.K. were opposed on the grounds that there were still outstanding inspections issues (Teixeira da Silva 2002, 210–11). One former UNSCOM official recalls that in mid-1998, the French and Russians "started really complaining about UNSCOM. They wanted sanctions lifted, so they shot the messenger [i.e., UNSCOM]."[29] An important background condition buttressing the pro-Iraq position was the growing number of voices questioning both the effectiveness and the morality of continued sanctions (Mueller and Mueller 1999; ICRC 1999).

By contrast, U.S. policy was becoming more bellicose. The leadership relied increasingly on the threat of military force to coerce Iraq. In February Albright had threatened a significant military campaign rather than a "pinprick" to punish Iraq for noncompliance (Marcus, *Boston Globe,* February 10, 1998). U.S. officials insisted that such actions were legal since Iraqi violations of UNSC resolutions revived the authorization to use force in 678. Undersecretary of State Thomas Pickering (1998) reasoned that any material breach by Iraq "would mean that the prohibition on the use of force, which arose as a result of the cease-fire, was no longer in effect." He further argued that the lack of a specific prohibition against unilateral force in resolutions such as 1154 constituted an implicit approval by other Security Council members of its use. The majority of the P5 disagreed with this logic and believed that previous resolutions could not be used to authorize armed action absent additional Council approval (Lobel and Ratner 1999, 124, 151–52). Resolution 1154 provides a microcosm of this broader debate. In the course of discussions on the day the resolution was passed, no Council member expressed the view that the resolution authorized the use of force in the event of Iraqi noncompliance, and, indeed, most argued that an additional resolution would be required for such enforcement (see UN Doc. S/PV.3858). After the meeting, however, Ambassador Richardson asserted that the resolution supplied the United States with a "green light" to attack Iraq if President Clinton judged that Saddam was not abiding by the agreement with Annan (Lobel and Ratner 1999, 124).

---

29. Author's interview with former senior UNSCOM official #2, New York, November 14, 2003.

These threats of force coincided with a regime-change policy emerging from Washington. On March 12, 1997, Secretary of State Albright had argued in a speech at Georgetown University that sanctions would likely remain in force as long as Saddam was in power. This was widely interpreted as reflecting an implicit policy of regime change, and it raised questions about the viability of continued inspections. How could Saddam be convinced to cooperate if the most powerful member of the Security Council was intent on removing him, regardless of the status of his WMD? Baghdad used the event to question U.S. motivations. As Butler recalls, "the Iraqis had just simply pocketed [Albright's] remarks, and repeated them and repeated them, because it served their purposes, and damage was done."[30] As another high-ranking UNSCOM official recalls, "Albright handed [the Iraqis] the excuse not to cooperate."[31]

The regime change approach was formalized with the Iraq Liberation Act of September 19, 1998, which stated that U.S. policy should aim at replacing Saddam and promoting democracy in Iraq.[32] Clinton administration officials increasingly spoke of toppling Saddam and supporting opposition groups (Gellman, *WashPo,* December 9, 1998). So while UNSCOM was hard at work trying to disarm Iraq, the United States was focused on another objective, removing Saddam, and its leadership increasingly expressed this objective publicly. It is fair to say that U.S. policymakers had introduced considerable ambiguity into the question of whether even a perfectly cooperative Saddam Hussein regime would be rewarded with an end to sanctions, a clear deviation from the formula expressed in Resolution 687.

Since it was not obvious that a failure to reach a mutually acceptable arrangement with inspectors would leave Iraq worse off,[33] Iraq's bargaining position vis-à-vis UNSCOM was greatly strengthened. As one UNSCOM official com-

---

30. Butler interview, p. 6.

31. Author's interview with a former UNSCOM commissioner and chief inspector, January 12, 2006.

32. The original push for this legislation came from a group of "neoconservative" thinkers, many of whom later occupied positions in the George W. Bush administration. Among those who drafted a letter to Clinton in January 1998 advocating regime change were Elliott Abrams, Richard Armitage, John Bolton, Paula Dobriansky, Zalmay Khalilzad, Richard Perle, Donald Rumsfeld, Paul Wolfowitz, and Robert Zoellick—all of whom held high-ranking positions in the lead-up to the Second Iraq War.

33. This problem went beyond the regime change policy. More generally, the Americans and British had shown inconsistency on the question of what conditions Iraq had to satisfy for sanctions to be lifted. At times, the bar seemed insurmountable. Tariz Aziz used the ambiguity of their position to criticize the inspections regime. In a letter to the Security Council in October 1997, Aziz complained that UNSCOM's policies constituted "a deliberate political approach aimed at maintaining the embargo on Iraq," and that "there is no clear prospect" for bringing the sanctions to an end (S/1997/789).

plained, the U.S. policy shift "changed the relationship with Iraq dramatically. Iraq had no incentive to cooperate. The whole relationship collapsed with UNSCOM."[34] From Saddam's perspective, the ambiguous criteria for lifting sanctions and the regime change threat dimmed the light at the end of the tunnel. Signals from Washington implied that whether or not he cooperated with UNSCOM, he was doomed.

The Endgame

In the wake of the failed Russian proposal to close the nuclear file in the summer of 1998, Iraq insisted in early August that no more disarmament could take place, that the executive chairman declare Iraq WMD-free, triggering the end of sanctions, and that UNSCOM's activities from that point forward be limited to monitoring (Krasno and Sutterlin 2003, 110, 134; Trevan 1999, 369–70; UN Doc. S/1998/719). Butler refused, and Iraq formally suspended cooperation with UNSCOM on August 5.

The Security Council responded to these events by passing Resolution 1194 on September 9, 1998. In so doing, however, its members managed only boilerplate language declaring Iraq's behavior "unacceptable"; they did not describe it as constituting a breach of previous resolutions and threatened no consequences. In other respects as well the resolution represented a victory for Iraq. The Council prescribed a "comprehensive review" of Iraq's compliance with the relevant resolutions, supporting a proposal by the secretary-general. This review proposal required UNSCOM to report to the Council on the state of each weapons file (nuclear, chemical, biological, and missile), to provide an estimate of what remained to be done and a time frame for its completion, and to provide evidence of Iraq's nonfulfillment of its commitments. Iraq would then be invited to provide its own "separate account" of its compliance.

According to Graham Pearson (1999, 53), the idea of such a review "does indeed put the activities of UNSCOM and the IAEA into the dock and, amazingly, in the light of the past and continuing record of Iraq, does not place the onus on Iraq to do what it has consistently failed to do over the past seven and a half years, provide a full, final and complete disclosure of its proscribed programme which can be verified by UNSCOM and the IAEA." The burden of proof had been reversed. From UNSCOM's perspective, having to defend its work and the legitimacy of its claims went even beyond the humiliation of the MOU episode. As the *Washington Post* (Gellman, *WashPo,* November 22, 1998)

34. Author's interview with a former senior staff member of UNSCOM, New York, November 14, 2003. See also Duelfer (2004, 10).

described the initiative when it began two months later, "Iraq's defenders in the U.N. Security Council are preparing an inquiry that will dissect and perhaps limit UNSCOM's work."

Iraq continued to deny all access, even for monitoring purposes, to UNSCOM in October. Requests for inspections and for documents were increasingly denied, tagged equipment was removed without explanation, and on several occasions UN personnel were threatened with physical harm (Krasno and Sutterlin 2003, 73–4). On October 31, 1998, Iraq announced that it was once again ceasing all cooperation, and on November 11 Butler reported to the Security Council and the secretary-general that he was withdrawing his entire UNSCOM team from Iraq (UN Doc. S/1998/1059). On the same day the United States began deploying additional forces to the region and threatened military action if Saddam continued to defy the UN. When Iraq agreed the next day to cooperate, Clinton called off an air strike within an hour of launching the first missiles (Goshko, *WashPo,* November 21, 1998). Inspectors resumed their work on November 17, but both Clinton and Blair made clear that the military option was still open and that the burden was on Saddam to show his benign intentions ("Survival as Victory" 1998).

During this phase, the P5 disagreed over whether the use of force was a proper response to Iraq's behavior. The United States pointed to the language in Resolution 1154 threatening "severest consequences," while France, Russia, and China consistently argued that there was no automatic trigger and that the UNSC would have to explicitly approve the use of force. When Butler reported to the Council on December 15, he pointed to progress and cooperation in some areas but also cataloged several instances of defiance, including denials of access and the prior removal of relevant materials (UN Doc. S/1998/1172). The Butler Report, as it became known, was used to justify a substantial bombing campaign—Operation Desert Fox, discussed at more length in the following section—by the United States and the U.K., which commenced on December 16. UNSCOM never returned to Iraq and was formally disbanded in December 1999.

Desert Fox and Its Aftermath

Operation Desert Fox lasted four days, from December 16 to 20, and involved more than 400 cruise missile strikes combined with about 650 aircraft sorties. From a diplomatic and operational standpoint, the operation was essentially unilateral. Beyond the British, there was no consultation or collaboration; neither allies nor the P5 were informed beforehand. In fact, other Security Council members learned of the campaign as they sat down to discuss the Butler

Report and its implications for how to proceed with inspections, a subject that was obviously superseded by events. Writing at the time, two international law scholars (Lobel and Ratner 1999, 154) described the event's significance: "The symbolism of the bombs falling in Iraq while the Council debated its response to a report from a UN special commission about Iraqi compliance with UN resolutions starkly illustrates the refusal of the United States to accept limits on its power."

For the United States, the costs of IO constraint, especially the prospect of further delay, were ultimately deemed too great; the result, consistent with hypothesis 4, was a more unilateral approach. U.S. policymakers and military planners felt a need to strike quickly and with as much surprise as possible. This would make it difficult for Iraq to move weapons and troops. Since a major goal of the attack was to hit military and security forces loyal to Saddam, any warning that would allow the occupants to flee or fortify themselves had to be avoided. Thus the military planners "put great emphasis on the desirability of surprise" (Gellman, *WashPo,* December 20, 1998).

In addition to these logistical issues, political exigencies favored a tight time frame. Support for a strike would be highest in the immediate aftermath of renewed Iraqi obstruction and the Butler Report; with time, in National Security Adviser Sandy Berger's words, support "would have dissipated" and the "predicate" for an attack would be less clear (Gellman, *WashPo,* December 20, 1998). More specifically, advance warning risked triggering a diplomatic intervention by France, Russia, or the secretary-general, which would delay and complicate matters. On a more general level, the experiences of 1998 had soured U.S. policymakers on hewing too closely to UN decisions in its Iraq policy. As one National Security Council official involved in Iraq policy complained in May of 1999, "We have been constrained by the UN in the Gulf. We waited while the Kofi Annan dance played itself out. Then we waited for the Butler Report."[35] As hypotheses 4 and 6 suggest, this desire for flexibility and speed made IO-based options—and the Security Council path in particular—less appealing in Washington.

For both U.S. and British officials, the stated goal of Desert Fox was to degrade Iraq's WMD capabilities and to set back its weapons programs. President Clinton's speech on the day the bombing began outlined the goals: "Earlier today, I ordered America's armed forces to strike military and security targets in Iraq. Their mission is to attack Iraq's nuclear, chemical and biological weapons programs.... Their purpose is to protect the national interest of the United States

35. Author's interview with a senior director, NSC, Washington, D.C., May 17, 1999.

and, indeed, the interests of people throughout the Middle East and around the world" (White House 1998). On the same day, Peter Burleigh, the acting U.S. ambassador to the UN, informed other members of the Council that the goal was to strike military targets. "We are focusing on Iraq's weapons of mass destruction programmes and its ability to threaten its neighbors" (UN Doc. S/PV.3955).

Running for UN Cover: U.S. Justifications and International Reactions

The American leadership relied heavily on the Butler Report to justify the use of force and framed the operation as legal and as fitting squarely under a UN mandate. In particular, they seized on language from Butler's concluding paragraph: "Finally, in the light of this experience, that is, the absence of full cooperation by Iraq, it must regrettably be recorded again that the commission is not able to conduct the substantive disarmament work mandated to it by the Security Council and, thus, to give the Council the assurances it requires with respect to Iraq's prohibited weapons programmes." This pessimistic assessment was used as evidence that Iraq was in breach of Security Council requirements and had refused a series of opportunities to come clean (see, e.g., Albright 1998). The British stressed the Butler Report as well. In a speech to the House of Commons the day after Desert Fox began, Tony Blair (1998) explained, "We are acting now because Butler's report...was so clear." He further stressed that the "evidence is clear, as set out by Butler," and that the report "was clear, and damning." The overarching goal of U.S.-British action, according to Blair, was to "seek genuine Iraqi compliance with the demands of the Security Council."

Despite Butler's conclusions, not all Council members were convinced that Iraq's behavior justified a forceful response. Meeting as the bombing commenced, the group was about evenly divided (see UN Doc. S/PV.3955). Representatives from five countries (Brazil, China, Kenya, Russia, and Sweden) spoke out against the campaign, four (Gambia, Japan, Portugal, and Slovenia) spoke in favor, and four (Bahrain, Costa Rica, France, and Gabon) made ambiguous or neutral statements. China and Russia were especially vocal in their opposition, and French officials later characterized the operation as hasty and counterproductive.

The British and American ambassadors obviously made arguments in favor of the use of force. The legal basis for their position—provided most eloquently by Jeremy Greenstock, the U.K. representative—lay in the Butler Report and in key resolutions from earlier in 1998: 1205 of November 5 had referred to Iraq's obstruction as a "flagrant violation of Resolution 687," and 1154 of March 2 had threatened "severest consequences" if Iraq violated the terms of the MOU.

Moreover, Iraq's violations of 687's requirements of disclosure and access on weapons matters, it was argued, implicitly revived resolution 678 authorizing the Gulf War. Because of Iraq's repeated violations, for the U.S. representative the argument was straightforward: "Coalition forces are acting under the authority provided by the resolutions of the Security Council."

Those opposed argued that there was simply no explicit UNSC authorization, and therefore that the Anglo-American bombing constituted, in the Russian ambassador's view, "a unilateral act of force." Boris Yeltsin characterized the bombing as "a gross violation of the UN Charter" that was not authorized by previous resolutions (Ismael and Kreutz 2001, 101) and expressed "the most serious concern, a feeling of dismay and deep alarm" ("Ingrates" 1999). In further protest, Yeltsin recalled his ambassador to Washington, and the Duma postponed the ratification of the second Strategic Arms Reduction Talks treaty (McKay 2005, 146–47). After the Security Council meeting, the Chinese ambassador stormed out and declared to the press that "there is absolutely no excuse or pretext to use force against Iraq" (Fidler, *FT*, December 17, 1998). He further accused the United States of violating the UN Charter and "the norms governing international law" ("Ingrates" 1999). The legal justification for Desert Fox was indeed questionable (White and Cryer 1999; Gray 2002, 11–12).

The French reaction was especially important: nobody expected the Russians and Chinese to support the use of force, but the French had participated in such actions in the past alongside the Americans and British. While his criticisms of the U.S. threats were more measured than those of his Russian and Chinese counterparts, Chirac had consistently argued throughout 1998 that force was not necessary or desirable as a coercive tool. This stance resonated with the French public. When asked about Chirac's decision not to support the United States' use of force against Iraq in December 1998, 75 percent of the French public expressed approval (BVA 1998). To further distance the French government from U.S. policy, Chirac announced that France was ceasing its participation in Operation Southern Watch, which, he argued, had changed from a surveillance and humanitarian operation to one with coercive intent.

Undermining the U.S. and British rationales for the bombing was the growing sentiment—in both the Security Council and the UN Secretariat—that Butler's steering of UNSCOM had become too aggressive with Iraq and too sympathetic to the U.S. position (Krasno and Sutterlin 2003, 32–35; Malone 1999, 393). Some critics even suggested that the language inserted into the final paragraph of his December report had been orchestrated by the Americans. The Russian representative, for example, argued in the Council that Butler was a puppet and that his report should be discounted as political. Indeed, it is apparently true that U.S. officials saw drafts of the Butler Report and played a role in shaping the text (Gellman,

WashPo, December 16, 1998).[36] In this way the Butler Report was turned against Washington rhetorically: it was portrayed as further evidence of American unilateralism and as supportive of Iraq's claims that UNSCOM was illegitimate.

For the Americans and British, the stress on Iraq's failure to cooperate with UNSCOM and on the conclusions of the Butler Report fit into a larger framing strategy that invoked the UN—its mandate and institutions—as frequently as possible in order to legitimize the resort to military force. The U.S. leadership repeated many of the same framing strategies that the Bush administration had used before and during the Gulf War to generate support, strategies that portrayed the United States as defending international rules and collective interests rather than narrow national interests. This was a confrontation, U.S. officials insisted, between Iraq and the international community, especially as represented in the Security Council.

Thus Albright (1998) referred to "the confrontation between Iraq and the UN Security Council" and argued that "U.S. policy is based on principles established by the Security Council in the aftermath of the Gulf War." Since Iraq was in violation of UN requirements, U.S. efforts should be understood as enforcement of compliance with legitimate rules. "I think that the point here is compliance, and the international community has demanded such compliance for the last seven and a half years." She continued: "The important point here is that Saddam Hussein get the message that the international community, through its Security Council resolutions, wants him to comply." Similarly, in Clinton's December 16 speech he framed U.S. actions as enforcing the requirements established by the international community through the Security Council. He relied heavily on the Butler Report to make his case and repeatedly framed the issue as one of compliance. In a three-and-a-half-page transcript of the statement, Clinton makes twelve references to UNSCOM, nine references to the UN or the Security Council, and five references to the "international community" (White House 1998). Consistent with hypothesis 3, in statements intended for public consumption we see an effort to repeat the same framing strategies that were used successfully during the Gulf War crisis.

With a more tenuous imprimatur and such a public split in the Council, however, these UN-based framing strategies were not as effective as they had been in 1990 and 1991. A CNN/Angus Reid Group (1998) poll conducted during and just after Operation Desert Fox assessed public reactions in eight countries. Not surprisingly, approval was high in Israel (83 percent) and the United States

36. One UN official reports seeing, from his office window, Butler walk across the street from the Secretariat building to the building housing the U.S. mission at least twice on the day the report was due. Author's interview with a UN Secretariat official, November 13, 2003.

(76 percent) and solid in Canada (60 percent) and the U.K. (61 percent). Publics disapproved in Russia (82 percent), Italy (57 percent), Japan (53 percent), and France (52 percent), while Germans were about evenly divided.[37] According to the *Guardian*/ICM opinion polls in the U.K., while 80 percent of Britons supported the use of force after the Gulf War was launched, only 56 percent supported Operation Desert Fox (Travis, *Guardian,* March 19, 2002).

Of course, these countries are mostly U.S. allies; in the wider international community, support was very slim. Arabs in particular reacted with anger. Demonstrations were held in Egypt, Jordan, Lebanon, Morocco, and Yemen, as well as in several European countries with large Muslim immigrant communities. Protesters attacked U.S. and British embassies in Damascus and clashed with Israeli troops in the West Bank and the Gaza Strip. As many as fifteen thousand Yemeni protesters marched through the streets of Sanaa shouting "America is the enemy of the Muslims," while Palestinian demonstrators called for "Death to America" (Cordesman 1999, 39). These domestic political dynamics help explain why several politically important governments in the region that had supported the Gulf War went on record as opposing the December 1998 bombing, including Egypt, Qatar, Saudi Arabia, Syria, and Turkey (BBC News 1998; Jehl, *NYT,* December 18, 1998). Egyptian president Hosni Mubarak, a key regional ally, urged Clinton to end the attack immediately (Williams, *WashPo,* December 20, 1998), and even Kuwait distanced itself from the action.

Especially with respect to these regional powers, the negative reaction to Desert Fox marked the ultimate failure of a sustained diplomatic strategy by Washington. Keeping key anti-Iraq allies in the Middle East on board was increasingly difficult as the 1990s wore on. As the former secretary of state explains the situation in 1998, "We also needed support from Arab states, although these governments tended to be ambivalent. Many were privately contemptuous of Saddam and would have been pleased to see him gone, but they worried that our threat to use air strikes was inflaming Arab public opinion. As a result, most were hard to pin down, especially in public" (Albright 2003, 278). Desert Fox, a sustained strike without UNSC authorization, made support for these leaders impossible from the perspective of their own domestic political needs. Hypothesis 3 stresses the importance of IO approval for generating permissive levels of support among foreign publics, an outcome that prevailed during the Gulf War and for several years thereafter. Consistent with this logic, support quickly evaporated once the United States began taking coercive actions that were opposed by many of its fellow Security Council members.

37. The Russian poll was conducted only in the city of Moscow.

Many politically important governments were concerned not just about domestic politics but also about the broader message being sent from Washington regarding its Iraq policy. Desert Fox signaled a willingness by the Clinton administration to disarm Iraq by force if necessary and, more generally, bred unease over U.S. intentions. As one reporter observed during the bombing campaign, many leaders, especially in the Middle East, "have watched the attacks with consternation, either from uneasiness about any nation that would take on itself the role of global policeman, or from concern about local repercussions, or from unanswered questions about what the United States is trying to achieve" (Schmemann, *NYT,* December 20, 1998). Iraq's disarmament seemingly had been subordinated to a more ambitious U.S. policy of containment, and possibly regime change, and no longer reflected the will of the broader international community (McKay 1999, 144–45). Consistent with hypothesis 2, as American actions became increasingly divorced from the UN process and its constraints, they were viewed as more threatening to international interests and thus less worthy of support.

Russia's reaction to Desert Fox is instructive in this regard. The extensive diplomatic efforts undertaken by Bush and Baker during the Gulf War crisis to assuage Soviet fears over U.S. intentions had produced a delicate accommodation between Moscow and Washington. This was shattered by Desert Fox. The bombing spurred Yeltsin to urge "common sense and restraint" and his defense minister, Igor Sergeyev, described the United States as "unpredictable" (Cordesman 1999, 31, 50). This contrasts with Gorbachev's satisfaction that the Bush administration exhibited self-restraint and sensitivity to international interests when it worked so carefully through the Security Council in 1990 and 1991.

The Consequences of Desert Fox

By most accounts, the four-day bombing campaign had only a modest impact on Saddam's military and weapons programs. While some WMD installations that UNSCOM had not dismantled were destroyed, most of these could be rebuilt (Krasno and Sutterlin 2003, 16). One Defense Department official involved in Desert Fox describes it as a "firepower demonstration" that didn't achieve much in terms of proscribed weapons capabilities.[38]

Most who were involved, and most outside commentators, viewed the operation as a politically counterproductive tactic as well. Indeed, Desert Fox may have played into Saddam's hands. According to one Arab newspaper at the time,

---

38. Author's interview with a Department of Defense intelligence officer, April 14, 2006.

"Saddam was ready for, perhaps even seeking a new confrontation which, in his own words, would achieve 'victory'" ("Survival as Victory" 1998). Enduring a few days of bombing was a small price to pay for shedding the yoke of intrusive inspections and demonstrating to his domestic audience—and Arab publics around the world—that he was willing to stand up to the Anglo-American powers.

The lukewarm international reaction was engendered by the widespread perception that the attacks were essentially unilateral. The U.S. framing campaign was countered by a variety of governments questioning whether the UN aegis covered the use of force under the circumstances. One Canadian diplomat involved in Iraq's disarmament argues that the campaign's unilateral nature undermined its effectiveness. If Saddam had responded to the bombing with concessions, "he would have been politically collapsing to the U.S. It would have been easier for him to politically collapse to the UN."[39] As a coercive tool, a modest bombing campaign conducted solely by the Americans and British was very weak, and it did not prompt Saddam to succumb to the Council's demands and readmit UNSCOM. On the contrary, Iraqi vice president Taha Yassin Ramadan vowed that the inspectors would never be allowed to return. "The issue of UNSCOM is now in the past, the commission of spies is now in the past," Ramadan told reporters. "[E]verything dealing with the inspections, monitoring and weapons of mass destruction, it's all behind us" (Robinson, *WashPo,* December 20, 1998).

Sergey Lavrov, the Soviet ambassador to the UN at the time, characterizes the December 1998 bombing as "a unilateral action, which undermined the unity of the Security Council and of the P-5," and argues that cooperation and "joint pressure" on Iraq would have continued without this resort to force.[40] This is partially misleading since there was little remnant of unity left in the Council, but Desert Fox did force the issue by provoking a public rupture among the P5 and making a return of UNSCOM inspectors a virtual impossibility. This was a high price to pay for a relatively ineffectual operation.

The most serious long-term cost was the absence of any monitors or inspectors in Iraq. With nobody on the ground, the international community was blind to any WMD-related activities in the country. Moreover, UNSCOM's mere presence had served as a brake on Iraq's weapons programs and as a deterrent against their reconstitution. As one analyst (Conetta 2003, 4–5) notes, "an ancillary effect of the inspections (together with outside surveillance activities) was that they served to impede any efforts to reconstitute a substantial weapons program and they precluded Iraq's testing or training with such weapons.... As long as an inspection or monitoring team was kept in place,...the United States and others

39. Author's interview with a Department of Foreign Affairs official, Ottawa, June 16, 2005.
40. Lavrov interview, p. 36.

would have had early warning of any attempt by Iraq to break out of the confines of the disarmament regime."

U.S. policymakers quickly came to learn that there was simply no substitute to having inspectors in country. This is a lesson that should have been learned in the first months of UNSCOM, when Iraq's chemical arsenal was found to be much larger than estimated before the Gulf War and its nuclear program much more advanced. And it was only with inspectors on the ground that the international community came to learn of Iraq's biological program in the mid-1990s. There was no remedy for this lack of eyes and ears. As one U.S. military intelligence officer involved in Iraq reported, "After we bombed them, we had no intelligence after that. We lost everything."[41] A Department of State official engaged in nonproliferation concurred with this assessment, recalling that "it was very useful having inspectors on the ground 24/7. It was very useful having neutral, unbiased information. We have had very little real information ever since."[42] A British diplomat heavily involved in Iraq diplomacy at the time also laments that the expert knowledge of UN inspectors, which had taken years to develop, was also lost from this point forward (Ross 2007). This ignorance was costly and came back to haunt the United States and Britain before, during, and after the 2003 invasion of Iraq.

The Evolution of U.S. Coercive Strategy

With the suspension of UN-based disarmament, the United States emphasized alternative forms of coercion that, while extant to varying degrees prior to Operation Desert Fox, were increasingly relied upon afterwards. Albright (2003, 287) describes this new approach, dubbed "containment plus" by the White House: "We counted upon allied military forces in the region to keep Saddam in his box, while we took other steps to weaken him. In practice, this meant stricter enforcement of the no-fly zones over northern and southern Iraq. When provoked, we did not hesitate to hit Saddam's radar and antiaircraft facilities.... We took steps to unite and strengthen the Iraqi opposition. And we adopted 'regime change' as an explicit goal of U.S. policy." At the same time, the United States advocated a shift toward "smarter" sanctions that would minimize the suffering of the Iraqi people while maximizing the pain felt by their regime.

Neither the no-fly nor the regime change policies, now central to U.S. statecraft, could be comfortably linked to a UN stamp of approval and were viewed

41. Author's interview with a Department of Defense intelligence officer, April 14, 2006.

42. Author's interview with a Department of State official in the Bureau for International Security and Nonproliferation, April 6, 2006.

unfavorably by most in the international community. Immediately following Desert Fox, the United States and the U.K. expanded the no-fly-zone patrols and relaxed the rules of engagement. Strikes against Iraqi targets, especially radar and surface-to-air missile sites, became routine—by August of 1999 more than a thousand sorties had been launched (Malone 1999, 403). U.S. policy also evolved to include an open-ended commitment to destroy any weapons facilities that Iraq attempted to reconstitute following Desert Fox. "If he rebuilds it," Berger warned, "we will come" (Slavin, *USA Today*, December 24, 1998).

In focusing on the patrolling of no-fly zones as a way to keep Saddam boxed in, U.S. and British officials continued to argue that enforcement of the zones—and the seemingly inevitable provocations and retaliatory strikes it entailed—was implicitly authorized by UNSC Resolution 688 (passed on April 5, 1991), which demanded an end to the Iraqi regime's repression of civilian populations and required Iraq to admit humanitarian aid groups.[43] However, as we have already noted, the resolution contained no language on no-fly zones (let alone the use of force to defend them) and in fact reaffirmed "the sovereignty, territorial integrity and political independence of Iraq." While the no-fly policy was widely accepted as long as its primary aims were humanitarian, support was replaced by widespread criticism in the late 1990s as the zones were expanded and as the frequency of patrols and bombing grew (Boileau 1997, 890–91).

The United States also stepped up its stress on regime change, largely through indirect measures such as supporting opposition groups. In a report to the Senate Committee on International Relations in March of 1999, President Clinton outlined this policy:

> As long as Saddam Hussein remains in power, he represents a threat to the well-being of his people, the peace of the region, and the security of the world. We will continue to contain the threat he poses, but over the long term the best way to address that threat is through a new government in Baghdad. To that end, we—working with Congress—are deepening our engagement with the forces for change in Iraq to help make the opposition a more effective voice for the aspirations of the Iraqi people. (U.S. House of Representatives 1999)

Beginning in early 1999, public consultations took place with opposition figures, and a new position was created within the administration to implement the Iraq Liberation Act. Emphasis on regime change had virtually no support outside the United States and Britain.

---

43. One U.S. diplomat directly involved tried to offer more precision on the basis for U.S. policy. "We don't claim that [patrolling the no-fly zones] 'is the UN,' but we say that it is necessary for

Outside the Security Council, it was diminishing support in the Arab world that was most politically damaging for the United States. Regional leaders became more actively opposed to U.S. actions. As two contemporaneous observers (Byman and Waxman 2000, 28) note,

> Egypt has led the effort to end containment. Saudi Arabia, Bahrain, and the United Arab Emirates (UAE) also have questioned sanctions and at times objected to certain U.S. military strikes against Iraq. Although the degree of Arab support for U.S. policies has varied according to the winds of domestic sentiment and the level of hostile Iraqi rhetoric, in general opposition to containment or other harsh policies has grown in recent years. Gulf allies are also wearying of the large American military presence.

While it had always been politically tricky, by the time of Desert Fox Washington struggled to maintain support among Arab nations for its containment policy toward Iraq.

This waning support for the United States' actions in the region, and for its highly visible military presence generally, was driven partly by the conveyor belt of domestic politics. Radicals and opposition groups began to pressure regimes friendly to the United States, threatening stability in countries like Egypt and Saudi Arabia. The Saudi government, for example, favored military action against Saddam through much of the 1990s but by the end of the decade could not allow U.S. strikes from its territory for domestic reasons (Lippman, *WashPo,* December 17, 1998). As U.S. policy evolved and as time passed, it became increasingly difficult for these leaders to invoke UN cover domestically and therefore to support American actions.

From the perspective of other leaders, the United States was displaying an increasing unwillingness to be constrained by the Security Council and by multilateral decision making more generally. In light of its actions, Washington's nods to the Council and its authority were viewed as mere cheap talk. "The refusal of the United States to accept limitations on its power by the Security Council thus depended on creatively interpreting the Council's resolutions to accord authority despite the contrary positions of a majority of its members" (Lobel and Ratner 1999, 125). The United States was no longer meaningfully constrained, which, consistent with hypothesis 2, raised fears about its ambitions in the region and the potential threat its policies posed to other government's interests.

In sum, by the end of the 1990s there was little support for the U.S. coercive strategy in Iraq, which was perceived as increasingly distant from the original

---

fulfilling the objectives of 688." Author's interview with a State Department official, Washington, D.C., January 11, 2000.

Security Council mandates and the dramatic events that produced them. Alongside and related to this skepticism of the U.S. approach was continually waning support for economic sanctions. While sanctions had helped constrain Iraq's military spending, they had proved ineffective as a way to undermine the regime. In fact, the civilian harm caused by sanctions was Saddam's most effective propaganda tool domestically, across the Arab world and in Europe, providing support for his argument that the United States was targeting Iraqi society—innocent Arabs and Muslims—as much as its government (Gause 1999, 56). Distaste for sanctions, along with a view that U.S. policy was now driven by anachronistic and parochial interests, undermined support for tough measures against Iraq. The broad coalition built so carefully by President Bush and Secretary Baker in 1990 had withered away.

Reviving Inspections: A Divided Council

The dust had barely settled from Operation Desert Fox when three of the five permanent members of the Council—Russia, France, and China—and many Arab governments called for lifting the oil embargo and disbanding or replacing UNSCOM. France led the way. With bombs still falling on Iraq, Foreign Minister Hubert Védrine called for a fresh approach: "We think it's time to move on to a mechanism more geared to the risk of future danger, rather than the systematic examination of what has happened in the past" (quoted in Diamond 1998). In January France advanced a proposal that labeled sanctions "the wrong tool to achieve the goals of the Security Council" and proposed a new weapons regime for Iraq that would focus on ongoing monitoring rather than on investigation and disarmament. The proposal called for a new commission to replace UNSCOM, one that would "have its independence insured and its professionalism strengthened"—language borrowed from Russian and Iraqi statements from the period and clearly intended to indict UNSCOM as a tool of the United States (Crossette, *NYT,* January 14, 1999).

While most UNSC members supported these ideas, the United States stuck to the (increasingly unpopular) position it had held throughout the 1990s. In one State Department official's formulation at the time, "there can be no sanctions relief absent a certification of Iraqi disarmament and... UNSCOM is the vehicle for making that assessment" (Gellman, *WashPo,* December 22, 1998). With support from the U.K. and the Netherlands, the U.S. argued that efforts should continue to be aimed at inspections and disarmament, not just OMV, and indeed that ongoing monitoring was useless without a reliable baseline assessment of the state of Iraq's programs (Teixeira da Silva 2004, 212). With no consensus on the

Council, the post-Desert Fox future of UNSCOM was up in the air. In David Malone's (1999, 398–99) assessment, UNSCOM had become a "political football. France, Russia, and China attacked Butler, calling for his resignation, for a lifting of the comprehensive sanctions regime against Iraq, and for UNSCOM to be recast completely. With little support for the bombing campaign among UN member-states, the USA was in a weak position to defend UNSCOM effectively."

On January 30, 1999, the Security Council established a panel to provide a "comprehensive review" of the status of Iraq's disarmament and to advise the Council on how to proceed. The resulting document, referred to as the Amorim Report after its chairman, Celso Amorim (Brazil's UN ambassador at the time), was transmitted to Annan and the Council in late March (UN Doc. S/1999/356). While it concluded that intrusive inspections in Iraq remained necessary, a nod to the U.S. and British position, it also recommended that disarmament and OMV be conducted simultaneously rather than sequentially, as provided in 687. To conduct this work, the report recommended a body substantially different from UNSCOM in composition and approach. A new organization should be embedded more thoroughly into the UN bureaucracy, with staff hired as international civil servants employed by the UN (rather than seconded from governments) and according to geographic distribution criteria. Further, to increase the body's independence, intelligence sharing should be "one-way only"—that is, information acquired from governments would not reciprocated. While inspections and monitoring should be "comprehensive and intrusive," they should also be conducted "with due regard to Iraq's sovereignty, dignity and sensitivities" (UN Doc. S/1999/356, 28–29). The new organization should be a more collegial and diplomatic body.

By the spring of 1999, there were three distinct approaches to Iraq's weapons being offered by the P5: one by the U.K. (in conjunction with the Dutch), one by Russia (supported by China), and one by France. And while the United States was generally sympathetic to the British-Dutch plan, it preferred to include an explicit policy of supporting opposition groups, a combination that represented in effect a fourth alternative (Diamond 1999). While the Iraqis did not express support for any of the draft resolutions, they clearly viewed the Russian-Chinese and French proposals most favorably.[44]

After several months of negotiations, Resolution 1284 was passed in December 1999 (see appendix). It began from the template of the British-Dutch proposal and was modified to reflect the preferences of Russia and France (Butler 2000, 224–28). It represented an imperfect compromise among the divergent positions

---

44. This is according to an interview with Iraqi foreign minister Said Al-Sahhaf in August of 1999. He was especially critical of the British-Dutch proposal. See Ezzat (1999).

on the Council. Building on the Amorim Report, the philosophy behind the resolution was that remaining disarmament tasks could be carried out in the context of a comprehensive and reinforced OMV regime. A new body, the UN Monitoring, Verification and Inspection Commission (UNMOVIC), was established to replace UNSCOM. UNMOVIC was built largely on the Amorim model in terms of staffing and its relationship to the Secretariat; it would be a true UN body. "The thrust of Resolution 1284, then, was to 'tame' UNSCOM, creating an inspection arrangement more integrated with the UN Secretariat and with closer political oversight by the Secretary General and members states" (Lipson 2006, 13).

Aside from the organizational changes, among the resolution's innovations was the offering of an additional carrot: if IAEA and UNMOVIC reports showed that Iraq had "cooperated in all respects" on disarmament, the UNSC could temporarily suspend nonmilitary sanctions for a period of 120 days and could renew this suspension based on further reports. This was a concession to France, Russia, and China, who had sought ways to reward Iraq throughout the second half of the 1990s. Echoing their clashes during the UNSCOM era, however, the P5 never agreed on precisely what this language meant. While the United States and the U.K. felt that only the completion of disarmament should trigger suspension of sanctions, the rest preferred that *progress* toward completion be sufficient (Teixeira da Silva 2004, 213). The language was left ambiguous in the resolution text offered—some argue prematurely—by the Americans and British for a vote.

While Resolution 1284 was successfully passed, Russia, China, France, and Malaysia abstained. And yet the United States certainly did not get what it wanted—an entity, like UNSCOM, that was nimble and separate from the UN bureaucracy and a continued focus on disarmament. The U.S. bargaining position was weakened as accusations of spying in UNSCOM were flooding the media during this period, beginning with a series of interviews by Scott Ritter in advance of his book's release. An article in the *Washington Post*, based on anonymous interviews with U.S. officials, filled in additional details. According to the article, the United States "infiltrated agents and espionage equipment for three years into United Nations arms control teams in Iraq to eavesdrop on the Iraqi military without the knowledge of the UN agency" (Gellman, *WashPo*, March 2, 1999). In the face of such reports, Washington was forced to make concessions. UNSCOM would have to be sacrificed.

In important respects, then, few on the Security Council were entirely pleased with the road map for confronting Saddam and reinvigorating inspections. In the wake of Desert Fox, nearly a full year of painstaking negotiations over sanctions and disarmament served only to expose differences among Security Council governments (Ross 2007, chapter 9). Asked a few months later if he had strong UNSC backing, the head of the newly created UNMOVIC, Hans Blix, equivocated: "Yes, I think there is strong support. It took a long time for the Security Council to work out that resolution. There are tensions between some of them as to how they interpret it; in principle, I think the support is strong, but the tensions ultimately lead to problems. I hope not."[45] His concerns proved prophetic.

Though UNMOVIC's structure addressed many of Iraq's concerns over its predecessor, Baghdad reacted with skepticism to Resolution 1284. The provision for a possible *suspension* of sanctions was viewed as a sign that the Council would never in fact lift them permanently. Iraq also believed the United States would never permit the lifting of sanctions as long as Saddam remained in power. Thus while the resolution included some favorable concessions, in the end "Iraq ignored its demands and also paid no further consequences. Clearly their strategy was to erode sanctions, and they saw no need to accept a new set of inspectors" (Duelfer 2004, 11).

UNMOVIC languished for almost two years. After the terrorist attacks of September 11, 2001, there was renewed energy to deal with Iraq. The United States engaged in a major diplomatic initiative in the Security Council to produce a resolution taking a tough stance on Iraq's WMD. Resolution 1441, passed on November 8, 2002, required that Iraq disclose any prohibited weapons and readmit inspectors. However, 1441 did not represent a robust new consensus on the Council, despite its unanimous passage. It papered over significant underlying disagreements with imprecise language (Byers 2004). Moreover, 1441 clashed in some respects with its predecessor, 1284, and the two resolutions represented dueling and often inconsistent mandates (Lipson 2006). This provided leaders—in UNSC states, in Iraq, and across the international community—with a menu of legal and political arguments they could use to justify their positions and behavior as inspections resumed and as the United States marched down the path to the Second Iraq War. Chapter 5 takes up these issues in more detail.

The period between the Gulf War and the Second Iraq War reflects a sort of hybrid political strategy for the United States, where UN-based policies were combined with unilateral threats and displays of force. Even the latter, however, were consistently—though not exclusively—couched in terms of the UN's authority, especially as embodied in Resolutions 678 and 687, the keystones of the Council's prewar and postwar collective mandates. Following the logic of hypothesis 1, UN approval was coveted as part of a political strategy by the Bush and Clinton administrations to reduce the international political costs of their actions.

---

45. Yale-UN Oral History Project interview with Hans Blix, May 11, 2000, p. 21.

Over time, as the link to a UN mandate became more tenuous, other Council members and the international community generally became increasingly skeptical of actions taken by the United States. Absent renewed and specific authorization for threatening and using force, and in the face of internecine and public quarreling in the Council, coercive U.S. actions—from sanctions to bombing—received less support from governments and diminishing public approval around the world. Moreover, the evidence reveals that levels of international support were driven to a large extent by the mechanisms identified in hypotheses 2 and 3: concerns by governments over U.S. intentions and doubts among foreign publics that U.S. policies were providing broad international benefits.

The chapter also provides evidence consistent with hypotheses 4, 5 and 6, which address the choices made by a coercing state. Early in the decade, with a unified Council, the constraints of channeling policy through the UN were low, making this an attractive option for the United States. Later in the decade, while the potential political costs of intervening in a politically sensitive region were still high, the degree of flexibility that had to be sacrificed in order to achieve further UNSC authorization grew too great. The result was a drift away from the UN toward actions conducted alone or with a small number of allies.

By all accounts, UNSCOM achieved considerable success in disarming Iraq and was on its way to establishing a comprehensive network of ongoing monitoring and verification. UNSCOM and the IAEA uncovered and then destroyed, removed, or rendered harmless fifty-seven prohibited missiles, fifty warheads (including thirty for chemical weapons), sixty-nine missile launchers, and all of Iraq's long-range "super-guns." Under the nuclear file, they sealed Iraq's uranium mine and destroyed sixteen buildings related to nuclear weapons programs, as well as 600 tons of alloys necessary for the production of nuclear weapons. In the biological area, they dismantled the entire al-Hakam biological weapons production facility and destroyed almost eighteen thousand kilograms of biological weapons growth medium. In terms of chemical weapons, they destroyed almost forty thousand chemical shells (some filled and some empty), as well as 760 tons of chemical warfare agents and more than 3,000 tons of precursor agents. Thousands of additional pieces of WMD-related equipment and components were also destroyed (Conetta 2003). A panel of experts established by the Security Council to assess the situation following UNSCOM's departure concluded that, "although important elements still have to be resolved, the bulk of Iraq's proscribed weapons programmes has been eliminated" (UN Doc. S/1999/356). We know now, of course, that no WMD remained.

In the end, however, the coercive strategies employed by the United States during the 1990s did not succeed in either verifiably disarming Iraq or deposing Saddam. The main stick employed by the international community, sanctions, served mainly to punish the Iraqi population; Saddam simply consolidated his domestic control and waited them out (Mueller and Mueller 1999).

The failure of peaceful, verified disarmament was primarily caused by the Iraqi leadership and its obstructionist tactics. However, the Security Council contributed to the failure of inspections as well. While UNSCOM was a generally faithful and hard-working agent, Council members failed to provide adequate support—political and material—for the disarmament task. At no time did UNSCOM have the benefit of both sufficient resources and sufficient unity of purpose on the Council (Thompson 2006b). In some instances, UNSCOM's mission and neutrality were directly challenged by UNSC member states—exemplified by the U.S. spying allegations. In short, the Council did not function well as a collective principal. Saddam learned over time that he was facing at best fragile unity, and he employed divide-and-conquer strategies accordingly. UNSCOM could not survive under these circumstances. As Krasno and Sutterlin (2003, 37) conclude, "The only leverage UNSCOM had was the authority to call on the Security Council to apply the threat of sanctions or military action on the one hand, or incentives on the other. When both its independence and the backing of the full Council dissipated, UNSCOM's ability to function, despite its remarkable accomplishments, was bound to dissipate as well." The very diversity that allows the Security Council to serve as an informative agent of the international community clearly has a downside when it must maintain unity over time to be effective, a point that extends beyond weapons inspections to realms such as sustained economic sanctions and extended peacekeeping missions.

By the time President George W. Bush entered office in 2001, the Security Council's position on Iraq had evolved considerably since his father's time in office. There was little enthusiasm among its members for continuing sanctions—let alone employing military coercion—against Iraq. Once the younger Bush made a decision to confront Iraq over its WMD capabilities, he set out to regain the imprimatur of the Council and the support of the international community.

5

THE SECOND IRAQ WAR

Down the UN Path, 2002–2003

Following the terrorist attacks against the United States on September 11, 2001, the international community responded with genuine compassion and an almost uniform desire to punish the groups responsible and any government sponsors. Capturing this sense of solidarity, the French newspaper *Le Monde* published an editorial two days later whose headline proclaimed "Nous sommes tous américains." For the first time in its history, NATO invoked Article 5, its collective self-defense provision, and the OAS passed a resolution declaring solidarity with the United States under the Inter-American Treaty on Reciprocal Assistance. The subsequent war against al Qaeda and the Taliban regime in Afghanistan received virtually unanimous support and was widely viewed as legitimate and legal—both as an act of self-defense and as a response to Security Council resolutions passed in the aftermath of September 11.[1]

Even with the Afghanistan campaign still under way, some members of the foreign policy team of President George W. Bush set their sights on another, more familiar target: Iraq. After a year of military planning and political maneuvering in both the domestic and international spheres, the Second Iraq War commenced on March 19, 2003. In this latest confrontation with Saddam Hussein's regime, important elements of the United States' coercive strategy were channeled through the UN, including a successful effort to obtain a Security Council

1. For a lengthier description of the international support for the United States after the September 11 attacks and the positive reactions of the international community to the Afghanistan war, see Beard (2002, 568–73).

resolution—1441, passed on November 8, 2002—designed to revive weapons inspections and threatening further consequences if Iraq did not disarm. The Bush administration also used the UN as its primary diplomatic forum for making its case against Iraq and generating international support. This included presentations before the General Assembly and the Security Council by Bush and his secretary of state, Colin Powell, and an effort in the final days before the war to obtain a resolution authorizing the use of force.

Agreement on such a resolution could not be forged. Bush and his advisers had always employed threats of force alongside their diplomatic initiatives and had repeatedly asserted their right to act alone—or preferably with a "coalition of the willing"—in the absence of UN consent. In the end, the war was conducted by the United States with a small group of like-minded states but with no IO approval and on shaky legal ground.

This chapter and the next trace and seek to explain the role of the Security Council in U.S. coercive policy leading up to the invasion. The episode is divided into two phases. This chapter asks, Why did the Bush administration initially channel its policies through the UN, launching a months-long and quite concerted effort to court the Security Council as it revived the confrontation with Iraq? Chapter 6 then asks why, after traveling some distance down the UN path, the administration ultimately chose to bypass the organization. I show how the political costs and benefits outlined in my information transmission argument help us understand the trade-offs and incentives behind these decisions.

To be clear, the focus here is not on *why* the Bush administration chose to go to war against Iraq in 2003, though perhaps it sheds some light in that direction. To address the book's theoretical arguments on coercion and IOs, the analysis concerns *how* statecraft leading up to the war was conducted, with emphasis on the role of the UN and multilateralism more generally in U.S. policy. As in the other empirical chapters, I thus offer a theory-driven "structured, focused comparison" (George and Bennett 2005, chap. 3) of key variables rather than a comprehensive historical account of the episode. This chapter focuses especially on the first three hypotheses outlined in chapter 2:

> Hypothesis 1 (Coercer's Motivation): *When powerful coercers work through IOs, they do so strategically to lower the international political costs of coercion.*
>
> Hypothesis 2 (Intentions Information): *Channeling coercion through an IO sends a signal of benign intentions to leaders of third-party states, thereby increasing the likelihood of international support.*
>
> Hypothesis 3 (Policy Information): *IO approval informs domestic publics abroad that the coercive policy has desirable consequences, thereby*

increasing the likelihood of international support by minimizing domestic opposition.

From September 11 to Iraq

The impact of the events of September 11, 2001, on the foreign policy of the George W. Bush administration cannot be overstated. In the first several months of his presidency, Bush had a modest foreign policy agenda focused mostly on ballistic missile defense and transformation of the military. Much of the administration's effort was devoted to disengagement from multilateral institutions such as the Kyoto Protocol, the International Criminal Court, and the Comprehensive Test Ban Treaty, as well as other arms control initiatives involving land mines, small-arms trafficking, and biological weapons.[2]

As for Iraq, though important members of Bush's team were preoccupied with it from the administration's earliest days,[3] no new plan was developed initially. In fact, Iraq policy was characterized by considerable continuity from the Clinton years, with funds allocated to opposition groups and efforts by Powell and the State Department to promote a modified, "smart sanctions" approach to economic containment. Terrorism also did not figure prominently on the agenda. It is fair to say that, in general, the administration did not have a clear or ambitious foreign policy blueprint before September 11, 2001. A focus quickly emerged after that date, with Afghanistan and Iraq as central elements. On the very afternoon of the terrorist attacks, Secretary of Defense Donald Rumsfeld ordered his staff to look into the possibility of an Iraq connection, and the next day he suggested to the war cabinet that the attacks might represent an "opportunity" to go after Saddam Hussein as well as al Qaeda (Woodward 2004, 25).

On September 15, 2001, key members of Bush's national security team—Powell, Rumsfeld, Vice President Richard Cheney, Deputy Defense Secretary Paul Wolfowitz, National Security Adviser Condoleezza Rice, Director of Central Intelligence George Tenet, and Chairman of the Joint Chiefs of Staff Richard Myers—met at Camp David, the presidential retreat. Iraq was a major topic of discussion. Wolfowitz in particular urged action against Iraq and argued that Saddam's government might have been involved in the 9/11 attacks, while Powell worried that the United States would lose its emerging international coalition, coalescing around the terrorist threat, if a country with no connection were

2. For overviews of these policies with additional context, see Malone and Khong (2003).

3. Iraq was apparently discussed at Bush's first National Security Council meeting (Suskind 2004, 72–75).

brought into the picture (Moens 2004, 164; Woodward 2004, 25–26). The latter urged Bush to "focus on the provocation"—that is, Afghanistan (Carney and Dickerson 2001, 103). While Bush decided at the time to put off a decision on Iraq, it remained on his mind; a few days later he told British prime minister Tony Blair he was determined to topple Saddam (Lantis and Moskowitz 2005, 95).

With the indirect but unequivocal support of the UN Security Council,[4] Operation Enduring Freedom was launched on October 7, 2001, with the goal of overthrowing the Taliban regime, destroying terrorist training camps, and capturing or killing al Qaeda operatives. With the Afghanistan war still under way, Bush ordered Rumsfeld in late November to begin generating war plans for Iraq, and efforts began soon thereafter on the intelligence side.

Concurrent with these secret planning efforts, Bush began to build a public case for turning the country's sights on Iraq. In his State of the Union address on January 29, 2002, Bush identified three states—North Korea, Iran and Iraq—as constituting an "axis of evil": "States like these, and their terrorist allies, constitute an axis of evil, arming to threaten the peace of the world. By seeking weapons of mass destruction, these regimes pose a grave and growing danger." By design he aimed his sharpest attack at Iraq, describing it as the most serious threat among the three (Frum 2003, 224).

The decision to launch a war against Iraq was made well before the important decisions on how to proceed in terms of political and diplomatic strategy. As early as April 2002, Bush reportedly indicated his intention to invade Iraq in a meeting with Blair, who in turn professed support but urged Bush to call for the return of UN inspectors (Sharp 2005, 114; Kampfner 2003, 167). However, the final decision on war was likely made in the summer of 2002. A slow process of troop buildup began in July, and in the same month the United States conducted covert air strikes on Iraq's communications infrastructure (Gordon, *NYT*, July 20, 2003). While not all key officials believed Iraq posed a threat sufficient to merit military force (Powell, Rice, and Tenet all expressed doubts), the dissenters were either convinced or overruled along the way. Richard Haass, director of policy planning in the State Department at the time, reported in an interview for the *New Yorker* magazine that by early July the decision to go to war had been made. From that point forward, in his words, "the agenda was not whether Iraq, but how" (Lemann 2003, 38). I now turn to this "how" question.

---

4. This support came in the form of Resolution 1368 (September 12, 2001), which, invoking Chapter VII, condemned the September 11 attacks as a threat to international peace and security and recognized the United States' inherent right of self-defense, and Resolution 1373 (September 28, 2001), which required states to take action against terrorism by disrupting their financing, training, and movement and by denying them safe haven.

Appealing to the General Assembly

With the war decision more or less a fait accompli, how would the Bush administration approach the conflict politically and diplomatically? This question pitted a generally multilateralist Powell against the more hawkish Cheney. The ensuing debate sheds light on the perceived trade-offs between the UN option and more unilateral alternatives. Cheney and his allies stressed the constraints—including freedom-of-action costs, organization costs, and delay[5]—that would result from working through the Security Council, while Powell's camp stressed the international political benefits in terms of increased support from foreign leaders and their publics.

At first the option of channeling policy through the UN seemed unlikely. This is certainly the atmosphere reported in what became known as the Downing Street Memo, which summarized a July 2002 meeting between Blair's advisers and their counterparts in Washington. This secret memo was obtained and then published by the *Sunday Times of London* on May 1, 2005. It reported a "shift in attitude" in the White House. "Military action was now seen as inevitable. Bush wanted to remove Saddam, through military action, justified by the conjunction of terrorism and WMD. But the intelligence and facts were being fixed around the policy. The [National Security Council] had no patience with the UN route, and no enthusiasm for publishing material on the Iraqi regime's record." From the British perspective, the approach appeared both precipitous and excessively unilateral. The memo characterizes Foreign Secretary Jack Straw as concerned that the case against Saddam was "thin" and that he posed less of a threat than Libya, North Korea, or Iran. It also reports that Blair suggested involving the UN to help provide a legal justification for the use of force.[6]

As the drumbeat of war grew louder, Powell led a group at the State Department calling for moderation and diplomacy. Powell also had allies outside the department, including many in the CIA as well as the British leadership. In general, the moderates pushed for a multilateral approach that included UN resolutions and renewed inspections as the best way to confront Iraq's WMD while reconstituting a semblance of the broad coalition that came together to confront Saddam in 1990 and for part of the ensuing decade. A particular concern was the risk of fanning hatred among Arabs and Muslims. Tenet, for example, worried that a new war with Iraq would aggravate anti-American terrorism and

---

5. See table 2.1 and the related discussion for an overview of these and other constraints presented by IO action.

6. The full text of the memo can be found at http://www.timesonline.co.uk/tol/news/uk/article387374.ece.

undermine U.S. security interests in the Middle East (Lantis and Moskowitz 2005, 98). UN cover would be the best way to mitigate these potential costs.

On August 5, Powell met with Bush and made the case that multilateralism was important for political reasons and that involving the UN in some capacity was the only effective way of achieving widespread international support (Woodward 2002, 332–34). Blair had been making similar arguments to Bush throughout the summer and suggested more specifically that the policy would have to be channeled through New York in order for British troops to participate in a potential war (Stothard 2003, 13). Powell then received unexpected support from senior figures in past administrations who chose to weigh in publicly on the Iraq issue. An August 12 opinion piece by Henry Kissinger in the *Washington Post* was generally supportive of war but advised against unilateralism. Extending Tenet's concerns to the broader war on terrorism, Brent Scowcroft, national security adviser during the Gulf War, warned in the *Wall Street Journal* on August 15 that "[o]ur pre-eminent security priority—underscored repeatedly by the president—is the war on terrorism. An attack on Iraq at this time would seriously jeopardize, if not destroy, the global counterterrorist campaign we have undertaken." Hasty and unnecessarily aggressive policy choices toward Iraq, these moderates argued, not only would grease the skids of terrorist recruitment but might also inhibit cooperation from other governments in this emerging global struggle.

Partly to counter the flurry of media coverage of those advocating multilateralism and patience, in late August 2002 Cheney used a speech to make the most unequivocal statement to that point about his administration's intentions, at least as he viewed them. In an argument against the diplomatic, multilateral track, he cautioned that "time is not on our side" and that "the risks of inaction are far greater than the risks of action." He specifically opposed renewed inspections as a viable approach, stating that they would provide "no assurance whatsoever" of Iraq's compliance. Referring to Saddam's Iraq as a "mortal threat" and erroneously asserting that "there is no doubt that Saddam Hussein now has weapons of mass destruction," he declared that the administration would "consider all possible options to deal with the threat that an Iraq ruled by Saddam Hussein represents" (Cheney 2002). Cheney had all but announced that the United States was planning to topple Saddam.

In the end, Bush was persuaded to channel his Iraq policy through the UN—at least initially. Powell's arguments about international costs combined with foreign leaders' concerns over their political situations at home to tip the balance toward formalized multilateralism. No leader was more important in this regard than Blair. An ICM Research poll conducted in late August revealed that 52 percent of Britons were opposed to Bush's policy toward Iraq; only 21 percent believed the policy was right and worthy of Blair's support (Travis and Watt, *Guardian,* August 28, 2002). Blair also faced "a growing revolt" within his own, generally dovish Labour Party (Stephens, *FT,* August 31, 2002; see also Gardiner 2002). Thus on a September 7 visit to Camp David, Blair urged Bush to seek the political cover of the UN (Sharp 2005, 118). Other leaders in the emerging coalition faced similar constraints. While offering their support in principle, Australian prime minister John Howard and Spanish president José María Aznar both urged Bush to seek UNSC approval. Shortly after Blair's Camp David visit, Bush decided to take his case to the UN General Assembly.

The decision to speak before the UN membership on Iraq having been made, there was still the question of what Bush would say. Cheney argued that he should simply make the case against Saddam and not ask for a new resolution, which would drag the United States into a slow diplomatic process. Indeed, Cheney argued that the president should explicitly affirm the right of the United States to act unilaterally. Cheney also urged the president to use the occasion to challenge UN members to reinforce earlier commitments on Iraq and not to appease Saddam once again, a rhetorical tack supported by Rice as well. The speech should be about the UN—its resolve and relevance—as much as it should be about Iraq. Powell disagreed. For the speech to be politically useful, Bush would have to identify a constructive role for the UN—specifically, he would have to ask for UN support. As Powell told his colleagues, "The UN would not just roll over, declare Saddam evil and authorize war. That approach was not salable. The president had decided to give the UN a chance and the only practical way to do that was to seek a new resolution" (Woodward 2004, 157, 175).

The outcome reflected both tactics. In his September 12 speech before the General Assembly, Bush first described the threat presented by the nexus of terrorism, WMD, and rogue regimes: "[O]ur greatest fear is that terrorists will find a shortcut to their mad ambitions when an outlaw regime supplies them with the technologies to kill on a massive scale." He then identified Iraq as the most immediate security concern, arguing, "In one place—in one regime—we find all these dangers, in their most lethal and aggressive forms, exactly the kind of aggressive threat the United Nations was born to confront." After describing the history of UN-based efforts to manage Saddam's defiance—his violation of UNSC resolutions, his obstruction of inspections, his covert weapons programs—Bush declared, "The history, the logic, and the facts lead to one conclusion: Saddam Hussein's regime is a grave and gathering danger."

Bush then turned the spotlight on his audience, presenting the situation as a challenge to the credibility of the UN: "All the world now faces a test, and the United Nations a difficult and defining moment. Are Security Council resolutions to be honored and enforced, or cast aside without consequence? Will the United Nations serve the purpose of its founding, or will it be irrelevant?" Finally, the president made it clear that unilateralism would be chosen in the absence of a concerted effort to confront the Iraq threat: "My nation will work with the U.N. Security Council to meet our common challenge. If Iraq's regime defies us again, the world must move deliberately, decisively to hold Iraq to account. We will work with the U.N. Security Council for the necessary resolutions. But the purposes of the United States should not be doubted. The Security Council resolutions will be enforced—the just demands of peace and security will be met—or action will be unavoidable. And a regime that has lost its legitimacy will also lose its power."[7] Thus while Bush satisfied Powell's preference by asking for a resolution, he also made it clear that his patience and restraint were limited.

For much of the world, Bush's September speech to the General Assembly seemed to signal a new openness to solving the Iraq crisis through multilateral channels. One newspaper account described a "collective sigh of relief" (DeYoung, *WashPo,* September 15, 2002) from an international community fearful of U.S. unilateralism. The response from capitals was largely positive. Reiterating parts of Bush's logic, French foreign minister Dominique de Villepin declared that "the status quo is unacceptable" and "we cannot agree to violations of any Security Council resolutions." Moscow displayed increased frustration with Iraq, and its strong antiwar stance seemed to soften. Even Secretary-General Kofi Annan agreed that if Iraq continued to violate UN resolutions, the Security Council "must face its responsibilities" (CNN 2002). The administration was beginning to see the benefits of channeling policy through the UN.

Given the positive reaction to Bush's General Assembly speech, on top of the already widespread pro-American sentiment following September 11, 2001, it is reasonable to conclude that opposition to the Second Iraq War was not a foregone conclusion. Rather, the degree of support from the international community was largely a function of the political approach adopted by the United States, especially the role granted to the Security Council, and shifted accordingly over the course of the episode.

Back to the Council: Resolution 1441

As attention turned to the more concrete concerns of drafting and generating support for a new resolution, the costs of IO constraint began to emerge

7. The full text of the speech is available at http://www.whitehouse.gov/news/releases/2002/09/20020912-1.html.

in ways that confirmed many of Cheney and Bush's fears. As discussion began in September over what would eventually become Security Council Resolution 1441, in several instances the UN process operated as an external check on U.S. policy options.

Two key issues drove the resolution debate in Washington and New York: the ground rules for reactivating inspections by UNMOVIC, which had lain dormant since its creation in 1999, and the question of what consequences would be threatened in the event of noncompliance. On the first issue, Cheney and Rumsfeld argued at first for a very stringent inspections regime, including the establishment of expanded no-fly and new no-drive zones to cover areas where the inspectors would be active, the elimination of any modalities for presidential and other sensitive sites, and, most dramatically, a provision whereby any P5 government could send its own inspectors along with UN teams. This last proposal would remove any notion of independence for UNMOVIC and thus was a nonstarter on the Council. It was also distasteful from the perspective of Executive Chairman Hans Blix and his UNMOVIC staff.[8]

On the second issue, the Bush administration advocated an automatic trigger that would authorize "all necessary means" if Saddam was found in material breach of any part of the new resolution. When this draft was circulated among Security Council representatives, it received no support; it was rejected even by those most supportive of U.S. Iraq policy, the U.K., Spain, and Romania (Woodward 2004, 220–21). The push for a trigger set off alarm bells for UNSC members concerned with American intentions. In order to constrain the most bellicose options, more moderate governments insisted on language that could not be interpreted as authorizing force on its own. As the *New York Times* (Preston, October 31, 2002) reported, the goal was "to force the United States to come back to the Council, after the inspections are under way, for a second round of decision-making if Mr. Hussein does not comply with the inspections."

In continuity from the interwar years, it was the French, Russians, and Chinese among the P5 who were most vocally against a military confrontation with Iraq in the absence of deliberation and authorization. They were wary of U.S. efforts to use the UN merely as a stepping-stone on the way to war, and thus the content of any new resolution on Iraq would have to be carefully guarded. De Villepin took the lead in this regard and, at a meeting of foreign ministers in September, insisted on a two-step approach: a first resolution to launch a new round of inspections, with an agreement to debate any violations, and a second

8. Author's interview with a senior UNMOVIC official, New York, November 13, 2003.

resolution to authorize force in the event of noncompliance.[9] The goal for Paris, Moscow, and Beijing was to produce a tough resolution that pressured Saddam while avoiding a "hidden trigger" that could be used by Washington to justify war (DeYoung and Lynch, *WashPo*, October 31, 2002).

In a more subtle maneuver during the resolution negotiations, the White House successfully advocated the inclusion of a declaration requirement whereby Saddam would be compelled to provide a detailed account of his prohibited weapons programs before inspections began. It was designed to place Saddam in a no-win situation: if he claimed he had no weapons, he would be lying and in violation of the new resolution, and if he declared prohibited weapons he would prove himself a serial liar in violation of previous resolutions. Either way he would be in material breach (Jordan, *CSM*, October 31, 2002).[10] Other UNSC members consented to this declaration requirement.

The effort to attain a resolution resulted in substantial organization and influence costs, as well as unexpected delay. The talks dragged on for more than seven weeks, leaving the White House exhausted and frustrated. In the end, eager to claim some diplomatic progress, Bush accepted an outcome filled with compromises. The most important of these—one that would come back to haunt the administration—was the two-resolution formula advocated by the French. Just a few weeks earlier Bush and Cheney had deemed the requirement for a second resolution "unacceptable" (Woodward 2004, 222) as it would entail further delay and an additional opportunity for rejection. They acquiesced in order to keep the Council on board.

Resolution 1441, passed on November 8, 2002, with a unanimous vote in the Council, was a milestone in the Iraq saga (see appendix). It began by recalling various prior resolutions concerning Iraq and by recognizing "the threat Iraq's non-compliance with Council resolutions and proliferation of weapons of mass destruction and long-range missiles poses to international peace and security." Invoking Chapter VII, it then declared Iraq in violation of the post-Gulf War disarmament requirements laid out in Resolution 687 and offered Iraq "a final opportunity" to comply with these obligations or else face "serious consequences." The

---

9. According to an official present at this meeting, Powell offered a message to his French counterpart in response to this formulation: "Don't vote for the first, unless you are prepared to vote for the second" (Weisman, *NYT*, March 17, 2003).

10. In his December 2, 2002, press briefing, White House spokesman Ari Fleischer used the same logic when asked about Iraq's weapons declaration, due a few days later. "Let's see what he says. If he declares he has [no weapons], then we will know that Saddam Hussein is once again misleading the world.... If Saddam Hussein indicates that he has weapons of mass destruction and that he is violating United Nations resolutions, then we will know that Saddam Hussein again deceived the world." http://www.whitehouse.gov/news/releases/2002/12/20021202-6.html.

resolution demanded that Iraq submit a "currently accurate, full, and complete declaration of all aspects" of its weapons programs within thirty days and then provide unconditional access to UNMOVIC and IAEA inspectors.

Paragraphs 4, 11, and 12 of the resolution deserve highlighting:

> 4. [The Security Council] Decides that false statements or omissions in the declarations submitted by Iraq pursuant to this resolution *and* failure by Iraq at any time to comply with, and cooperate fully in the implementation of, this resolution shall constitute a further material breach of Iraq's obligations and will be reported to the Council for assessment in accordance with paragraphs 11 and 12 below;
>
> 11. Directs the Executive Chairman of UNMOVIC and the Director-General of the IAEA to report immediately to the Council any interference by Iraq with inspection activities, as well as any failure by Iraq to comply with its disarmament obligations, including its obligations regarding inspections under this resolution;
>
> 12. *Decides to convene immediately upon receipt of a report* in accordance with paragraphs 4 or 11 above, *in order to consider the situation* and the need for full compliance with all of the relevant Council resolutions in order to secure international peace and security. (Emphasis added)

The language in these passages represented a victory for the multilateralist forces on the Security Council. While the Americans had preferred to use the word "or" in paragraph 4, the French insisted on "and" so that an incomplete or false declaration alone could not be used as a *causus belli;* a failure to cooperate with inspectors would also be needed. Paragraphs 11 and 12 left that latter determination up to UNMOVIC and the IAEA, who were required to report to the Security Council on Iraq's compliance. Paragraph 12 was explicit: the UNSC must convene and consider the situation before further action could be taken.

Thus while the passage of the resolution represented a victory for the United States and its efforts to mobilize the international community against the Iraq threat, the details reflected the interests of the more moderate forces on the Council. In many ways, the Bush administration was becoming mired in the UN process—precisely what some of its principals had feared.

Renewed Inspections

Iraq formally accepted the conditions of Resolution 1441 on November 13, and active inspections resumed on November 27. Because 1441 linked even the possibility of considering the use of force to Iraq's compliance with the inspections process, the activities of UNMOVIC were carefully watched by all sides and provided the fuel for a political firestorm in the run-up to war.

On December 7 the Iraqi government submitted its 1441-mandated weapons declaration, a twelve thousand-page report that did not disclose any prohibited WMD or programs. While many in the Bush administration and abroad, confident of intelligence estimates, felt it was incomplete and false, this act alone was not sufficient legal grounds to abandon inspections in favor of war (for reasons rooted in the language of 1441, as noted above). Many in Washington viewed the declaration as an insult: Saddam was thumbing his nose at the international community and at the Bush administration in particular. "There was a feeling that the White House was being mocked," recalled one U.S. official. "A tinpot dictator was mocking the president. It provoked a sense of anger inside the White House" (Graham, *FT,* May 27, 2003).

The structure and mandate of UNMOVIC also posed challenges for Washington that were not present during the era of the Special Commission in the 1990s. As noted in chapter 4, Resolution 1284 of December 1999 replaced UNSCOM with an organization far more rooted in the UN bureaucracy and less subject to the influence of UNSC member states. The most important difference was that UNMOVIC staff were UN employees subject to Article 100 of the charter; they were not seconded by and did not receive instructions from governments. Blix used his leadership position and discretion to take this independence even further, orienting UNMOVIC around the more diplomatic language of 1284 rather than the more confrontational 1441 (Lipson 2006). This created conflict with the Bush administration, which felt the later resolution should supplant the earlier one and that Blix should take a more aggressive approach toward Iraq. Blix also preferred not to share information or otherwise work closely with national intelligence agencies, especially the CIA, in order to maintain neutrality (Blix 2004, 92–93). (Unsatisfied with this arrangement, U.S. intelligence agencies spied on Blix and the inspectors to maintain awareness of their activities and findings.) Finally, compared with its UNSCOM predecessor, UNMOVIC had the advantage of more resources at its disposal, with a staff of about 250, including 100 trained inspectors, and a budget of about $80 million for its first year of operations.[11] The budget was tied to Oil-for-Food revenue, which had increased substantially since the UNSCOM years, and was essentially guaranteed.[12] This provided additional insulation against political pressure from governments.

---

11. Author's correspondence with Ewen Buchanan, UNMOVIC Public Information Officer, January 27, 2006.

12. Iraq's oil exports in 2002 were double their amounts in 1998, at the time of UNSCOM's demise. See table 4.1. This translated directly into a larger inspections budget, which was based on

The inspections began well. Blix (2004, 110) reports that December was an extremely productive month, with UNMOVIC ramping up its capabilities and Iraq offering substantial cooperation. By early January, however, Bush was growing impatient; he felt the inspectors were not assertive enough and that the international consensus behind Resolution 1441 was attenuating. Bush told Rice in a private meeting that Saddam was growing more confident and was manipulating the international community. "Time is not on our side," he told her (Woodward 2004, 253–54). Rice met with Blix on January 14 to urge him to move more quickly and more aggressively—for example, by interviewing Iraqi scientists outside the country, a tactic that Blix was reluctant to employ (he believed the interviewees would be recalcitrant with their families back in Iraq vulnerable to retribution). On the same day, Bush publicly expressed impatience: "The world came together, and we have given [Saddam] one last chance to disarm. So far, I haven't seen any evidence that he is disarming. Time is running out on Saddam Hussein—he must disarm" (quoted in CNN 2003b).

Bush's impatience was not widely shared at the international level. At a press conference in Paris on January 17, Blix, IAEA director general Mohamed ElBaradei, and French president Jacques Chirac displayed a united front in calling for more time. All three stressed the importance of avoiding war if possible. ElBaradei said that "if we can avoid [war], even spending a few more months to do our job, that is time well-spent" (Sciolino, *IHT,* January 18, 2003). Chirac echoed the sentiment: "The inspectors have asked for more time [and] wisdom dictates that we accede to their request and give them the necessary time." He added that war "is always the acknowledgment of failure." Chirac also reiterated the necessity of returning to the Council: "We consider that if there were to be military action, this could be decided only by the Security Council on the basis of the inspectors' reports" (Embassy of France 2003).

The contrast with U.S. rhetoric at the time could not have been greater. Earlier in the week, the White House seized on the inspectors' discovery of eleven empty chemical warheads in southern Iraq, which dated to the 1980s, calling the finding "troubling and serious" and a sign that Iraq had not disarmed. Others were less concerned. Even Blair's spokesman warned of a "rush to judgment" and adopted the position that the inspectors should be given the time they needed to investigate the warheads' origins. A French diplomat simply commented, "I have only one thing to say—empty" (Bumiller and Sciolino, *NYT,* January 18, 2003).

The French had emerged as the greatest champions of the inspections process and continued to insist that a second resolution was legally necessary. On

---

the same fixed percentage (0.8) of oil revenues as established in 1996 when the Oil-for-Food Program was created.

January 20, de Villepin used the occasion of a Security Council ministerial-level meeting on terrorism to outline France's position on Iraq in advance of UNMOVIC's first report, scheduled for presentation to the Council a week later. At a press conference afterwards he sharply criticized Washington's policy. A military intervention without UNSC authorization would represent "a victory for the law of the strongest" (Schmemann, *NYT,* January 26, 2003). In his view, Saddam's actions and the available WMD evidence simply did not justify military action. He also pointed to the value of having inspectors in country, a luxury the international community had lacked since 1998. As a result of UNMOVIC's activities, he argued, Iraq's weapons programs were "largely blocked, even frozen. We must do everything possible to strengthen this process" (Kessler and Lynch, *Toronto Star,* January 21, 2003).

Powell was apparently surprised and disappointed at de Villepin's comments. At the January 20 meeting he admonished his UNSC counterparts: "We must not shrink from our duties and responsibilities when the material [the first UNMOVIC report] comes before us next week." He added, "If the United Nations is going to be relevant, it has to take a firm stand." But France was in good company. Among the Council's foreign ministers, only Britain's Jack Straw openly supported the U.S. view that further inspections were futile and that Saddam's "last chance" was evaporating—though even his statement was accompanied by a call for a second resolution authorizing force. Foreign Minister Joschka Fischer of Germany captured the sentiment of most Council members when he argued that the inspections "are moving in the right direction" and that "they should have all the time which is needed." In the same spirit, Chinese foreign minister Tang Jiaxuan acknowledged the inspectors' request for more time and expressed approval: "I think we should respect their opinion and support their work."[13]

Following the timetable laid out in 1441, Blix delivered his first official report to the Security Council on January 27. He criticized Baghdad for not being forthcoming enough in its December 7 declaration and in particular for not explaining the status of various unresolved issues identified by UNSCOM upon its departure from Iraq. The general tone of Blix's report was tough and critical, repeatedly noting instances where question marks remained and where Iraq had not actively sought to provide necessary evidence or access to appropriate individuals. At one point, he all but accused the government of hiding documents from UNMOVIC.[14]

---

13. The quotations in this paragraph, along with an account of the January 20 Security Council discussions and press statements, can be found in Kessler and Lynch, *WashPo,* January 21, 2003.

14. The text of Blix's January 27 briefing is contained in the Security Council meeting record for that day (UN Doc. S/PV.4692). ElBaradei also reported to the Council that day on the IAEA's nuclear

U.S. and British officials reacted strongly to Blix's report as evidence of Iraq's failure to comply with 1441. Even before it was delivered, they had urged their counterparts in the UN to view the January 27 briefing as the beginning of the end of inspections, triggering a process that would lead to the use of force if necessary. But most viewed January 27 as simply one important date in a complicated process. Tang characterized Blix's report as "not a full stop of the inspections work, but rather a new beginning," and Fischer urged, "Blix and his team should have all the time that is needed" (Nichols, *USA Today,* January 21, 2003). After the Blix report was released, de Villepin continued to reject the idea of a deadline. "Let us stay within resolution 1441, which established the appropriate framework for the international community," he argued. "The resolution sets no deadline" ("International Reaction," *Irish Times,* January 28, 2003). Even Blair had stated that he did not view the report as a deadline that could trigger conflict (CNN 2003b).

Nevertheless, the U.S. leadership continued to seize on the report much as it had with Richard Butler's final UNSCOM report, used to justify the Operation Desert Fox campaign of December 1998. On February 5, Powell made his famous intelligence presentation to the Security Council with the goal of demonstrating that Iraq possessed WMD and was actively concealing them from UNMOVIC inspectors. He used Blix's own words from the January 27 report to preface his remarks: "As Dr. Blix reported to this council on January 27th, 'Iraq appears not to have come to a genuine acceptance, not even today, of the disarmament which was demanded of it.'" To the extent possible, he framed the case for war in terms of the UN, focusing especially on Resolution 1441. "Resolution 1441 gave Iraq one last chance, once last chance to come into compliance or to face serious consequences," Powell noted. Then, echoing Bush's September General Assembly speech, he challenged his colleagues to uphold the Security Council's credibility. "Iraq has now placed itself in danger of the serious consequences called for in UN Resolution 1441. And this body places itself in danger of irrelevance if it allows Iraq to continue to defy its will without responding effectively and immediately," he warned.[15] Powell was trying to use Blix's report to establish Iraqi noncompliance and thus to initiate the "serious consequences" threatened in the resolution.

The United States and Britain may have made a tactical mistake by seizing too readily on Blix's January report as a catalyst for war. Their zeal caused other

---

inspections. His report was very positive ("We have to date found no evidence that Iraq has revived its nuclear program") and he was more forthright than Blix in demanding more time from the Security Council. The text of his briefing is available in the same UN document.

15. Powell's presentation is available at http://www.state.gov/secretary/former/powell/remarks/2003/17300.htm.

governments to dig in their heels and may have convinced Blix that he should be more cautious in the future so as not to provide ammunition to the hawks. Indeed, Blix's next briefing to the Council, delivered on February 14, was much more positive and contained no clear condemnations of Iraq—and no sound bite the White House could use against Iraq. He focused mostly on describing UNMOVIC's activities and successes and avoided specific references to noncompliance on Iraq's part. He stated that UNMOVIC had not found any proscribed weapons or programs and that the Iraqis had been largely cooperative. "Since we arrived in Iraq, we have conducted more than 400 inspections covering more than 300 sites. All inspections were performed without notice, and access was almost always provided promptly." He went so far as to characterize some of Iraq's behavior as "indicative of a more active attitude focusing on important open issues." Blix conveyed the impression that inspections were paying off, telling the Council, "Inspections are effectively helping to bridge the gap in knowledge that arose due to the absence of inspections between December 1998 and November 2002." While not all previously identified WMD had been accounted for, he urged governments not to "jump to the conclusion that they exist."

In an unusually direct rebuff, Blix also addressed Powell's February 5 intelligence presentation, noting that truck movements at weapons cites—which Powell portrayed as an effort to clean up or remove WMD—could just as easily have been "routine activity." He added a more indirect barb at Powell and U.S. intelligence claims more generally: "Governments have many sources of information that are not available to inspectors. Inspectors, for their part, must base their reports only on evidence, which they can, themselves, examine and present publicly. Without evidence, confidence cannot arise."[16] Blix was clearly frustrated that his repeated appeals to Washington to provide "actionable intelligence" to UNMOVIC had resulted in little aid. Bush and his advisers were hesitant to cooperate in this way, arguing that it was incumbent on Iraq, not the United States, to provide information on the whereabouts of any proscribed weapons (some U.S. officials also did not trust UNMOVIC staff with highly classified information). In the end, Blix did receive some intelligence from the United States and other governments on the suspected locations of WMD, though none of these sites revealed evidence of proscribed weapons or programs (Blix 2004, 93).

The second Blix report further emboldened the war's opponents. Most directly, it gave them an occasion and a forum to make their views known in the most public manner possible. As the foreign ministers of each UNSC member state offered a statement that day, following Blix, it became clear that there was

16. The text of Blix's February 14 Security Council briefing is contained in UN Doc. S/PV.4707.

no stomach for war without further diplomatic efforts, inspections, and authorization. De Villepin declared that "there is an alternative to war, disarming Iraq through inspections," and he was greeted with applause in the Council chamber. He was backed up by strong speeches from the Russian and German ministers supporting continued inspections. Powell argued that day that Iraq "has failed to comply with resolution 1441" but the tide was turning away from such condemnatory sentiments, and Blix's presentation had provided no new fodder for proponents of war.[17]

Moreover, Saddam began cooperating more actively with UNMOVIC, destroying missiles and handing over documents (Daalder and Lindsay 2003, 143). While this newfound eagerness was undoubtedly a calculated move to deflate American and British rhetoric, it seems to have been real and substantive as well. This is confirmed by one UNMOVIC inspector, who had the impression that by late February the Iraqis were "falling all over themselves to find new evidence to convince us they had no weapons."[18] A credible threat of force from Washington certainly had its benefits, but in a perverse way this disarmament success, combined with Blix's fairly positive February 14 report, was viewed as a setback in Washington. As the BBC (2003c) reported, "from that point on, somehow the momentum slipped away from the Americans."

With little support for the notion that Resolution 1441 alone justified force, it was clear that a second resolution would be needed for intervention to be deemed acceptable by the international community. It was also clear that much convincing and diplomacy would be required of the United States to bring the Security Council on board.

A Second Resolution?

As the inspections process was unfolding, action on the diplomatic front continued. The main objective for U.S. diplomats was to pursue a second resolution explicitly authorizing force. While this was seen as a difficult task, it was not deemed impossible until fairly late in the game. Many governments had called for more time for inspections, yet most on the Security Council had not ruled out war as an option if the inspectors reported significant violations by Iraq. Thus the prospect of a second resolution remained.

One reason for confidence was that throughout the fall the French indicated they would support force if inspections failed. As late as mid-December, a senior

---

17. The various February 14 statements can be found in UN Doc. S/PV.4707.

18. Author's interview with a former UNMOVIC inspector, Ottawa, June 15, 2005.

French military officer informed the Pentagon that his country would actively participate in the invasion if it had UNSC authorization (Kitfield 2003, 2338). The conventional wisdom within the Bush administration at the time was that France would consent to a second resolution. Indeed, in early January Chirac warned his armed forces "to be ready for anything," implying that he had not ruled out force (Mallet, *FT*, January 14, 2003). The French were apparently concerned about being cut off from the United States—and, by extension, any decision making regarding the use of force in Iraq—if they were too categorical in their opposition (BBC News 2003a).

At the same time, the French insisted that a decision on force could be made only by the Council with an additional resolution, and that such a decision should be, in the words of Defense Minister Michele Alliot-Marie, "based on the work of the inspectors" (Mallet, *FT*, January 14, 2003). The French objection to war was not categorical, and this left room for hope. This hope was further magnified by Blix's January 27 report, which seemed to indicate that he was taking a tough line with Saddam and that it was only a matter of time before Iraq was deemed in material breach.

Thus a second resolution was both necessary—if the United States wanted a clear UN mandate—and plausibly achievable. However, Bush was opposed to a second resolution, and, in a rare case of agreement, so were both Cheney and Powell. All felt that the first resolution could be used as justification, and in any case they recoiled at the thought of weeks of diplomacy that promised to be even tougher than the 1441 negotiations. In the end, it was pressure from Blair that made the difference. He framed a resolution as an "absolute political necessity" at home, and Bush in turn promised an all-out effort to help his British counterpart (Woodward 2004, 297). Without the U.K., the United States would be practically alone going into battle.

However, as the Anglo-American axis began pushing for a second resolution, a coalition was forming against any momentum toward war. In particular, Germany's opposition was becoming more vocal and, after it assumed a rotating seat on the Council in January, more politically salient. During the first half of January, with the French still equivocating, German chancellor Gerhard Schroeder was among the most antiwar of European politicians. When Chirac and Schroeder met in Paris on January 22, the Frenchman revealed to the German that, after months of leaving his options open, he had decided to join him. At a joint press conference after the meeting, Chirac made it clear that his policy was now aligned with Germany's, saying that war "is always the worst of solutions. And hence everything must be done to avoid it.... France and Germany have a judgment on this crisis that is the same." He added that "any decision [on war] belongs to the Security Council, and to it alone" (Tagliabue, *NYT,* January 23, 2003). France and Germany now stood in coordinated opposition to the United States.

Echoing its role in the run-up to the Gulf War, Russia consistently pushed for a diplomatic solution in order to avoid war. In mid-January Alexander Saltanov, the deputy foreign minister, traveled to Baghdad for talks. Speaking at the UN on January 21, Foreign Minister Igor Ivanov warned of the risks of going to war. "Terrorism is far from being crushed.... We must be careful not to take unilateral steps that might threaten the unity of the entire anti-terrorism coalition. In this context we are strictly in favor of a political settlement of the situation revolving around Iraq" (Kessler and Lynch, *WashPo,* January 21, 2003).

These three countries—France, Germany, and Russia—coalesced in their views and emerged as the key anti-American coalition. On February 10, Chirac, Schroeder, and Putin issued a joint statement declaring, "Nothing today justifies war." They called for enhanced inspections as an alternative: "Russia, Germany and France are in favor of pursuing inspections with a substantial strengthening of human and technical capacity by all means and in consultation with the inspectors, within the limits of resolution 1441" (CNN 2003a). China publicly endorsed the statement, such that a majority of the P5 were now lined up against the U.S. push for war in the near term. It is important to note, however, that none had yet explicitly threatened to veto a new resolution, though Paris had all but declared this its policy.

As hope faded of bringing the French on board, Washington pursued a two-pronged approach to its Security Council diplomacy. The first element involved convincing the Russians that they should support—or at least not veto—a resolution declaring Iraq in breach and authorizing force. If Russia went along, most believed that China would also acquiesce, not wanting to be alone with the French in scuttling the effort. The second element involved generating support among the nonpermanent members. If the United States could show that nine out of fifteen members—the threshold required for passage of a resolution—supported a war authorization, France would again be isolated. Such an outcome would be politically, if not legally, important, and the intervention policy might benefit from some legitimation effect.

By the end of February, however, Russia, after equivocating for weeks, came out in clear opposition to war and threatened to veto a new resolution. Ivanov declared, "Russia has the right to a veto in the U.N. Security Council and will use it if it is necessary in the interests of international stability.... Russia will not be in favor of any new resolution which allows the use of military force directly or indirectly to solve the Iraqi issue" ("The Iraq Crisis," *Houston Chronicle,*

February 28, 2003). China made its veto threat explicit shortly thereafter (Gee, *Globe and Mail,* March 7, 2003). The first element in the two-pronged approach was failing.

Attention thus turned to the nonpermanent members. By late January, Syria and Germany were considered firmly in the opposition camp while Bulgaria was in support. That left six undecided countries on the Council: Pakistan, Chile, Mexico, Cameroon, Guinea, and Angola. Pakistan reportedly would have gone along if it had been the ninth and thus deciding vote (Weisman, *NYT,* March 17, 2003). The United States would therefore need to convince Chile, Mexico, and two of the three African countries in order to achieve the nine-out-of-fifteen threshold, and it engaged in a diplomatic push to achieve this. The French and Germans responded in kind. "Over the next six weeks, Messrs. Chirac and Schroeder worked the phones, visited foreign capitals and called in diplomatic chits. Their goal: nothing less than the reining in of what they saw as a rogue superpower" (Champion et al. 2003). By the end of February, nothing had changed; the same six countries remained officially undecided. Table 5.1 lists the Security Council members and their positions in the run-up to war.

A February 24 draft resolution being circulated by the United States, Britain, and Spain declared bluntly that Iraq had failed to disarm and was thus subject to the serious consequences threatened in 1441. This amounted to a declaration of war. With at least five countries explicitly opposing the resolution's formulation, the British, loath to launch war without UNSC authorization, were left "grasping for a compromise" (Gee, *Globe and Mail,* March 7, 2003). Inspired by a Canadian compromise proposal, Straw began airing the possibility of establishing specific benchmarks for Iraqi disarmament and a deadline for their accomplishment. The hope was that fence-sitting countries would find it more palatable to vote for a resolution that did not directly authorize war—they would be supporting only a deadline. If enough of them could be brought into a coalition of nine affirmative votes, perhaps the French, Russians, and Chinese would abandon their veto

Table 5.1. Security Council positions on war, February 2003

SUPPORTIVE	UNDECIDED	OPPOSED
United States[a]	Angola	France[a]
United Kingdom[a]	Cameroon	Russia[a]
Bulgaria	Chile	China[a]
Spain	Guinea	Germany
	Mexico	Syria
	Pakistan	

[a]Permanent member.

threats (most likely with abstentions). Even with a veto, at least the war's proponents could claim meaningful support on the Council.

Thus in a last-ditch effort to garner votes, the British, supported by the United States and Spain, introduced a revised draft resolution on March 7. It noted "that Iraq has submitted a declaration pursuant to [UNSC] resolution 1441 (2002) containing false statements and omissions and has failed to comply with, and cooperate fully in the implementation of that resolution," and imposed a March 17 deadline on Iraq and the Security Council. In the operative paragraph, the Security Council

> Decides that Iraq will have failed to take the final opportunity afforded by resolution 1441 (2002) unless, on or before 17 March 2003, the Council concludes that Iraq has demonstrated full, unconditional, immediate and active cooperation in accordance with its disarmament obligations under resolution 1441 (2002) and previous relevant resolutions, and is yielding possession to UNMOVIC and the IAEA of all weapons, weapon delivery and support systems and structures, prohibited by resolution 687 (1991) and all subsequent resolutions, and all information regarding prior destruction of such items.[19]

However, most Council members were holding out for a plan that would ensure UNMOVIC several weeks to perform its task. The final nail in the coffin came on March 10, when Chirac announced he would veto a second resolution "in all circumstances."[20] A week before the March 17 deadline, the number of countries on the Council committed to war remained at four—the United States, Britain, Spain, and Bulgaria (Weisman and Barringer, *NYT,* March 10, 2003). On March 12, Bush made one last effort to garner the politically important Latin American votes. He called Vicente Fox of Mexico and Ricardo Lagos of Chile to ask them how they would vote. Lagos told Bush no; Fox did not call back (Woodward 2004, 344–45).

On March 15, France and Germany, again supported by China, issued a declaration stating, "We reaffirm that nothing justifies in the present circumstances putting a stop to the inspection process and resorting to the use of force." While they expressed support for a timetable for disarmament, they would not agree to any resolution that contained an explicit or implicit trigger for war (Housego

19. The full text is available at http://news.bbc.co.uk/2/hi/middle_east/2831607.stm.

20. In fact, the French might have preferred to avoid the whole issue of a second resolution, settling instead on a more ambiguous outcome whereby the United States used 1441 to justify war and the French grumbled but were not compelled to openly threaten a veto. Hoffmann (2004, 15) suggests that French leaders hoped for precisely this outcome until the Americans and British pushed for a second resolution, forcing their hand.

2003). On March 16, Bush, Aznar, and Blair met in the Azores Islands, purportedly as a last-ditch effort to seek a solution but more realistically to demonstrate solidarity and to publicly make their case for war one last time. The draft second resolution was officially withdrawn on the morning of March 17. In a speech that evening, Bush issued a public ultimatum to Saddam and his sons: leave Iraq within forty-eight hours or face attack.

Explaining U.S. Motivations

Having outlined the role of the Security Council in prewar statecraft, I now address what motivated U.S. policymakers to go so far down the UN path and discuss implications for the book's first three hypotheses. While the United States ultimately chose to bypass the Council, a decision discussed at length in the next chapter, my hypotheses on why powerful states work through IOs should shed light on the elements of diplomacy that did center on the UN.

Strategically Minimizing International Costs

Hypothesis 1 predicts that states work through IOs as a calculated strategy to minimize the international political costs of coercion. This requires ruling out several alternative motivations—namely, (1) a logic of appropriateness, (2) material necessity, and (3) domestic politics at home. While we should not be surprised to find these factors present, support for my argument requires that they not be the primary driving force behind the U.S. decision to seek UN approval.

First, there is little evidence that the Bush administration turned to the UN out of an internalized desire to behave legitimately (this is the "strong" version of the legitimacy logic, in the terminology of chapter 2). Rather, the decision was based on a calculation of political costs and benefits; the UN was a means, not an end. Powell and others pushing for a multilateral approach stressed the political costs of proceeding without UN support and made arguments in consequential rather than normative terms. In the National Security Presidential Directive that outlined the goals and strategy in Iraq, the foreign policy principals in the administration agreed that they would act with a coalition "if possible" but alone "if necessary." The choice would be a matter of political expedience (Woodward 2004, 155).

In general, the U.S. approach to dealing with proliferation threats and WMD in the post-September 11 era has been flexible and politically pragmatic, emphasizing legal and normative principles only when convenient. In the words of one State Department official, "we have a range of options and we want to maximize the use of those options."[21] This is consistent with the underlying attitude driving Bush administration foreign policy vis-à-vis IOs, which Richard Haass, the State Department's director of policy planning at the time, famously characterized as "à la carte multilateralism" (Shanker, *NYT,* July 31, 2001). It is clear that Bush—like Clinton and the senior Bush in their confrontations with Iraq—treated the role of the UN as a calculated choice in a manner consistent with hypothesis 1.

Second, during the coercive phase of the confrontation the United States did not seek UN involvement primarily for purposes of burden sharing or aggregating power.[22] Material cooperation from a small number of states was indeed highly valued; in particular, regional partners were coveted for basing and overflight rights, and British forces took on a significant burden. However, most of these contributions were assured through bilateral arrangements that had little to do with the UN process. Moreover, for the most part this assistance was desirable for war-planning purposes but not necessary. Military planners hoped to launch a second front from Turkish territory, but the initial phase of the war was a spectacular success without this luxury. Even the British were not viewed as crucial from a military standpoint, a reality underlined by Rumsfeld's infelicitous comment on March 11, 2003, that British participation would be "helpful" but that "there are work-arounds" if Blair could not muster domestic support to participate in the war. American forces would simply proceed on their own.[23]

The minimal concern for burden sharing was largely the product of two variables: the overwhelming relative power of the U.S. military and the lessons of the Afghanistan war. The Iraqi military was about half its 1991 size and was in very poor condition following a decade of sanctions.[24] The United States would be virtually unchallenged in the air and at sea—indeed, not a single Iraqi plane took to the air during the war, heeding the American motto "If they fly, they die." This resulted in a lopsided campaign: the regime was toppled and the country occupied in about twenty-seven days, all with minimal casualties. The United States simply did not need much help to get the job done. Moreover, a central lesson from the 2001 Afghanistan war was that the lone superpower did not need help to conduct successful wars. The United States did not seek any material assistance from NATO in Afghanistan largely because the Europeans had little to

21. Author's interview with a State Department official in the Bureau of International Security and Nonproliferation, Washington, April 6, 2006.

22. This was not true in the postinvasion period, when the United States desperately sought partners to help defray the costs of rebuilding Iraq and providing security.

23. This comment provoked a "mixture of panic and fury" in London (Burkeman and Norton-Taylor, *Guardian,* March 12, 2003), as it made Blair's considerable—and politically risky—efforts to support the United States appear unappreciated. See also Kearney (2003, 88–89).

24. On the state of Iraq's military, see Pauly and Lansford (2005, 116) and Adams (2003, 109).

offer. Alexander Moens (2004, 146) notes that "there simply was not much NATO could do.... Europe did not have the precision-guided munitions, the high-tech air power, nor the necessary logistics and intelligence to be a full partner." Success in Afghanistan implied little need to seek widespread material assistance in the run-up to Iraq. In David Lake's (1999) terminology, the UN was not used to capture "joint production economies" in war fighting but rather for political reasons, as emphasized in hypothesis 1.

A third plausible alternative to hypothesis 1 is that domestic politics drove the U.S. decision to channel policy through the UN. Indeed, before the war two-thirds of the American public wanted the president to seek the support of the international community and specifically to wait for UN approval before using force.[25] As with his father in the Gulf War, however, President Bush was not terribly concerned with public opinion because he could count on a substantial rally once war was initiated. The rally effect was in fact strikingly similar across the two cases: 76 percent of Americans supported the use of force against Iraq on April 9 of 2003 (three weeks into the second war), versus 77 percent in late January of 1991 (two weeks into the first war) (Pew Research Center 2003b). Thus the 2003 rally drowned out a prewar desire for UN authorization and involvement. President Bush ended up with a clear majority supporting war and "with little need, as far as domestic politics is concerned, to seek authorization from the United Nations Security Council" (Asmus, Everts, and Isernia 2004, 75).

In fact, the rally effect is so powerful that for some people it overrides concerns over the policy itself. A Program on International Policy Attitudes poll conducted just after the war began showed that, of those who approved of the war, 18 percent said they supported the decision not because it was "the best thing for the U.S. to do" but because they "support Bush's decision because he is president." Twenty-one percent of respondents did not agree with Bush's decision to invade unilaterally but nevertheless indicated that they "still support the President" (PIPA 2003, 4). These data suggest that Bush could count on support from many who did not even agree with the substance of the policy.

There is also little evidence that Bush needed the UN in order to persuade Congress to support the war. To be sure, Bush's General Assembly speech in September did help build momentum in Congress for a bill empowering the president to pursue a military option (Balz and VandeHei, *WashPo,* September 13, 2002). Tom Daschle, the Democratic leader of the Senate, gave Bush credit for a "strong" speech and said he was "encouraged by his express desire to go to the

25. For similar results along these lines, see Los Angeles Times Poll (2002), conducted in December of 2002; and Tyler and Elder, *NYT,* February 14, 2003 (reporting a *New York Times*/CBS News poll).

international community" (Mitchell, *NYT,* September 13, 2002). But Congress did not vigorously push the UN path. Joseph Biden, the Democratic chairman of the Foreign Relations Committee, even hinted in September at the possibility of bypassing the UN: "The worst option is going it alone, but it is an option" (quoted in Pauly and Lansford 2005, 72). The House and the Senate passed Iraq war resolutions on October 10 and 11, respectively, by wide margins (296 to 133 and 77 to 23). This was a month before the passage of Resolution 1441 showed widespread international support for pressuring Saddam.

The Bush administration was simply not very concerned about bringing Congress along. The White House asserted in late August that it did not need authorization from Congress to establish a domestic legal basis for war (Allen and Eilperin, *WashPo,* August 26, 2002). After months of discussions on the *international* aspects of Iraq policy, including the possible role of the UN, the Bush foreign policy team devoted only one principals meeting to strategizing on the *domestic* politics. With congressional elections coming up, and with memories of 9/11 still fresh, it was easy to generate support on Capitol Hill for a war resolution. Rice suggested that a congressional resolution, while not necessary, would strengthen the administration's hand at the UN and therefore could be helpful (Woodward 2004, 167–68). Thus contrary to the conventional wisdom in the literature, that IO approval can help overcome congressional opposition (Schultz 2003; Cortell and Davis 1996), in this case the causal mechanism seems to have operated in the opposite direction. The Bush team was not using the UN primarily for domestic purposes.

Signaling Intentions and Appeasing Publics Abroad

Hypotheses 2 and 3 compel us to consider the more specific motivations that drove the UN-based approach for several months. Hypothesis 2 focuses on intentions information: Coercing states channel power through IOs in order to signal benign intentions to other leaders, thereby increasing the likelihood of their support. Hypothesis 3 focuses on policy information: IO approval informs domestic publics abroad that the coercive policy has desirable international consequences, thereby reducing domestic opposition in third-party states. We see both dynamics in the lead-up to the Second Iraq War, with emphasis on sending intentions information early in the episode and a focus on policy information and domestic publics as time went on.

Initially, Powell and his moderate allies preferred to operate through the UN for the purpose of greasing the wheels of diplomacy and keeping other countries, especially European allies, on board. Bush's post-9/11 rhetoric about preemption and regime change—what had emerged as the new "Bush Doctrine"—was viewed as highly ambitious and potentially threatening to other states, even allies. These concerns were aggravated by the United States' unmatched power. "[G]iven America's overwhelming military dominance," Graham Allison (2004, 127) notes, "it had the power to topple other regimes unilaterally, without requiring others' assistance or asking their permission." In this context, operating through the UN was initially seen as a way to counteract the image of the United States as hasty and aggressive in its approach to Iraq, an image aggravated by Cheney's hawkish speech from August 2002. To generate international support, the United States would have to demonstrate that it was willing to be constrained by allies and other Security Council members.

This is precisely the signal that was sent with Bush's September 12 speech to the UN and, more important, with the much more costly negotiation and passage on November 8 of Resolution 1441, which required substantial compromise on Washington's part and seemed to rule out unilateral options in the near term. Some in the Bush administration wanted to utilize 1441, with its declaration that Iraq was in material breach of previous resolutions and its threat of serious consequences, as a trigger for war. This position gained force when Iraq submitted its incomplete weapons declaration on December 7. However, on both occasions the White House chose to stay with the UN and to support renewed inspections for fear that doing otherwise "would be seen as too provocative and too much evidence of American desire for war" (Weisman, *NYT,* March 17, 2003). Thus repeatedly during the fall of 2002 the United States chose to tie itself to the UN process in order to maintain international support for applying pressure on Iraq. These actions follow the logic of hypothesis 2.

Over time, however, the leadership grew tired of waiting and proved itself increasingly unwilling to compromise and to accept the costly constraints of working through the UN (a trend discussed more in the following section). It is perhaps surprising, then, that they adhered to the IO-based process by accepting renewed inspections and by pursuing a second, authorizing resolution. Consistent with hypothesis 3, the evidence indicates that they did so with a specific audience in mind: domestic publics in key third-party states. Publics around the world doubted the desirability of an Iraq war; appealing to them with a UN endorsement was the only way to build support by freeing governments from this domestic constraint. At the very least it might dampen overt opposition by other states and mitigate anti-American resentment.

There is ample evidence that domestic publics abroad affected the strategic calculations of the United States. In an article written just before the outbreak of war, Fareed Zakaria (2003) argued, "Countries are furtive in their support for the administration not because they fear Saddam Hussein but because they fear their own people. To support America today in much of the world is politically dangerous." The U.S. government responded accordingly. From his view inside the administration, Haass confirms that these considerations motivated policy-makers. "In any event," he recalls, "we ended up going for the second resolution, quite honestly, not because we needed it. It was seen as nice to have, from our point of view. It was seen as desirable. But it was something that Tony Blair and others felt very strongly that they needed in order to manage their domestic polities" (quoted in Lemann 2003, 39). One U.S. official, who served as a political officer in an important eastern European embassy during the run-up to war, confirms that domestic public opinion in potential coalition partner countries was a major preoccupation for the State Department. He recalls that "we definitely spent effort tracking public opinion" and also tried to shape it by making speeches to certain organizations and by making sure local journalists "had the right information."[26]

Blair had already seen the benefits of a UN imprimatur. The passage of Resolution 1441 had a positive effect of several percentage points on approval for an intervention in Iraq (Thompson 2005, 31). But this effect wore off as the policy veered away from the UN, and by early 2003 Blair was facing the largest antiwar demonstrations in Britain's history. More than 80 percent of Britons polled in mid-January felt that "it is essential for Britain and America to get a fresh mandate from the UN before they launch military action against Iraq."[27] Blair desperately pressed the White House to go the extra step in the Security Council. On January 31, he visited Bush with the primary objective of obtaining U.S. support for a second resolution. While the Americans were reluctant to go this route, "in Britain, political pressures were taking their toll on the prime minister. Opposition to war was hardening among the public, within his party and even in the cabinet" (Baker et al., *FT,* May 29, 2003). In the end Washington joined the cause for a second resolution in order to assist Blair with his political situation. As one U.S. official put it, "it's increasingly obvious to folks in all capitals that a new resolution would be a very good thing. And it has to be said that Blair politically really needs it" (Frankel, *WashPo,* February 19, 2003).

The prospects for a war authorization from the Council looked bleak in early March, prompting the British to propose their revised draft resolution on March 7. As late as March 12, a week before the war started, Blair, sensing trouble in Parliament and with upcoming elections, was imploring Bush to stick with the UN path (Woodward 2004, 342). During this period, the United States was forced to contemplate war without the U.K. by its side. As the prospects of a second

26. Author's interview with a State Department political officer, June 15, 2005.

27. According to an ICM/*Guardian* poll conducted between January 17 and 19, 2003, http://www.icmresearch.co.uk/reviews/2003/guardian-poll-jan-03.htm.

resolution faded, it was not clear whether Blair could defy a rebelling Parliament and public opinion by joining the intervention. His defense secretary was obliged to warn the White House that Britain might not be able to participate in the war after all (Kearney 2003, 88).

Blair was not alone. Bush's two other staunchest allies, Aznar of Spain and Howard of Australia, were similarly torn between international and domestic interests. Aznar consistently supported the war but worked tirelessly to promote UN authorization in order to appease his domestic political audience. More than 90 percent of Spaniards were against the war, with only 5 percent expressing support.[28] When he announced to the Spanish parliament that he was scaling back earlier pledges and would not send combat troops to join the United States (he instead sent medical and mine-clearing units and three ships for support roles), the news was met with cheers in the chamber (CNN 2003c). For Australians, UNSC authorization was critical: on the eve of war, just 25 percent of Australians supported a war without UN authorization, compared with 61 percent who supported a UN authorized war.[29] On February 5, the Australian senate went so far as to pass a motion of no confidence in the prime minister's handling of the Iraq crisis and also formally censured his government.

I suggest in chapter 2 that the framing strategies of leaders provide additional observable implications for hypothesis 3. If leaders believe that public support hinges on IO approval, in statements intended for public consumption we should see them frame their actions in terms of the IO and especially its informative properties—that is, its independence and its internationally representative membership. Indeed, all the public efforts to justify the Iraq war by the key governments involved were in terms of the UN and its imprimatur. Even once hope was gone for a formal authorization, there was still a systematic effort to frame the war in terms of compliance with UNSC resolutions. The news conference given jointly by Bush, Blair, and Aznar on March 17 provides typical examples. In Bush's words, "The United Nations Security Council, in Resolution 1441, has declared Iraq in material breach of its longstanding obligations, demanding once again Iraq's full and immediate disarmament, and promised serious consequences if the regime refused to comply. That resolution was passed unanimously and its logic is inescapable: the Iraqi regime will disarm itself, or the Iraqi regime will be disarmed by force. And the regime has not disarmed itself.... The world has spoken. And it did it in a unified voice." For his part, Aznar declared that his

28. According to an Instituto Opina/*El Pais* poll conducted on March 26 and 27, 2003, reported in Center for Public Opinion and Democracy (2003b).

29. These are the results of a Newspoll survey reported in the *Sydney Morning Herald* on March 18, 2003, available at http://www.smh.com.au/articles/2003/03/18/1047749732511.html.

coalition allies wanted nothing more than "for UN resolutions to be respected." Finally, Blair touched on the same themes: "So now we have reached the point of decision, and we make a final appeal for there to be that strong, unified message on behalf of the international community that lays down a clear ultimatum to Saddam that authorizes force if he continues to defy the will of the whole of the international community set out in 1441."[30]

These public statements shed light on the political calculations of the leaders. Just as in the Gulf War and Operation Desert Fox, the intervention was framed in terms of the UN to the greatest extent possible. Specifically, Bush, Aznar, and Blair argued that the Security Council represented the "will of the international community" and that, through Resolution 1441, "the world has spoken." The implicit argument was that because of its diversity, the UN's alleged stamp of approval should be meaningful to publics around the world concerned about whether the use of force was justified. Thus a war against Iraq would be in the interests of the international community; no reference was made to the national interests of the intervening states themselves. This was part of a systematic effort—in the end, largely unsuccessful—to appeal to domestic publics around the world.

Shortly after the attacks of September 11, 2001, and the subsequent war in Afghanistan, the administration of President George W. Bush focused its energy on Saddam Hussein, reviving a confrontation that began in August of 1990 with the invasion of Kuwait. During the ensuing months, the administration channeled important aspects of its Iraq statecraft through the UN. These efforts included the use of the General Assembly and Security Council as the primary forums for making the case to the international community that Iraq, because of its purported possession of WMD and potential links to terrorists groups, posed a threat to the international community. In November of 2002, the Security Council backed up U.S. concerns by passing Resolution 1441, which threatened "serious consequences" if Iraq did not disarm and resurrected the weapons inspections process.

U.S. decision makers chose the UN path because they worried about the international political costs of intervening in Iraq—and the Middle East more generally—without a sound legal basis or at least a multilateral stamp of approval. Security Council authorization was especially coveted in this regard and was sought for two reasons in particular. First, as in the Gulf War case, working through the Council would demonstrate to the international community

30. A transcript of the news conference is available at http://www.whitehouse.gov/news/releases/2003/03/20030316-3.html.

that the United States was willing to be constrained and to accommodate the interests of others. This would diminish the threat posed by a U.S. intervention in the region to the interests of various politically important governments. Second, and most important, the Bush administration was concerned with the reactions of domestic publics abroad. Key members of the emerging anti-Iraq coalition, including the governments of Australia, Spain, Turkey, and the U.K., faced substantial political barriers at home to supporting an increasingly aggressive U.S. policy in Iraq. Security Council approval would signal to these publics that the coercive policy being pursued was designed to provide broad international benefits—beyond the narrow interests of the United States. Among the key decision makers, Colin Powell was especially forceful in pushing for a UN-based policy that, he argued, would provide these political benefits.

The prewar diplomacy of 2002 and 2003 offers a powerful illustration of how important foreign publics are in the politics of military intervention. A strong argument can be made that Bush and his advisers were more concerned about legislatures and citizens abroad than they were about Congress and the American public, a dynamic that the international relations and foreign policy literatures have largely overlooked. While international public opinion was still generally supportive of U.S. policy after Bush's speech to the General Assembly in September of 2002, opinion polls revealed increased skepticism about the war option as the year drew to a close. On the eve of war, in early 2003, large majorities opposed forceful intervention. It was in this context, and especially in response to the domestic backlash facing Prime Minister Tony Blair, his staunchest ally, that President Bush channeled policy through the UN for so long. In the end, this included an attempt to achieve a second, authorizing resolution from the Security Council.

As the next chapter demonstrates, this effort ultimately failed because the United States was not willing to countenance the delay and compromise that would have been required to bring the diverse nations of the Council on board. The war option was pursued without the political benefits of IO approval.

6

THE SECOND IRAQ WAR

Bypassing the Security Council

The Second Iraq War began on March 19 (the early morning of March 20 in Iraq) of 2003 with a flurry of cruise missile attacks in and around Baghdad designed to target Iraq's leadership. Additional air strikes and cruise missiles were used to take out Iraq's air-defense systems, artillery batteries, and command-and-control centers. The Pentagon had dubbed this a "shock and awe" bombing strategy, design to weaken enemy resolve and dissuade resistance. By the third day of the war, ground forces were moving northward into Iraq from Kuwait and Saudi Arabia, and a far more substantial air campaign was launched at targets throughout Iraq. On April 5 U.S. soldiers took control of the Baghdad airport, and by April 9 they had moved into central Baghdad. With the fall of Tikrit, Saddam's hometown, on April 14, the occupation of Iraq was complete. On May 1, from the deck of the aircraft carrier USS *Abraham Lincoln*, President George W. Bush declared an end to "major combat operations" in what amounted to a victory speech.[1]

U.S. and British forces did suffer from a few modest setbacks: dust storms, unexpected resistance from the paramilitary fedayeen, and a brief slowdown in late March as the advance outstripped supplies. For the most part, however, military opposition melted away and progress was swift, reflecting the utterly lopsided stature of the opposing forces. Even the best Republican Guard divisions, to say nothing of the regular army, lacked both the skills and the firepower to

1. For more comprehensive histories of the invasion, see Gordon and Trainor (2006); Keegan (2004); Cordesman (2003); and Murray and Scales (2003).

pose a serious challenge to U.S. and British forces. Their poor organization and outdated equipment "condemned them to be massacred" (Keegan 2004, 192). "As expected," John Mueller (2005, 120) notes, "the Iraqi military disintegrated under the onslaught and seems to have lacked any semblance of a coherent strategy of resistance." As noted in the previous chapter, sufficient material power and success in defeating the Iraqi regime were never in question.

In this chapter, I explore why the United States ultimately chose to bypass the United Nations and what the consequences of that decision were. These questions bear directly on the theoretical arguments of the book. While chapter 5 had its most direct implications for hypotheses 1 to 3, here I mostly address the last three hypotheses, on flexibility, anticipated costs, and forum shopping.

> Hypothesis 4 (Flexibility): *When coercers place a low value on flexibility (i.e., are less sensitive to the costs of constraint), they are more likely to turn to IOs.*
> Hypothesis 5 (Anticipated Costs): *When coercers anticipate high international political costs for taking action, they are more likely to turn to IOs.*
> Hypothesis 6 (IO Forum Shopping): *When coercers place a low value on flexibility (i.e., are not sensitive to the costs of constraint) and anticipate high international political costs, they are most likely to turn to the Security Council. When only one of these conditions is met, they are more likely to turn to regional organizations.*

To preview my conclusions, consistent with hypothesis 5, U.S. policymakers were indeed concerned about international political costs—hence the concerted effort to bring the UNSC on board. But these concerns were in the end overshadowed by a very high sensitivity to the costs of IO constraint, which they were simply not willing to pay. This led them to veer away from the UN, as hypothesis 4 predicts. Thus the dual conditions outlined in hypothesis 6, present in the Gulf War, did not exist in the 2002–3 episode. Taken together, and given that there was no regional IO alternative (an important factor addressed in more detail below), the outcome follows my theoretical predictions: a strong urge to work through the UN in order to minimize international costs was ultimately outweighed by an unwillingness to pay the attendant costs, leading to intervention without IO approval.

Much of this chapter thus focuses on the issue of flexibility and the perceived constraints of IO-based action in the case of the Second Iraq War. I outline the various costs involved in working through the UN during late 2002 and early 2003 and then identify three factors that led the Bush administration to value flexibility over the benefits of a multilateral umbrella: (1) the feeling of vulnerability produced by the September 11 attacks, (2) the neoconservative and nationalist ideologies of key officials, and (3) the lessons derived from interventions in the recent past, especially Kosovo, which soured many decision makers on multilateral approaches.

After explaining U.S. political strategy vis-à-vis the UN, a final section addresses the consequences of acting without an IO mandate. Consistent with my information theory, the United States suffered a backlash by governments concerned about U.S. motivations and foreign publics highly skeptical that intervention was justified and serving broad international interest. The costs of acting alone were—and continue to be—substantial.

Was It a "Unilateral" Policy?

The Second Iraq War is often portrayed in the media as the archetypal case of unilateralism and of a go-it-alone foreign policy. But we should not take this popular impression for granted. Before I discuss the motivations behind the choice to bypass the UN, I first establish that the United States did indeed operate without UN approval and consider whether the policy was nevertheless multilateral in a meaningful sense. These assessments help us place the intervention on the continuum of independent approval discussed in chapter 2 and portrayed in figure 2.3. While the Gulf War case presented in chapter 3 was fairly straightforward in this regard—UNSC approval was explicit, thus placing the case on the far right end of the continuum—the Second Iraq War, much like Operation Desert Fox in 1998, is more ambiguous.

The legal argument made by the United States and the U.K. to justify force was based on extant Security Council resolutions and had two related components. First, they argued, a material breach of Resolution 687—the 1991 ceasefire resolution imposing disarmament obligations—revived the authority to use force under Resolution 678, the Gulf War authorization. They then referred to language in Resolution 1441, of November 8, 2002, accusing Iraq of being in material breach of 687. Second, they pointed out that 1441 gave Iraq a "final opportunity" to comply with its disarmament obligations or else face "serious consequences," and then described Iraq's behavior since 1441 as noncompliant and argued that the use of force constituted a legitimate serious consequence.[2] (The appendix contains the texts of these resolutions.)

---

2. The legal arguments made by the United States are most clearly expressed in the March 20, 2003, letter from U.S. ambassador to the UN John Negroponte to the president of the Security Council. See UN Doc. S/2003/351. See also Taft and Buchwald (2003) (both were legal advisers in the State Department at the time of the war). The definitive British legal argument was made in a March 17,

These arguments rely on the notion of "implied authority" in the absence of specific authorization. That force was authorized by past resolutions surrounding the Gulf War (i.e., 678 and 687) is doubted by most law scholars. Resolution 678 clearly refers to Iraq's invasion of Kuwait as the relevant threat to international peace and authorizes member states "cooperating with the Government of Kuwait" to use all necessary means. Thus the authorization is expressly limited to the situation at hand in 1990 and does not countenance future possibilities. Resolution 687 is similarly framed in terms of the threat posed by Iraq to Kuwait. And while the American and British governments argued that violations of 687 "revived" 678 and its authorization of force, there is no mention of this possibility in the text of 687.

Resolution 1441 also does not provide a solid legal basis for war. First, even if we accept that Iraq's behavior was noncompliant, the resolution threatens only "serious consequences" in such a circumstance. This phrase is not the standard UNSC language for war—the accepted phrase being "all necessary means (or measures)." Second, an even more central problem is that 1441, as noted in chapter 5, explicitly calls for the Security Council to reconvene to "consider the situation" in the event of Iraqi noncompliance. It requires an additional decision to initiate war, which is why the diplomatic push for a second resolution was so important. Third, the expressed intent of Council members throughout its drafting history and on the day of the vote was not to pass a resolution authorizing war (Murphy 2004, 172), a point reaffirmed by almost all Council members during the subsequent months. Indeed, previous drafts of the resolution promulgated by the United States contained language—including the phrase "all necessary means"—that would have authorized war in the event of further material breach by Iraq. With most members opposed, the Council *consciously chose to exclude* any such formulation (Conte 2005, 160). Finally, Resolution 1441's ambiguity makes it a weak legal foundation for war. While the resolution was adopted unanimously, it masks fundamental differences among Council members over the seriousness of the threat posed by Iraq, the proper role of inspections, the consequences of Iraq's failure to comply with its 687 obligations, and more generally the circumstances under which force should be used (Byers 2004).

In any case, there is no doubt that the overwhelming impression of leaders and their publics around the world was that the war was fought without Security Council backing and, indeed, that it was fought against the vocally expressed wishes of most UNSC member states. Thus both legally and practically, it is

---

2003, public statement by Attorney General Lord Peter Goldsmith. For the full text, see http://www.guardian.co.uk/Iraq/Story/0,2763,1471659,00.html.

safe to characterize the Second Iraq War as having been conducted without IO approval.

The theoretical discussion in chapter 2 suggests that simple multilateralism—that is, action conducted by a group of states—can confer some political benefits even when policies are not channeled through an IO. Depending on its size and diversity, a coalition can send politically meaningful information to the international community by constraining the leading coercer and by certifying that the policy serves broader collective interests. This leads us to the question of how "multilateral" the intervention was. In terms of figure 2.3, how far to the left of the continuum should the Iraq 2003 case be placed?

The Bush administration made the case that it was acting with a very large coalition indeed. The State Department published a list of forty-six countries that supported the war. In his address to the nation on the day the war began, Bush declared that more than thirty-five countries were "giving crucial support." Top administration officials repeatedly claimed that the coalition was larger than its Gulf War counterpart.

Ivo Daalder (2003) vigorously challenges these assertions by focusing on the substance of the support offered to the invasion: "The administration is trying too hard to prove something that isn't. By insisting that the 'coalition of the willing' is larger, deeper, and wider than is in fact the case, the administration only emphasizes the extent of its own isolation. Only Britain is offering meaningful support." Most contributions to the war were largely symbolic, as in Palau's offer of access to its harbors and airports. Some members of the coalition expressed support for the United States but simultaneously worked strenuously to avoid a war. Others expressed support only secretly, which was not helpful from a political standpoint. The invading coalition itself comprised about 250,000 U.S. combat personnel, joined by 45,000 British, 2,000 Australians, and 200 Poles. This is in contrast to the 160,000 coalition troops that fought alongside the United States in 1991. Another angle of comparison between the Gulf War and the Second Iraq War is the degree of condemnation. In 1991, only a handful of countries, such as Cuba, Yemen, and Jordan, openly opposed the war. In 2003, opposition was widespread, even among allies such as Canada, Mexico, France, and Germany.

Even if the size of the coalition as presented by the Bush administration could be taken at face value, a certain qualitative dimension was lacking. U.S. allies, UNSC member states, and even coalition members did not get the sense that U.S. policy was multilateral in any meaningful way, and engagement with other governments was largely perfunctory—they were given the option of going along, induced by a mixture of carrots and sticks, but were not expected to offer their input. As Chancellor Schroeder complained, the message coming from

Washington was "we are going to do it, no matter what the world or our allies think" (quoted in Rubin 2003, 50). Even the British did not elicit any substantial compromises from Washington. As one commentator notes, "there is precious little evidence that [Blair] secured more than marginal influence over the course of U.S. policy" (Andrews 2005, 75; Sharp 2005, 134–35).

The bottom line from a political standpoint is that, notwithstanding the presence of a modest coalition, the United States was widely viewed as having behaved in a lawless manner by imposing a might-makes-right, unilateral solution (Trachtenberg 2005, 214–15). While the policy was not strictly unilateral, its multilateral nature was circumscribed to the point that it transmitted little or no beneficial information regarding U.S. intentions and policy consequences to the international community. Few political benefits could be derived from such an approach.

The Costs of Working through the UN

Returning to the central themes of the book, I argue that the Bush administration chose to take action against Iraq without UNSC approval because it deemed the costs of working through the UN too high in the end. Chapter 2 outlines several costs of constraint imposed by independent IOs on even the most powerful coercing states (these are summarized in table 2.1). As U.S. policymakers and military planners started down the UN path, they faced many of these costs and could see others on the horizon. The divergence in policy preferences over Iraq that plagued the Security Council in the late 1990s became ever more salient as the prospect of war grew more real, and this imposed organization costs (as others were brought on board and tried to influence the course of policy) and delay at various stages (as diplomacy and formal procedures slowed the pace of policy implementation). It became increasingly clear that letting UNSC governments drive the policy might reduce U.S. freedom of action substantially and very possibly lead to undesirable outcomes, including that feared most by the Bush administration: leaving Saddam Hussein in power. They were not willing to pay these actual and prospective costs.[3]

Vice President Dick Cheney's opposition to the UN route was premised largely on the constraints that such a political strategy would entail. In mid-August of 2002 he warned the administration's other foreign policy principals that going to

---

3. One of the costly IO constraints identified in chapter 2, scrutiny, was not an important factor in the episode at hand and is thus left out of the discussion. Because the events were so highly publicized and controversial, there was little the Security Council could add in this regard.

the UN "would invite a never-ending process of debate, compromise and delay. Words not action" (Woodward 2004, 157). What Cheney, Defense Secretary Donald Rumsfeld, and eventually Bush feared the most was a political strategy based on "process"—synonymous, for them, with the UN option—rather than a set of more definitive decisions. These types of concerns are consistent with the delays and organization costs theorized in chapter 2. As I outline in the previous chapter, the United States devoted considerable effort to mobilizing support and achieving necessary voting thresholds in the Security Council. In addition to the delay and diplomacy, an important product of organizing coercion under the UNSC umbrella was what I term "influence costs"—the complications that arise as each IO member state seeks to impose its own interests on the organization's decisions.

From the moment the Bush administration set its sights on Iraq, delay emerged as a concern for both practical and political reasons. From a war-fighting perspective, waiting too long was risky. While much of the wait leading up to the Gulf War had been needed to position troops and equipment, this was far less true in the later case. By the end of 2001, General Tommy Franks had devised more flexible, "rolling start" war plans that could be launched as soon as the following spring or summer—almost a year before the war actually started—and by February 2002 Franks informed Bush that he could go "anytime the president chooses" (Woodward 2004, 60, 101, 118). Especially because the troops would be wearing chemical protective gear, military planners preferred to launch the invasion during the cooler winter months, extending through March. And the Iraqi army's training schedule meant they would be least prepared in the winter as well. These factors led the Pentagon to prefer an invasion in January or February, or March at the latest (Woodward 2004, 99–100, 214).

Against this background, acquiring the appropriate Security Council resolutions for action against Iraq was potentially costly since it would require substantial and time-consuming diplomacy and negotiations. It took weeks, from September to November, for Resolution 1441 to be secured, and while many in the Bush administration viewed this as a victory in rallying the world against Iraq, from the perspective of most other governments it was only the beginning of a strategy to pressure Iraq and readmit inspectors, this time from UNMOVIC. These disparate goals led to various compromises in the language of 1441 that set in motion an indefinite inspections process combined with open-ended criteria for the use of force. From this point forward, keeping the rest of the P5 on board, especially France, would require continued patience and compromise.

By December of 2002, as the inspections process was being revived, there was a substantial American military buildup and a growing sense that troops could not remain deployed indefinitely, in terms of both morale and logistical support. However, the inspections developed a momentum that was difficult for the White House to stifle. Resolution 1441 did not specify a timetable for inspections. Hans Blix, the executive chairman of UNMOVIC, therefore drew up a plan in mid-January for the conduct of the inspections operation, including the establishment of additional infrastructure and the generation of a list of "tasks" to be completed before Iraq could be considered disarmed (and therefore eligible for the lifting of sanctions). According to the Blix plan, the list was to be drawn up by March 27, a date selected to be consistent with the schedule laid out in the much earlier Resolution 1284, which established UNMOVIC in 1999 (see appendix). Resolution 1284 was more specific than 1441 about the timetable for inspections, and, to the annoyance of Washington, Blix viewed it as still operative. The Americans immediately balked at such a delay. Rice and Negroponte became "alarmed that Mr. Blix's view could slow the inspections" and expressed their concerns privately to Blix and in public statements (Preston, *NYT*, January 16, 2003; Usborne and Grice, *Independent*, January 17, 2003).

In both their January 27 and February 14 presentations to the Security Council, Blix and Mohammed ElBaradei, head of the International Atomic Energy Agency, called publicly for more time to complete their tasks. This placed Bush, who at this point was more focused on how to force an endgame, in a difficult political position. On March 5, Blix made matters worse for the United States when he said that Iraq was showing "a great deal more cooperation" and asked for more time (Gee, *Globe and Mail*, March 7, 2003). And in a March 8 interview, ElBaradei stated again that there was no evidence of a nuclear program and reiterated his desire to have more time—"at least two to three months"—to make a definitive judgment (Weisman and Barringer, *NYT*, March 10, 2003). To end the inspections by using force would be to flout the independent assessments of ElBaradei and Blix, inviting an international backlash.

On March 11, the six "undecided" members of the Security Council—Cameroon, Guinea, Angola, Mexico, Chile and Pakistan—requested that the U.S.-British ultimatum deadline (set for March 17 in the revised draft resolution from the previous week) be extended to give Iraq an additional forty-five days to disarm. While the British had an open mind to some additional delay, the White House was "alarmed at the extent to which the British government is prepared to be flexible in offering compromises" and rejected the proposal as "a non-starter" (MacAskill, Norton-Taylor, and Borger, *Guardian*, March 12, 2003). The contrast to Gulf War diplomacy is instructive. In that case the United States showed a willingness to delay the deadline to allow further diplomacy by France and Russia and to secure a favorable vote on Resolution 678. In 2003, this flexibility was not repeated.

While the Bush administration was willing to countenance delay and some compromise earlier in the standoff, these organization costs were now viewed as a threat to the ultimate policy objective of overthrowing Saddam by force. Just as many proponents of the Gulf War had worried about the diplomatic costs of delay, the junior Bush and his advisers worried that, as time passed, the willingness of the international community to stand up to Iraq would dissipate from its zenith with the passage of 1441. "Time is not on our side here," Bush warned Rice. He felt Saddam was becoming more confident and was manipulating the international system into a position where it would accept a less-than-comprehensive solution to the Iraq problem (Woodward 2004, 254).

If the UN process were allowed to continue, U.S. freedom of action would be affected through significant policy modifications, including the possibility that the war option would be taken off the table entirely. The Bush administration was not willing to compromise on this goal, and the inspections regime emerged as the single most important threat in this regard. Cheney warned Bush repeatedly that inspections would complicate the task of taking out Saddam, and by late January even Powell was worried that some Council members viewed inspection as an end in itself and doubted whether they were serious about holding Saddam accountable (Kessler, *WashPo,* January 24, 2003). UNMOVIC's work was viewed by many in Washington not as a possible path to peace but as an obstacle to a fait accompli—an obstacle that would have to be either undermined or circumvented.

Two episodes in particular illustrate the United States' unwillingness to be flexible when it came to war. First, in early February an emissary from the Egyptian government met with Bush in secret to discuss the possibility of exile for Saddam in a neighboring country such as Saudi Arabia, Jordan, or Turkey. Despite several earlier public statements by administration officials that this might be an option for averting war, Bush threw cold water on the Egyptian proposal, and it was stillborn (Woodward 2004, 314). Later, the president of the United Arab Emirates reportedly worked out an eleventh-hour deal with Saddam offering him refuge. Saddam agreed in principle but asked for certain guarantees in return, including immunity from prosecution and an Arab League resolution approving the exile arrangement (Fattah, *NYT,* November 2, 2005). The League could not agree on a resolution, at least not in time, but the United States apparently did not earnestly pursue the possibility. According to a senior State Department official, "they didn't believe Saddam would really step down" and therefore did not seriously consider this alternative solution (CNN 2005).

Second, in late February the Canadian government, torn between its traditional multilateralism and a desire to maintain good relations with its powerful neighbor, suggested a compromise designed to find a middle ground between the UNSC's rival camps. This "bridging the divide" proposal set specific benchmarks—based on substantive accomplishments, not just procedural obedience—that Iraq would have to achieve by March 28, after which the Security Council would approve "all necessary means" if inspectors reported noncompliance.[4] While many Council members—including the U.K., which suggested similar language two weeks later—viewed this as a promising way forward, it was rejected out of hand by Washington. When Undersecretary of State John Bolton was asked about the Canadian plan, he simply repeated his government's official line: "Our view is that Iraq has failed to take advantage of the final opportunity that was presented to it" (CBC News 2003). The Bush administration did not engage the Canadian government at all on the proposal and did not offer a formal response, instead allowing its media statements to send the message of rejection.[5]

To be sure, there is no guarantee that either alternative, exile or the Canadian proposal, would have succeeded even with a more receptive United States. The point of these anecdotes is that the U.S. leadership had concrete possibilities to pursue had there been a real desire to find common ground and avoid war—but categorically chose not to. The Bush administration was willing to be flexible earlier in the episode as long as its central policy strategy and war planning were not affected. However, when the compromises and delay became too costly and began to substantially implicate U.S. freedom of action, the administration was no longer willing to abide the constraints required to maintain UNSC support. Doing so would have required, as Harold Koh (2003, 1520–21) notes, "genuine strategic multilateralism," a method deemed incompatible with the more aggressive approach preferred by the Bush administration.

Sensitivity to IO Constraints

The previous section outlined the meaningful constraints imposed on the Bush administration—and the prospect of additional ones on the horizon—as it channeled its Iraq policy through the UN during the second half of 2002 and early 2003. These costs ultimately convinced Bush and key advisers to abandon the UN process. While understanding these costly constraints helps explain the choice to bypass the UN, it still raises the question of why U.S. officials decided these costs were too high to pay. Why were they so sensitive to the costs of IO

4. While Canada was not a member of the Security Council at the time, the Mexican delegation expressed willingness to forward the proposal.

5. Author's interview with a senior Canadian diplomat, New York, November 13, 2003.

constraint? Getting at this issue addresses hypothesis 4 in more depth and helps explain why the United States eschewed IO-based action despite a concern with the international political costs of operating alone.

I argue that three factors combined to generate a very low tolerance for costly constraints in the confrontation with Iraq. First, the events of September 11, 2001, produced a newfound sense of vulnerability in Washington that served to diminish patience in dealing with foreign threats, actual and potential. Second, several key administration officials were ideologically predisposed toward unilateralism and aggressive foreign policies, and September 11 strengthened their hand and allowed them to impose their policy preferences. Third, recent experiences of multinational war fighting had soured policymakers, especially in the Pentagon, on actions implemented through IOs. The 1999 Kosovo intervention, conducted with NATO, was especially salient in this regard and had convinced many that coalitions added little in terms of usable power and subtracted much by complicating and politicizing operations.

The Influence of 9/11

The end of the Cold War had brought about what James Baker (1996, 30) describes as "a general reduction of the strategic stakes for the great powers," who no longer viewed every threat and local conflict through the lens of a global power struggle. The 2001 attacks on New York and Washington forced an abrupt end to this mind-set and profoundly altered thinking inside the Beltway. September 11 appears to have had an important impact on Bush himself, who prior to his presidency had advocated less involvement abroad and a "humble" approach to wielding U.S. power.[6] Indeed, as noted in chapter 5, the Bush administration's pre-9/11 policy toward Iraq displayed considerable continuity with its predecessors'. The terrorist attacks were a catalyst for change.

The most important source of change was a new sense of vulnerability: suddenly it was demonstrably possible for a foreign adversary to inflict massive civilian casualties on U.S. soil. Despite its immense power, one historian (Lundestad 2005, 17) notes, the United States now "feels itself to be uniquely vulnerable." Fueling this sense of vulnerability was the fact that such adversaries did not require great strength to cause harm. As the Bush administration's 2002 National Security Strategy warned, "even weak states and small groups could

6. In his second presidential debate with Vice President Al Gore during the 2000 presidential election campaign, Bush, asked how the rest of the world should view the United States and its unmatched power, advocated humility: "If we're an arrogant nation, they'll resent us. If we're a humble nation, but strong, they'll welcome us."

attain a catastrophic power to strike great nations" (White House 2002, 13). The potential threats to the United States were difficult to detect and almost limitless in number.

Vulnerability to small, almost invisible, and potentially suicidal enemies, especially ones able to acquire unconventional weapons, rendered irrelevant much of the strategic culture and lessons of the Cold War. Hegemony was no longer a guarantee of safety, and traditional deterrence would be largely unworkable. The strategic value of multilateralism and international institutions was further questioned by an already skeptical Bush administration following September 11. Rumsfeld captured the administration's thinking in a *New York Times* editorial entitled "A New Kind of War," published on September 27, 2001. In his words, "This war [on terrorism] will not be waged by a grand alliance united for the single purpose of defeating an axis of hostile powers. Instead, it will involve floating coalitions of countries, which may change and evolve. Countries will have different roles and contribute in different ways. Some will provide diplomatic support, others financial, still others logistical or military.... In this war, the mission will define the coalition—not the other way around." The implication was that solutions to serious security threats would not be held hostage to mere diplomatic niceties.

From a U.S. perspective, multilateralism was also less attractive because the potential partners did not necessarily agree on the nature and magnitude of the threat. The strategic assessments and perceived vulnerability of the United States after September 11 were simply not shared by the Europeans and other allies (see Pond 2005, 31). This divide served to increase the costs of working multilaterally and especially through IOs, where the interests and influence of other states are formally integrated into the decision-making process.

Bush Administration Ideology

Of course, the response of Bush administration officials to September 11 was also a function of existing biases and predisposition—and a sense that the terrorist attacks would unleash executive power and allow various foreign policy goals to be pursued. In other words, 9/11 not only changed the mind-set of Bush administration officials, but it provided a strategic opportunity. Rice made precisely this point when, reflecting on the post-9/11 atmosphere during an interview with the *New Yorker* magazine, she stated that it was "important to try to seize on that and position American interests and institutions and all of that before they harden again" (quoted in Cirincione 2003, 4).

The foreign policy team assembled by Bush combined a set of idealistic goals with an appreciation for realpolitik methods based on the exercise and threat of military power. Much has been made of the influence of neoconservatives in the Bush administration. It was a group of neocon thinkers, all members of the Project for a New American Century (PNAC), who sent a letter to Clinton in January of 1998 advocating regime change in Iraq. Among those who signed the letter, several went on to hold high-ranking foreign policy positions under George W. Bush, including Rumsfeld, Wolfowitz, Elliott Abrams, Richard Armitage, John Bolton, Paula Dobriansky, Zalmay Khalilzad, Richard Perle, and Robert Zoellick.[7]

The neocons believed that American values—especially freedom and democracy—should be spread actively around the world. Added to this Wilsonian idealism (see Zakaria 2002) was the notion that the United States' unparalleled military power was a legitimate tool for achieving this goal and for confronting regimes that challenged U.S. values and interests. The neocon philosophy combined a strong belief in American exceptionalism with a willingness to challenge others, if necessary through the application of military force. This confidence was matched by "a skepticism about the ability of international law and institutions to solve serious security problems" (Fukuyama 2006, 4). The UN was subject to the most pointed derision.

The neocon critique of President Clinton had always been one of wasted opportunities: he was unwilling to use American power on behalf of a coherent, principled project (Farer 2004, 44). September 11 allowed this group to activate American muscle and thereby set their idealism in motion. As Elizabeth Pond (2005, 30) describes it, "The neoconservative policy shift after 9/11 transformed the United States from being the guarantor of the status quo, its traditional role, into a revolutionary power and supplanted the USA's collaborative Cold War leadership with a more muscular, unilateral, and crusading exercise of hegemony." Beyond Afghanistan, Iraq was fingered as the best candidate for the spread of American values in the Middle East.

Cheney, arguably the pivotal foreign policy player of Bush's first term, was not a neoconservative per se; he was in Daalder and Lindsay's (2003, 15) terms an "assertive nationalist" in the mold of more traditional, hard-line conservatives. What he and the neocons had in common after 9/11 was a willingness to use military power to defeat even indirect threats to U.S. security. He therefore did not stand in the way of—and indeed encouraged—the neoconservative focus on Iraq. Cheney and Bush also had in common with neocons a strong distrust of

---

7. There is a considerable literature on the influence of neoconservatives on Bush's foreign policy. See, for example Nuruzzaman (2006); Davis (2006); Fukuyama (2006); Packer (2005, chap. 1); and Daalder and Lindsay (2003).

multilateral institutions, which they believed stood in the way of U.S. interests more often than they promoted them.

The confluence of neoconservative ideology with the lessons of September 11 led to two powerful new sets of ideas in the Bush administration: the "nexus argument" and the preemption doctrine. The first held that the primary threat to U.S. national security was the potential for terrorists to acquire weapons of mass destruction and for "rogue" regimes to facilitate this acquisition. Bush's invocation of an "axis of evil"—comprising North Korea, Iran and Iraq—during his 2002 State of the Union address was based on this logic. He proclaimed, "States like these, and their terrorist allies, constitute an axis of evil, arming to threaten the peace of the world. By seeking weapons of mass destruction, these regimes pose a grave and growing danger."

This nexus argument was coupled with an emerging doctrine of preemption, the most important element of what came to known as the Bush Doctrine. In June of 2002, Bush used a commencement address at the West Point military academy to outline his post-9/11 strategic doctrine. He declared that new threats require new thinking, and continued: "We cannot defend America and our friends by hoping for the best. We cannot put our faith in the word of tyrants, who solemnly sign non-proliferation treaties, and then systematically break them. If we wait for threats to fully materialize, we will have waited too long.... We must take the battle to the enemy, disrupt his plans, and confront the worst threats before they emerge. In the world we have entered, the only path to safety is the path of action. And this nation will act."[8] The 2002 National Security Strategy (White House 2002, 6) lays out the notion of preemption in more formal terms. The document promises to defend "our interests at home and abroad by identifying and destroying the threat before it reaches our borders. While the United States will strive to enlist the support of the international community, we will not hesitate to act alone, if necessary, to exercise our right of self-defense by acting preemptively against such terrorists, to prevent them from doing harm against our people and our country." The Cold War mainstays of deterrence and containment were declared obsolete.

The idea that threats would have to be confronted before they materialized—really a doctrine of preventive action rather than of preemption—would make multilateralism difficult to implement. The implication was that coalitions that imposed constraints on U.S. freedom of action would not be practicable. This

8. The text of the West Point speech is available at http://www.whitehouse.gov/news/releases/2002/06/20020601-3.html. Bush had used very similar language in his State of the Union speech six months earlier, insisting that "I will not wait on events, while dangers gather. I will not stand by, as peril draws closer and closer."

approach fit comfortably with the unilateralist predisposition of many Bush administration officials.

The Lessons of Kosovo

The Kosovo intervention in 1999 was authorized by NATO and conducted in conjunction with several NATO allies. While this regional cover certainly offered political advantages to the United States, the episode was viewed in a negative light by many in Washington who were frustrated by what they viewed as an excessively democratic and deliberative approach to the conflicts in the former Yugoslavia. The Kosovo experience has been underappreciated in the academic literature as an influence on the Bush administration's approach to the subsequent wars in Afghanistan and Iraq.

While the Kosovo intervention was ultimately successful in ending Serbian aggression and preserving the autonomy of Kosovo, the military campaign was significantly hampered by problems associated with multinational planning and command and control. This is perhaps not surprising since this was NATO's first joint combat mission.

Problems arose even before the operation began, as NATO governments found it difficult to share intelligence effectively. Once the campaign was launched, policymakers became mired in the organization's inefficient consultation and decision-making procedures (Kay 2004). This was important since the original plan was for an operation of a few days; as the operation wore on for several weeks, countless ad hoc decisions had to be made on a timely basis. On paper, the nineteen NATO governments addressed this problem by delegating authority to Secretary-General Javier Solana during the first week of the war. But several leaders could not resist having control, and thus a "management committee" was formed of the most involved NATO countries—the United States, Britain, France, Italy, and Germany. This was literally a war run by committee. From the perspective of the United States, one partial solution to the collective action problem was to progressively shift responsibility to the more agile U.S. joint task force, but this effectively "created two command structures, which occasionally worked at cross-purposes" (Thomas 2000, 47). It also drew the ire of other NATO governments, especially the French.

From the Pentagon's perspective, by far the most frustrating aspect of coalition warfare in Kosovo was the selection of bombing targets. The U.S. military bridled at European meddling in the Kosovo bombing campaign (Peterson 2003). Not only was the process slow and complicated, it was highly political, such that targets could be removed from the list for a wide variety of reasons. In his exhaustive analysis of the operation, Anthony Cordesman (2001, 66) concludes,

"The most serious single problem in coalition warfare affecting the execution of the air and missile campaign was political and not a matter of resources and capabilities. NATO targeting and operations were so tightly constrained by individual European countries that they exerted a veto power over both the kind of targets that could be attacked, and even over individual missions." Some governments vetoed targets at the last minute, forcing planes to abort missions already under way. This created logistical complications and risked pilots and airplanes in fruitless missions.

Imbalances between U.S. and European capabilities also created problems. Many of the European allies lacked the advanced avionics, the secure communications, the electronic warfare capabilities, the precision munitions, and the training needed to strike specific targets, especially in bad weather and given the desire to limit collateral damage (Cordesman 2001, 64). This wide disparity in usable military power had two implications. First, it meant that the United States bore most of the burden by necessity. Second, it created friction in terms of interoperability, which degraded the alliance's war-fighting effectiveness (Department of Defense 2000, 24–26).[9]

In the aftermath of Kosovo, according to one analyst, U.S. leaders took away two main lessons: "First, it reinforced the idea that war by multilateral committee is a bad idea. The U.S. military also had more serious doubts about the reliability of its allies. Second, Kosovo showed Washington that the U.S. could do it alone" (de Jonge Oudraat 2004, 179–80). One Defense Department official involved in planning the operation recalls that he felt "bogged down in this political NATO-approval nightmare."[10] The same official concludes that "the net effect of NATO as a military alliance was negative" and reports that after Kosovo, "at DOD we're saying to ourselves 'forget it, we're never going to go through that again.'"

Thus it became clear soon after September 11 that, despite NATO's invocation of Article 5 and offers of support from the Europeans, the Afghanistan operation would be conducted by the United States with minimal input from others. NATO was not directly involved for reasons rooted in the Kosovo experience (Gordon 2001–2, 92). From Washington's perspective, Operation Enduring Freedom further illustrated the utility of relying almost exclusively on U.S. planning and operations and confirmed many of the perceived lessons learned in Kosovo.

In the lead-up to the Iraq war, there remained fears over the potential for international political interference that might compromise the military mission. Recalling the multilateral efforts in Kosovo and Bosnia in the 1990s, Bush

---

9. For a discussion of this issue with less blame placed on the Europeans and NATO, see Daalder and O'Hanlon (2000, 220–23). See also Clark (2001).

10. Author's interview with a Department of Defense intelligence officer, April 14, 2006.

Pentagon officials cringed at the thought of fighting another "war by committee" (Champion et al. 2003). And indeed, during the war-fighting stage, there were clear benefits to working alone. As I showed in chapter 3, the large UN coalition of the Gulf War actually degraded the United States' ability to prosecute the war, an outcome repeated in Kosovo. By contrast, acting on its own in 2003 the United States was "freed from the perceived constraints of a multilateral military coalition," and military planners were afforded "wide latitude to formulate and implement their preferred strategy" (Pauly and Lansford 2005, 107). A larger coalition—especially one working under a UN mandate—would have imposed much greater checks on U.S. flexibility.

Combined with the influence of the September 11 attacks on the strategic mind-set in Washington and the ideological predispositions of key players in the Bush administration, the Kosovo experience heightened the United States' sensitivity to the costs entailed in IO-based action. As a result, the constraints outlined in the previous section were deemed too much to bear in the end. This helps explain the choice to bypass the UN despite concerns about the international political costs of doing so.

Regional Options: Constrained Forum Shopping

I argue in chapter 2 that coercing states are most likely to turn to the Security Council when they have low sensitivity to being constrained and when they anticipate potentially high political costs for taking action. Hypothesis 6 predicts that when one but not both of these conditions are met, states are more likely to turn to regional IOs for approval. This brief section considers the regional option in the case of the Second Iraq War.

As it turned its sights once again on Iraq in 2002, the United States was highly constrained in its IO options since there was no natural institutional choice in the region. This made the Persian Gulf, and the Middle East more generally, unlike theaters such as Europe and Latin America, where NATO, the Organization for Security and Cooperation in Europe, the Organization of American States, and other IOs could be activated by the United States. Endorsement from a local bloc such as the Arab League—composed of "preference outliers" with respect to a U.S. intervention—would have been ideal and exceptionally informative to the international community. But such an endorsement was never in the cards.

Nevertheless, consistent with the expectation of hypothesis 6, the United States did seek to involve NATO indirectly in the lead-up to war. Even if NATO could not formally back the mission, it could provide at least a modicum of political cover with an endorsement of the policy (as it did in Afghanistan in 2001) or by deploying troops in indirect support of the Iraq operation. In January 2003 the United States asked NATO to deploy hardware—including planning facilities, surveillance planes, minesweepers, patrol ships, and missiles—to the border with Turkey, a NATO member, in the event of Iraqi aggression to the north. The request was couched as part of a prudent contingency plan to defend an ally if it became necessary (Usborne, *Independent*, January 16, 2003).

However, most governments viewed this request as a thinly disguised effort to gain tacit NATO approval of the impending war. Germany, France, and Belgium quickly announced that they would veto any such proposal in the North Atlantic Council, the alliance's main political forum. Some NATO members reportedly felt spurned when the alliance was not meaningfully activated for the Afghanistan operation (Champion et al. 2003). With the help of George Robertson, NATO's secretary-general at the time, the United States and U.K. maneuvered the issue into NATO's Defense Planning Committee (DPC), of which France is not a member. After two weeks of discussion, Germany and then Belgium acquiesced to revised language that referred to "defensive" support for Turkey and provided for the deployment of AWACs planes and theater missile defense systems. An affirmative vote was secured in the DPC on February 16, temporarily repairing one of the most serious rifts in NATO history.

Given that the two most resistant countries on the Security Council, France and Germany, were also members of NATO, and that NATO's political decisions operate on the basis of unanimity, there was no possibility of formal authorization from NATO once the UNSC option was rejected. Therefore, the effective choice facing the Bush administration was between staying with the UN and operating with an ad hoc coalition in the absence of IO approval. Nevertheless, it is interesting to note that Washington did engage in a concerted effort to involve NATO, if only indirectly, and valued any role it could play.

International Reactions to Iraq 2003

What were the consequences of launching the 2003 invasion of Iraq without Security Council approval? This chapter has so far examined the trade-offs involved in deciding whether to work through the UN and how these trade-offs influenced Bush administration statecraft during the coercive, prewar phase of the conflict. My theoretical arguments also have implications for the *consequences* of these decisions. Most generally, hypothesis 1 implies that, ceteris paribus, international support should be lower when interventions are conducted without IO approval. I thus compare support for the Second Iraq War with support of the Gulf War. Hypotheses 2 and 3 suggest specific types of reactions to the war. First, without a signal of benign intentions to third-party governments, we should see concern over U.S. motivations and less support of the policy for this reason. Second, we should see certain responses from publics in third-party states. They should be disinclined to support the war, and, further, we should see evidence that this lack of support results from the absence of UN approval. Without the independent certification of an IO, publics should also be suspicious of the justifications and predicted consequences of the war as outlined by the United States in its public rationale for war. Finally, following the two-level logic of my argument, we should find that public reluctance acts as a constraint on governments as they decide whether or not to support the intervention.

Lack of UN Approval and International Support

From the beginning, virtually every U.S. ally expressed a strong preference for a UN-based approach. Most western European governments linked their support for military action to "a clear UN mandate" (BBC News 2003b). The United States' most vital partners were urging Bush to pursue a Security Council authorization. For example, Prime Minister Recep Tayyip Erdogan said Turkey would not participate in an invasion unless it was approved by the UN, and that Turkey was "obliged by the United Nations' decisions" (Alemdar, Associated Press, November 4, 2002). Even the most enthusiastic supporters of the war coveted a UN mandate and urged the White House to pursue one vigorously, as we have already seen in the case of Blair. Italian prime minister Silvio Berlusconi signaled his support for a U.S. intervention in late 2002 but "hastened to add that Italy supported a UN resolution to provide the necessary mandate and international legitimization" (Nuti 2005, 194).

It is no surprise, therefore, that international support for the war was low. I have already outlined the modest size of the coalition of the willing gauged in terms of active contributions to the invasion—only the U.K., Australia, and Poland provided combat troops, while Denmark and Spain offered token forces for noncombat roles. This can be compared with more than thirty countries that contributed to Operation Desert Storm. And while eight governments contributed tens of billions of dollars to defray the costs of the 1991 war, not a single government pledged financial support for the 2003 invasion.

Further comparison of the two wars also reveals that several politically key countries which supported the first did not repeat their endorsements for the second. There was a glaring lack of support from neighbors and allies such as Germany, France, Canada, and Mexico and from Security Council veto wielders China and Russia. And Arab hearts and minds were clearly skeptical: not a single Arab nation was a public member of the U.S.-led coalition in the Second

Iraq War. The situation was very different in 1991, when Bahrain, Egypt, Kuwait, Oman, Qatar, Saudi Arabia, Syria, and the United Arab Emirates all contributed personnel (including tens of thousands of combat troops), equipment, or both to the military operation. Indeed, about a hundred countries offered political support—defined as either material assistance or rhetorical approval—to the 1991 war, compared with only three dozen or so in the 2003 case (McCartney, *WashPo,* March 21, 2003; Thompson 2005).

The White House did receive two very public displays of support from European governments before the war. The first was the Letter of Eight, orchestrated by the U.K. and Spain and also signed by the leaders of Denmark, the Czech Republic, Hungary, Italy, Poland, and Portugal. It was published in the *Wall Street Journal* and several European newspapers on January 30, 2003. While it expressed solidarity with Bush's efforts to "rid the world of the danger posed by Saddam Hussein's weapons of mass destruction," it stopped short of endorsing a war in the near term. The second was the letter of the so-called Vilnius 10, a group of central and eastern European leaders, published on February 5, the same day as Powell's intelligence presentation to the Security Council. On closer inspection, it is doubtful whether the Vilnius 10 letter reflected heartfelt backing of the war. The text, which professed strong support for the United States, was presented to these leaders as a take-it-or-leave-it offer (with a suggestion that they not leave it) by an American with close ties to the Pentagon and in consultation with the Bush administration. All ten countries were candidates for NATO membership, and they were presented with the letter just weeks before Congress was to vote on their candidacy. Further evidence of U.S. influence came in the text itself: it contained a reference to Powell's "compelling evidence," even though none of the signatories had yet seen that evidence.[11]

It is notable that most supporters of the war were from smaller states. These governments—and they were especially numerous in eastern and central Europe, including Estonia, Lithuania, the Czech Republic, Hungary, Poland, and Romania—seem to have felt a need to display loyalty to the United States, on which they were dependent for security and to whose political influence they were highly vulnerable (Schuster and Maier 2006). Slovakia's prime minister, for example, clarified that his decision to sign the Vilnius 10 letter "was not only about Iraq, but also about Slovakia's future direction and about its chances to become a part of the democratic world" (quoted in Pauly and Lansford 2005, 96). Naturally, the United States actively attracted these states with various inducements (see Slavin, *USA Today,* February 25, 2003). More generally, many small

11. For a history of these two letters, on which this paragraph draws, see Baker et al., *FT,* May 28, 2003.

countries that joined the "coalition of the willing" were the target of economic linkage, both positive and negative, from Washington, producing what some have called a "coalition of the bribed and bullied" (Newnham 2008).

Concerns over U.S. Intentions

As Washington's attention turned to Iraq during the course of 2002, a primary concern for governments around the world was the extent of U.S. ambitions—in Iraq, in the broader Middle East, and beyond. The standoff with Iraq was not an isolated issue; it had to be considered in light of the emerging preemption doctrine and the vast capabilities available to the United States to realize its interests. America was potentially threatening because it did not need anybody's assistance to act aggressively against distasteful regimes. A P5 ambassador involved in the Iraq diplomacy placed it in this larger geopolitical context. "The whole debate is about two issues," he observed. "One is Iraq. The other is U.S. power in the world. The second issue is the bigger part of the debate" (Kessler and Pincus, *WashPo,* October 30, 2002).

States in the region had a distinct set of concerns with respect to U.S. intentions, many of which echoed those present in the lead-up to the Gulf War. Even before the confrontation with Iraq was rekindled, many feared the United States had ambitious goals to dominate the region, altering the strategic landscape to its advantage. At the very least, local governments were looking for a sign that the United States was truly a liberator and not merely the latest in a long line of Western occupiers. The fact that the United States acted without a constraining coalition, let alone with IO involvement, did nothing to mollify these fears. As Shibley Telhami (2003) assessed the regional mind-set after the war, "Most are…concerned that the war in Iraq was merely the opening move in a larger strategy; they ask themselves which country will be next." Indeed, Syria and Iran were subsequently targeted by U.S. diplomacy and sanctions, and the United States has never denied that permanent military bases in Iraq were an intended legacy of the intervention. Majorities in seven of eight Muslim populations polled by the Pew Research Center (2003c) in May 2003 considered the United States a military threat to their country.

The heavily ideological rhetoric used by the Bush administration aggravated apprehensions in the region. Bush portrayed his Iraq policy as part of a grand vision of spreading democracy throughout the region and described the enemy in religious terms, as "Islamic extremists" and "Islamic fascists." He and his advisers may not have realized how such rhetoric played in the rest of the world, especially in the Middle East. Indeed, de Villepin fanned these fears and gained support in the Security Council by "warning that the United States had dreams of remaking the Middle East in its own image of democracy" (Weisman, *NYT,* March 17, 2003). The Bush administration also may have misread the extent to which the United States' authoritarian allies in the Middle East viewed aggressive democracy promotion as a threat to their interests. Regimes in places like Egypt and Saudi Arabia "were less fearful of an Iraq that had not threatened its neighbors with direct military invasion since the end of the Persian Gulf War in 1991 than they were of the democratic empowerment of restive populations" (Pauly and Lansford 2005, 52). This was especially true where relatively secular governments faced more religious populations. Images of a crusading United States had a powerful impact.

The United States' traditional allies in Europe were also keen to discern U.S. intentions, though they were driven by a different set of concerns. Without a common enemy to the east, the world's only superpower was no longer obligated to work with its partners on the Continent. If the United States exercised its primacy through unilateral means, this would relegate the Europeans—with their conspicuous dearth of hard power—to the sidelines.[12] At stake was thus the possibility of a world dominated by a single power. In German foreign minister Joschka Fischer's formulation, Europeans faced nothing less than the "question of a new world order after the end of the Cold War" (quoted in Beste et al. 2003).

European governments also had more specific concerns about the emerging policy. They worried that a U.S. invasion, far from bringing peace and democracy to the region, would aggravate the Israel-Palestinian conflict, ignite further terrorism, strengthen Iran's influence, and generally result in a more destabilized Middle East. Indeed, the prevailing view was that Saddam's suspected WMD would pose a threat only if he were invaded, an event that would give him an incentive either to use the weapons himself or to share them with terrorists.[13] A U.S.-led invasion of Iraq thus posed a risk to European interests, in the region and potentially at home.

The French felt particularly threatened by the events unfolding in 2002 and early 2003. Since the mid-1990s, French leaders had consistently stressed the objective of checking American influence on international politics and balancing U.S. power by promoting multilateralism. A preventive war on Iraq conducted outside the framework of the Security Council would violate this French vision of a multipolar world. As one French commentator notes, for Paris "'multipolarity' is not meant to enhance or even to modify the global role of the United States,

12. Alexander and Garden (2001) argue that Europe simply lacks the military wherewithal to make partnerships appealing from Washington's perspective. Kosovo and Afghanistan offer cases in point.

13. Pond (2005, 34–35) provides a concise summary of Europeans' security concerns over a potential war.

but to reduce it, because American power and policy are currently regarded as excessive and unbalanced" (Soutou 2005, 115). The divisive power of the Iraq issue within Europe added to these French concerns, as the EU is viewed as an important vehicle for French influence on the world stage. To the extent that the war jeopardized the EU's role as a coherent and important global actor, it threatened long-term French interests.

It should be noted that the British government, generally committed to multilateral cooperation and institutions, was unsettled by U.S. unilateralism from the early days of the Bush administration despite a close relationship (Wallace and Oliver 2005, 168). Even with their inclination to maintain good relations with Washington, the British leadership was looking for evidence of U.S. restraint. Indeed, part of Blair's stated rationale for joining the United States in Iraq was to avoid the even more distasteful outcome of encouraging American unilateralism. As he warned the House of Commons on the eve of war, "And if our plea is for America to work with others, to be good as well as powerful allies, will our retreat make them multilateralist? Or will it not rather be the biggest impulse to unilateralism there could ever be" (Blair 2003).

None of these fears—in the Arab and Muslim world, and in Europe—were allayed by the U.S. approach, which failed to signal benign intentions. The war was launched without UN approval, and the United States showed little willingness to accept meaningful constraints on its policy. By mid-January, more than one hundred thousand U.S. troops had been deployed to the region. From that point forward (and possibly sooner), suspicions that the Bush administration was not seeking alternatives to war in good faith were likely well founded.[14] As one French envoy to Washington reported back to Paris in mid-January, his feeling was that the United States would go to war "no matter what" (Champion et al. 2003). These impressions were confirmed by the White House's own public admissions that it would not be satisfied with disarmament absent an overthrow of Saddam Hussein, a goal that was incommensurate with any reasonable interpretation of extant UN resolutions.

Domestic Publics and International Support

Public opinion abroad was a key factor driving U.S. policy in Iraq, and its effect on the broader international politics of the episode should not be underestimated. Its importance stems from a simple reality: most publics did not support

14. By early January 2003, Bush had privately decided to go to war in the near term—something he shared with his close advisers as well as Saudi ambassador Prince Bandar (Woodward 2004, 254, 256, 262–74)—even though publicly he was still professing a desire for alternatives.

war without UN authorization, and governments that disobeyed their publics tended to be punished. Thus international reactions were largely driven by domestic politics.

Governments around the world were constrained by domestic politics as they decided whether or not to support the Iraq intervention. There was a systematic link between public opinion on the war and government positions on both direct participation in the war and indirect participation through political support of the United States (Schuster and Maier 2006; Chan and Safran 2006). Several governments were inclined to support the cause but backed away because of public opposition. Vicente Fox of Mexico was interested in cultivating his relationship with Bush but was "too boxed in politically" to support the U.S. war policy—both the war and Bush were unpopular in Mexico (Weisman, *NYT,* March 17, 2003). A similar situation existed in Turkey, where Erdogan hoped to please the United States but faced a skeptical parliament and a hostile population, 90 percent of which opposed the war. This explains why the United States was allowed to launch planes from Turkish soil but not a ground invasion.

Among friendly Arab states, Hosni Mubarak's situation before the 2003 war was typical: he began to side with the United States but was constrained from doing so by a domestic backlash, including public protests and accusations that he was an American lackey. In the end, he criticized the war on the grounds that it played into bin Laden's hands by stirring anti-Western sentiment ("Those Awkward Hearts and Minds" 2003). Saudi Arabia was in an especially difficult position. The Saudi king was already the subject of criticism in the Muslim world for allowing the U.S. military to use the Holy Land as a base of operations during the Gulf War and to maintain an indefinite presence thereafter. This fueled fundamentalist anger—indeed, Osama bin Laden had used the existence of U.S. bases in the region and the complicity of the Saudi royal family as a rallying cry. For these reasons, supporting the United States in a new war against Iraq was a risky proposition, and the regime chose against it.[15]

Those who proceeded to support the war despite the absence of a UN mandate were in some cases compelled to modify the degree and nature of their support. I have already described the domestic pressure facing Bush's allies during the diplomacy stage. As one commentator writes with regard to Berlusconi, "Italy nevertheless found itself in a difficult spot when the United States and its

15. Arab regimes were in an especially difficult position domestically because Saddam had carefully positioned himself as a champion of Arab nationalism, not only by defying the United States during the 1990s but also through more specific strategies. For example, he began paying stipends to Palestinian families of suicide bombers and of those killed during Israeli incursions and supported the Palestinian Authority with hundreds of millions of dollars.

closest allies decided to go to war without a second UN resolution backing their intervention. The Berlusconi government was placed in the embarrassing position of maintaining support for Washington without actually participating in the war, since anti-war rallies were already drawing hundreds of thousands of demonstrators in the streets and squares of Italy" (Nuti 2005, 194–95). Despite José María Aznar's decision to scale back the Spanish contribution to a modest, noncombat role, only 14 percent of his public approved of his position once the war began.[16] And while Poland contributed two hundred special operations forces, it did so covertly. Once the Polish public learned of their country's participation, opposition mounted quickly. By spring of 2004, almost two-thirds of Poles wanted their twenty-five hundred post-conflict troops withdrawn from Iraq as soon as possible.[17] This led to successive reductions in the size of the Polish contingency, to only nine hundred by early 2006.

While some supporters of the coalition of the willing were punished at the polls, those who opposed the war were often rewarded. Incumbent chancellor Gerhardt Schroeder was in a close reelection battle in the summer of 2002. The more he criticized the United States and adopted an antiwar platform, the more his popularity rose, and in the end he secured a come-from-behind victory over his center-right rival in September. Other politicians "could observe the potential political payoff from opposing U.S. war plans" (Champion et al. 2003). For example, when Aznar faced reelection in early 2004, his socialist opponent, José Luis Rodríguez Zapatero, ran on a platform of withdrawing Spain's troops from Iraq, a promise he promptly fulfilled upon taking office. Zapatero then aligned himself squarely with Paris and Berlin, joining them to rebuff a U.S. request to have NATO provide a stabilization force in postinvasion Iraq.

International Public Opinion and the UN Effect

Many more opinion surveys were conducted around the world at the time of the Second Iraq War than during the Gulf War crisis or the interwar years. In particular, we have the advantage of large cross-national surveys with uniform questions for the more recent case. They paint a picture of publics generally skeptical of war, with UN approval acting as a key variable in shaping attitudes.

The Pew Research Center (2002, 3) reported surveys from early November 2002 in six countries as part of its Global Attitudes Project. While the U.S. public was supportive of using force to remove Saddam (62 percent in favor, 26 against)

16. According to an Instituto Opina/*El Pais* poll conducted on March 26 and 27, 2003, reported in Center for Public Opinion and Democracy (2003b).

17. According to a Public Opinion Research Center poll, cited in Pond 2005, 54.

Table 6.1. Support on eve of war

COUNTRY	FAVOR (%)	OPPOSE (%)	DON'T KNOW (%)
United States	59	30	11
Join the war?			
Britain	39	51	10
Italy	17	81	2
Spain	13	81	7
Poland	21	73	6
Support the war?			
France	20	75	6
Germany	27	69	4
Russia	10	87	3
Turkey	12	86	2

Source: Pew Research Center (2003a).

and the British were split (47 in favor, 47 against), strong opposition was voiced in France (33 in favor, 64 against), Germany (26 in favor, 71 against), Russia (12 in favor, 79 against), and Turkey (13 in favor, 83 against). Another Pew poll conducted a week before the war shows even less enthusiasm for war (Pew Research Center 2003a). Four members of the coalition of the willing were asked if they favored or opposed *joining the war,* while publics in four other politically important countries were asked if they *supported the war.* Table 6.1 displays the results. A majority of Britons now opposed war, as did large majorities in coalition members Italy, Spain, and Poland, and antiwar positions had hardened in France, Russia, and Turkey. Of course, in November 2002 there was still hope that the war would be conducted under a UN umbrella; by the time of the later poll, such hopes had all but disappeared.

Similar attitudes prevailed around the world. A Gallup survey conducted in January 2003 asked samples in thirty-nine countries and territories, "If military action goes ahead against Iraq, do you think your country should or should not support the action?" Majorities in the United States and Australia and pluralities in Romania, the U.K., and Canada responded favorably; the other thirty-four populations objected to supporting the war, with an average result of 21 percent for and 68 percent against (Gallup International 2003a). The apparent ease and success of the invasion did not significantly swing publics in favor of the war. In late March, only 14 percent of Indians supported the war, with 86 percent against,[18] and 71 percent of Canadians had by June come to the opinion that

18. According to a Centre for Forecasting and Research/*Outlook Magazine* poll conducted on March 26 and 27, 2003, reported in Center for Public Opinion and Democracy (2003a).

Prime Minister Chrétien was justified in not supporting the United States.[19] This of course stands in contrast to the widespread—though by no means universal—international public support enjoyed by Washington before, during, and after the Gulf War.

These findings are consistent with hypothesis 3, which suggests that publics in third-party states should be skeptical of coercive policies not approved by an IO. Even more to the point, however, we should observe that lack of UN approval was a key factor in diminishing support.

The Gallup International (2003a) Iraq Poll 2003 is helpful in this regard. It asked publics if they favored military action under two conditions: "if sanctioned by the UN" and if conducted "unilaterally by America and its allies." The results give us a better grasp of the influence of UN approval. Table 6.2 presents the data with additional columns reporting what I term the "UN effect." The third column shows the absolute difference between the percentages in favor with and without a UN sanction. In cases where support for war is very low, however, this can be misleading since the change reported is constrained to be small in absolute terms (for example, Spain drops from 13 to 4, a difference of only 9). I thus also report, in the fourth column, the UN effect as a percentage change between the two conditions.

The numbers are striking. In all thirty-eight countries UN approval increases support for war, with an average UN effect of twenty percentage points in absolute terms. Moreover, publics in every region represented—western Europe, eastern Europe, the Americas, Asia-Pacific, and Africa—display a strong preference for UN-based action over a coalition approach. The UN effect measured as a percentage change is even more dramatic—and arguably more meaningful. All but seven of the thirty-eight countries show a UN effect of 50 percent or greater, and more than half show an effect of 70 percent or greater. The average change is 64 percent, ranging from a regional average of 38 in the Americas to 78 in Asia-Pacific and 73 in western Europe. This means that in every corner of the globe, governments are virtually guaranteed to face much lower domestic constraints to supporting military action when it is approved by the Security Council.

This UN effect is profound and remarkably uniform in Europe, where, I would argue, a Security Council authorization would have swung the continent into line behind the United States. A survey by EOS Gallup Europe (2003), also conducted in January of 2003, asks a somewhat different set of questions and allows us to calculate a different type of UN effect. The two relevant questions

---

19. According to an Ipsos-Reid/CTV/*Globe and Mail* poll conducted in June 2003. See Ipsos-Reid News Release, "Seven in Ten (71%) Now Feel Prime Minister and Canada Justified," June 15, 2003, http://www.ipsos-na.com/news/pressrelease.cfm?id=1845.

Table 6.2. Support for war and the UN effect

Question: Are you in favor of military action against Iraq?

COUNTRY	ONLY IF SANCTIONED BY THE UN (%)	IF UNILATERALLY BY U.S. AND ALLIES (%)	UN EFFECT (DIFFERENCE)	UN EFFECT (% CHANGE)
Western Europe				
Denmark	38	10	28	74
Finland	44	37	7	16
France	27	7	20	74
Germany	39	9	30	77
Iceland	36	7	29	81
Ireland	50	8	42	84
Luxembourg	34	5	29	85
Netherlands	51	7	44	86
Portugal	29	10	19	66
Spain	13	4	9	69
Switzerland	45	5	40	89
U.K. (excluding Northern Ireland)	39	10	29	74
Regional average	*37*	*10*	*27*	*73*
Eastern Europe				
Albania	36	7	29	81
Bosnia & Herzogovina	16	9	7	44
Bulgaria	28	5	23	82
Estonia	20	9	11	55
FYR Macedonia	13	4	9	69
Georgia	18	9	9	50
Romania	38	11	27	71
Russia	23	7	16	70
Yugoslavia	20	8	12	60
Regional average	*21*	*7*	*14*	*58*
The Americas				
Argentina	4	3	1	25
Bolivia	25	9	16	64
Canada	46	10	36	78
Colombia	25	15	10	40
Ecuador	19	3	16	84
Uruguay	10	9	1	10
USA	34	33	1	3
Regional average	*20*	*10*	*10*	*38*
Asia-Pacific				
Australia	56	12	44	79
India	29	8	21	72
Malaysia	12	3	9	75
New Zealand	52	8	44	85
Pakistan	16	3	13	81
Regional average	*33*	*7*	*26*	*78*
Africa				
Cameroon	38	9	29	76
Nigeria	35	10	25	71
Kenya	28	17	11	40
South Africa	20	9	11	55
Uganda	27	20	7	26
Regional average	*30*	*13*	*17*	*54*
Overall average	***30***	***10***	***20***	***64***

Source: Gallup International (2003a); and author calculations.

both ask, "Do you consider that it would be justified or not that your country participate in a military intervention in Iraq?" Question 7e then offers the condition "If the United Nations Security Council decides on a military intervention in Iraq," while Question 7d offers "If the United States intervenes militarily in Iraq without a preliminary decision of the United Nations." By comparing the results, we can generate UN effect scores in the same manner as table 6.2 does, this time focused on the question of national participation rather than more abstract approval and disapproval of the policy. Table 6.3 presents the results.

The overall averages reported at the bottom of the table again indicate great reluctance to participate in a war that is not endorsed by the Security Council, with only 13 percent in favor. The effect of UN approval is again striking, with support jumping to 44 percent when this condition is introduced. The UN effect, expressed as both an absolute difference and a percentage change, is even greater than in the European results reported in table 6.2, implying that the choice to take national action in support of an intervention is even more sensitive to the UN variable than more abstract preferences over the policy. Once again, western Europeans value the UN imprimatur somewhat more than the former communist populations. Thus while reluctance to participate in an unauthorized war was unanimous among European publics, the EU candidate countries of eastern and central Europe (most of which are now members) had somewhat more domestic political leeway than their counterparts to the west. This is consistent with the East-West disparity in European support exhibited throughout the crisis.

Beyond the survey data, interviews with officials from two politically key third-party states, Turkey and Canada, confirm that the lack of a UN mandate suppressed international governmental support through the conveyor belt of domestic public opposition. As one Turkish diplomat notes, contrasting Turkey's unwavering support of the Gulf War with its reticence in 2003, "a resolution gives us something to work with domestically; we just didn't have that in the second case."[20] A U.S. diplomat stationed in Ankara during the run-up to war is confident that the government would have eagerly consented to facilitating a ground invasion from Turkish soil if a second UNSC resolution had been secured.[21] The Canadian government wavered for months, neither definitively condemning nor supporting U.S. policy in Iraq. In the end, however, domestic politics drove the government's choice to reject the war option. According to a

20. Author's interview with a Turkish diplomat, New York, November 13, 2003. The interviewee was confident that UN authorization of the 2003 intervention would have swayed public opinion sufficiently to achieve a favorable vote in parliament on the question of whether the U.S. could use Turkey as a base of operations for ground troops.

21. Author's interview with a State Department official, August 8, 2003.

Table 6.3. Europe: Support of national participation and the UN effect
Question: Do you consider that it would be justified or not that our country participates in a military intervention in Iraq?

COUNTRY	WITH UN APPROVAL (%)	IF U.S. ACTS WITHOUT UN APPROVAL (%)	UN EFFECT (DIFFERENCE)	UN EFFECT (% CHANGE)
EU 15				
Austria	19	8	11	58
Belgium	56	13	43	77
Denmark	71	13	58	82
Finland	31	7	24	77
France	67	13	54	81
Germany	45	10	35	78
Greece	25	9	16	64
Ireland	51	13	38	75
Italy	66	18	48	73
Luxembourg	63	13	50	79
Netherlands	68	13	55	81
Portugal	56	16	40	71
Spain	45	12	33	73
Sweden	39	9	30	77
United Kingdom	79	27	52	66
EU 15 average	*52*	*13*	*39*	*74*
EU candidates				
Bulgaria	29	6	23	79
Cyprus	9	2	7	78
Czech Republic	71	30	41	58
Estonia	28	8	20	71
Hungary	30	8	22	73
Latvia	24	7	17	71
Lithuania	33	12	21	64
Malta	17	4	13	76
Poland	52	21	31	60
Romania	50	16	34	68
Slovakia	60	41	19	32
Slovenia	22	8	14	64
Turkey	33	11	22	67
Candidate average	*35*	*13*	*22*	*66*
Other				
Norway	63	7	56	89
Switzerland	30	8	22	73
Other average	*47*	*8*	*39*	*81*
Overall average	***44***	***13***	***32***	***71***

Source: EOS Gallup Europe (2003); and author calculations.

Canadian Department of Foreign Affairs official, "The UN mandate's effect on public opinion was the key variable in Iraq I versus Iraq II."[22] Several Canadian officials indicated that Chrétien's preferences would have been to find a way to please Washington but that in the end doing so was deemed politically perilous. A U.S. official in the Ottawa embassy agreed and went further. "Public opinion was very important. The government was on shaky ground to begin with in terms of support for the war. Without a resolution authorizing the use of force, Canada had no choice [but to reject the war]."[23]

It should be noted that gaining international support is not just a question of unilateralism versus multilateralism. Consistent with the information theory presented in chapter 2, approval by a standing IO has added value beyond multilateral support alone. The Iraq Poll 2003 (Gallup International 2003a) offered action by "America and its allies"—that is, ad hoc multilateralism—as the alternative and still found substantially higher support with UN approval, as reported in table 6.2. Further evidence is offered by a February 2003 EKOS poll, which asked Canadians if they would support or oppose their country's participation in the war under two conditions: if the United States acted "with its major allies" and with UNSC support, and if it acted with its allies without UNSC support. Under the first condition, 63 percent supported and 35 percent opposed, while under the second condition 25 percent supported and 74 percent opposed.[24]

Thus in the Second Iraq War multilateralism by itself was not sufficient to generate support. This confirms one of the central themes of this book, that support from a group of like-minded states—a coalition of the willing—is not informative to the international community because it does not impose constraints on a coercing state and does not provide an independent assessment of the policy. Only an IO can perform this function effectively.

Washington's Policy Justifications: Skeptical Publics Abroad

Individuals by necessity look for information shortcuts to assess international affairs and the foreign policies of governments. When IOs endorse a state's policy, this informs publics around the world that the action is likely to have beneficial consequences that provide international benefits beyond the narrow interests of the state conducting the policy. Absent such an endorsement and the policy

22. Author's interview with a senior policy adviser in the Canadian Department of Foreign Affairs, June 15, 2005.

23. Author's interview with a U.S. embassy official in Ottawa, June 15, 2005.

24. According to an EKOS/CBC/SRC/*Toronto Star*/La Presse poll, February 21, 2003, http://www.ekos.com/admin/articles/21feb2003.pdf.

information it conveys, hypothesis 3 suggests, publics should be skeptical of such actions, especially when they involve the use of force by a powerful state.

Once it was clear that the United States planned to act without Security Council authorization, publics around the world were highly skeptical of the intervention policy. They believed the United States was too eager to use force and should have waited, they were cynical about U.S. motives, they did not believe the world would be safer as a result of the war, and they believed the war would have negative consequences for their own country. In short, they did not view the policy as providing any sort of collective international good.

In Gallup International's Post War Iraq Poll, released on May 13, 2003, publics in all but three of forty-five countries surveyed felt that the United States was "too keen to use military force in other countries" (the three exceptions were Malaysia, Georgia, and the United States itself). Some of the strongest sentiments on the question were expressed in key U.S. allies and other politically important states, including France (87 percent), Russia (87 percent), and Turkey (75 percent) (Gallup International 2003b). Not only was the United States perceived as acting too aggressively in Iraq, but its expressed motivation—to remove a threat posed by Iraq's possession of WMD—was widely doubted (even before it became clear that Iraq did not in fact possess such WMD). When asked if oil was the main motivation for the United States, sizable majorities in all thirty European countries surveyed agreed (EOS Gallup Europe 2003). Indians were also skeptical that the United States was motivated by genuine security concerns. Asked "What do you think is America's reason to invade Iraq?" 61 percent named oil. Only 14 percent pointed to terrorism and 13 percent to disarmament, roughly the same percentage (12) who felt that Bush went to war to boost his reelection chances.[25] Even Canadians were more likely to point to "strategic oil interests in the Middle East" (39 percent) than to the "threats of terrorism and WMD" (30 percent) as Washington's motive for war.[26] In the end, as one survey of world public opinion concludes, most were convinced that the war was not based on "persuasive reasons" (Bernstein, *NYT*, September 11, 2003).

These perceptions led people around the world to doubt whether the war policy was designed to serve broad interests. After Bush announced the end of major combat operations on May 1, citizens in forty-two of forty-five countries surveyed felt the world was a more dangerous place than before the war, and majorities in only two of these countries thought the threat of terrorism had

25. According to a Centre for Forecasting and Research/*Outlook Magazine* poll conducted on March 26 and 27, 2003, reported in Center for Public Opinion and Democracy (2003a).

26. According to an EKOS/CBC News Sunday Poll, "Perceived American Motives for War in Iraq," March 9, 2003, http://www.cbc.ca/sunday/polls/mar9.pdf.

been reduced (Gallup International 2003b; see also Roy Morgan Research 2003). Not only were these international benefits absent in people's minds, but publics in all eight countries surveyed by Pew in March felt that American foreign policy actually had a negative effect on their country (Pew Research Center 2003a).[27] In sum, in the wake of Iraq few viewed the United States as a benevolent hegemon sensitive to the interests of the international community.[28]

The International Political Costs of the War

This subsection considers some of the political costs suffered by the United States as a result of its decision to bypass the Security Council, beyond the low support for the invasion itself. Evidence of such international costs would support the general proposition of the book—and the specific contention of hypothesis 1—that IO approval is an important variable in determining the political consequences of intervention.

Because of its material dominance, the United States presents us with a hard case for finding substantial costs imposed by other states. Most states simply lack means to punish the superpower. Nevertheless, while there have been no formal alliances created to balance American influence, some internal balancing has taken place, most notably in China with its annual double-digit increases in military spending over the last several years. In a June 2005 speech, Rumsfeld (2005) expressed concern—and disingenuous bewilderment—over this trend: "China appears to be expanding its missile forces, allowing them to reach targets in many areas of the world. . . . China also is improving its ability to project power, and developing advanced systems of military technology. Since no nation threatens China, one must wonder: Why this growing investment?" Other countries chose to balance by accelerating their nuclear programs, with North Korea and Iran as the most prominent examples. Most observers agree that these actions were in part a response to U.S. policy in Iraq.

Most costs of the Second Iraq War are indirect and political and fall under the category of soft balancing. Robert Pape (2003) warned as the war was under way that "the use of international institutions, economic leverage, and diplomatic maneuvering to frustrate American intentions will only grow." There is evidence

27. The countries surveyed were Britain, France, Germany, Italy, Spain, Poland, Russia, and Turkey.

28. A TNS Sofres polled conducted in the fall of 2003 found that only 11 percent of Europeans felt the United States "respects the interests of the rest of the world." See http://www.tns-sofres.com/etudes/pol/291003_cnn_r.htm.

of precisely this trend. Stephen Walt (2005, 126–78) provides several examples, including conscious coordination of diplomatic action designed to thwart U.S. objectives, deliberate decisions not to cooperate with the United States, efforts to restrain U.S. power through international institutions and norms, and strategies of publicly delegitimizing the United States and its behavior. In a more recent example of such balancing, Putin visited Iranian president Mahmoud Ahmadinejad in October of 2007 to forge an agreement among the five countries bordering the Caspian Sea—Russia, Iran, Azerbaijan, Kazakhstan, and Turkmenistan. In addition to reasserting control over the sea's resources, the five governments agreed not to let any country use their soil for an attack against the other four, a move that was obviously aimed against growing U.S. influence—and military bases—in the region.

I suggest three specific areas where the United States has incurred international political costs: the transatlantic rift, lack of cooperation over postinvasion rebuilding in Iraq, and the tarnished image of the United States around the world, which may in turn exacerbate the threat of international terrorism.

The Transatlantic Rift

First, relations with Europe have certainly been strained as a result of the war. One study (Lundestad 2005, 11) of transatlantic relations concludes that the Iraq episode has engendered a fundamental shift, "from a relationship characterized by periodic crises of high politics toward a greater overall drift and distance between Alliance partners." Henry Kissinger (2003) refers to the "gravest crisis within the Atlantic Alliance since its creation five decades ago." While there is debate over the intensity and probable duration of soured relations between the United States and Europe, a variety of observers agree that the 2003 Iraq war has driven these allied governments apart and poses a serious threat to their relationship (Cox 2006; Trachtenberg 2005; Gordon and Shapiro 2004; Asmus 2003). While the United States and Europe were arguably drifting apart before the Iraq crisis erupted again in 2002, the war has pushed the development of new European security institutions and identities in a more explicitly anti-American and counterhegemonic direction (Hopf 2005).

Perhaps most worrisome are the trends in public opinion outlined in the previous section. While several European governments supported the war, at least rhetorically, publics were not nearly so divided. Virtually every European public, including those in central and eastern Europe, was very skeptical about the Bush administration's Iraq policy and highly critical of the U.S. role in the world. Remarkably, 78 percent of Europeans reported in June 2003 that they viewed U.S. unilateralism as an "extremely important" or "important" threat to Europe, a threat judged comparable to North Korean and Iranian WMD (German Marshall Fund 2003). Never has public opinion in Europe been so universally negative toward Washington (Lundestad 2005, 10).

Rebuilding Iraq

Second, the United States faced a political backlash when it came to generating support for the nation building and reconstruction phase of the Iraq intervention. I have already outlined the efforts by Berlin and Paris to balance the United States' political influence in the Security Council during the prewar phase. This strategy continued with the war under way, as France and Germany pushed for isolation of the United States and for a strong UN role in Iraq after hostilities. In mid-April, they succeeded in enlisting Russian President Vladimir Putin to call for multilateral management of postwar political development and reconstruction. The three leaders argued that "[o]nly the United Nations has the stamp of legitimacy and impartiality essential to creating a broadly backed government" (Wines, *NYT,* April 12, 2003).

The White House and Pentagon instead chose to maintain tight control of Iraq. Early indications were that the United States would involve the UN more thoroughly in rebuilding efforts—Bush spoke repeatedly of granting the UN a "vital role" in postwar Iraq, a formulation that gave U.S. allies some reason for optimism. As events unfolded, it became clear that the Coalition Provisional Authority (CPA)—the governing authority established by the United States and headed by Ambassador L. Paul Bremer—would grant the UN only a minor role. While the CPA coveted the UN's involvement as a way to legitimize the occupation and political reform efforts, Bremer worked to limit the UN's mandate so that the United States could retain as much control as possible. Despite the considerable nation-building expertise of the UN mission staff in Baghdad, Bremer tended to ignore their advice and tolerated their presence only as long as they supported U.S. activities (Diamond 2005, 54–55).[29]

In general, governments were reluctant to offer support to an operation conducted without a UN mandate and harbored lingering resentment of the U.S. approach to war. After the passage of UNSC Resolution 1483 on May 22, 2003, which recognized the occupation and requested international assistance, dozens of countries did eventually contribute to postwar reconstruction and security. But

29. Larry Diamond (2005) offers many other examples in which the CPA, and Bremer in particular, tried to circumscribe the UN's influence. A bombing on August 19, 2003, destroyed the UN compound and killed twenty-two of its staff, including the head of the mission, Sergio Vieira de Mello. All permanent UN staff left Iraq after this point.

for the most part Resolution 1483 did not have the desired effect—at least not to the extent hoped for by the Americans. It was a case of too little, too late from the perspective of the international community. In terms of troop contributions from postwar cooperators, most were very small contingents, which the U.S. military lumped into a single multinational division. Confused chains of command and an almost complete lack of interoperability rendered this division the "shakiest part of the coalition" with "little or no fighting capability" (Woodward 2006, 292). Many states that were nominally part of the coalition of the willing were not willing to contribute forces to help with postwar stability, and overall the contributions were far below what the White House was requesting from its allies (Pauly and Lansford 2005, 125–26). In contrast to its vital role in stabilizing postwar Afghanistan, NATO agreed only to a modest training mission to assist Iraq's security forces.

India provides a case in point. In the summer of 2003, the Indian government seriously considered deploying a full army division, about seventeen thousand troops, to assist the United States in Iraq—far more than any other country's contribution. However, the proposal generated intense opposition in India and, with elections a year away, the ruling party worried about the political consequences of supporting the postwar effort. In the end, India decided against sending troops. "Were there to be an explicit UN mandate for the purpose, the government of India could consider the deployment of troops to Iraq," the foreign minister explained (Baruah, *Hindu,* July 15, 2003).

The lack of postwar contributions was indeed costly for the United States because troop levels were desperately low (Packer 2005, 244–47). As one CPA official commented, "We did genuinely need the foreign troops. We had too few American divisions [in Iraq]."[30] The security situation quickly spun out of control and remained dire for years after the invasion (see Iraq Study Group 2006). Perhaps this is not surprising: a comprehensive survey of nation-building efforts from World War II through Iraq conducted by the RAND Corporation concludes that multilateral approaches are more successful and cost-effective than unilateral efforts (Dobbins et al. 2005). And for a variety of cultural and geopolitical reasons, Iraq is an exceptionally difficult nation-building challenge for the United States (Edelstein 2004).

The Damaged U.S. Image and the War on Terrorism

Third and finally, the Iraq war generated international political costs in the form of degrading the United States' image around the world. Ronald Asmus (2003,

30. Author's interview with a former CPA official, June 15, 2005.

21–22) provides a stark assessment of the war's effect in this regard: "The [Bush] administration's behavior helped unleash the largest wave of anti-Americanism in decades.... Whereas U.S. military prowess may be at an all-time high, Washington's political and moral authority has hit a new low." The sympathy and support that followed the September 11, 2001, attacks dissipated in the aftermath of Iraq, replaced by widespread sentiment that the United States was driven by aggressive and unilateral—even imperial—tendencies.

The Pew Global Attitudes Project tracks favorable attitudes toward the United States over time. Table 6.4 shows the dramatic effect of the Second Iraq War on these trends. Without exception, the image of the United States suffered after the war, in many cases dramatically. Publics in NATO allies were not immune: only 50 percent of Poles, 34 percent of Italians, 31 percent of French, 25 percent of Germans, 14 percent of Spaniards, and 12 percent of Turks had a favorable image of America in 2003. Muslim countries held the dimmest view and also exhibited the largest drops in favorability. With the exception of Morocco and Lebanon (both at 27 percent), no other Muslim population displayed a percentage higher than 15, and only 1 percent of Palestinians and Jordanians reported a favorable image of the United States.

Public attitudes in the Muslim world became (and continue to be) especially extreme. In April of 2003, the *Economist* reported "a wave of anger against the war, and against America and its allies in general, in the Muslim world" ("Those Awkward Hearts and Minds" 2003). Among Turks, 60 percent believed in March 2003 that U.S. military action against Iraq was part of a broader U.S. war against unfriendly Muslim nations (Pew Research Center 2003a). Following the war, the United States' image among Muslim countries declined further. A May 2003 poll conducted by the Global Attitudes Project showed fear of the United States, mistrust of President Bush, and weakening support for the war on terrorism. In seven of eight Muslim countries surveyed, majorities expressed fear of a U.S. military threat to their country (Pew Research Center 2003c).

These shifts in public opinion were not merely an ephemeral effect of the war. In January of 2007, the BBC World Service (2007) surveyed more than twenty-six thousand people across twenty-five countries, representing every region of the world.[31] Respondents were asked if the United States has a "mainly positive" or "mainly negative" influence in the world. The results are striking: the average percentage indicating a positive influence was only 32, with majorities in only

31. The countries included in the survey were Argentina, Australia, Brazil, Chile, China, Egypt, France, Germany, Great Britain, Hungary, India, Indonesia, Italy, Kenya, Lebanon, Mexico, Nigeria, the Philippines, Poland, Portugal, Russia, South Korea, Turkey, the United Arab Emirates, and the United States.

Table 6.4. Damage to the United States' image (percentage of population with favorable opinion)

COUNTRY	1999–2000	2002	2003
West Europe			
Germany	78	61	25
Great Britain	83	75	48
Italy	76	70	34
Spain			14
France	62	63	31
East Europe			
Poland	86	79	50
Russia	37	61	28
Conflict area			
Turkey	52	30	12
Pakistan	23	10	13
Egypt		6	13
Lebanon	35		27
Palestinian Authority		14	1
Jordan		25	1
Americas			
Brazil	56	52	34
Canada	71	72	63
Asia			
Indonesia	75	61	15
South Korea	58	53	46
Africa			
Morocco	77		27
Nigeria	46	77	61

Source: Pew Research Center, Global Attitudes Project, various reports.
Note: Pew conducted two surveys in 2003, in March and May. For countries that were included in both surveys, the earlier figure is reported.

Kenya, Nigeria, and the Philippines feeling this way. This reflects a downward trend: 36 percent reported a positive influence in 2006 and 40 percent did so in 2005. Thus, far from dissipating, the negative effect of the war continues to be seen in public attitudes. The same BBC poll shows that 73 percent of the global public continued to disapprove of U.S. policy in Iraq four years after the invasion.

Negative public opinion abroad does affect U.S. national interests. Evidence indicates that increased resentment toward the United States over Iraq has had a detrimental effect on the war on terrorism, for example. Al Qaeda and other terrorist organizations found a ready-made rallying cry in Iraq. The International Institute for Strategic Studies in London issued a report arguing that the risk of anti-Western terrorism increased after the Iraq war began in March 2003. The

Table 6.5. Perceived sincerity of U.S. war on terrorism

COUNTRY	A SINCERE EFFORT TO REDUCE TERRORISM	NOT SINCERE
U.S.	67	25
Britain	51	41
Russia	35	48
France	35	61
Germany	29	65
Turkey	20	64
Morocco	17	66
Jordan	11	51
Pakistan	6	58

Source: Pew Research Center (2004).

war "had galvanized the transnational Islamic terrorist movement and probably increased terrorist activity worldwide" (IISS 2004, 169). Beyond fueling anti-American resentment, according to the report the war provided al Qaeda with a potent recruitment tool, swelling its ranks to eighteen thousand within a year. According to U.S. government figures, the number of "significant" terrorist attacks increased threefold between 2003 and 2004 (from 175 to 655), and the number continued to mount dramatically through 2006, a year that witnessed 14,338 "terrorist incidents."[32]

The damage caused by the Second Iraq War may also damage international cooperation, over terrorism and other issues, with friendly governments. As table 6.5 demonstrates, citizens in key allies in the war on terrorism are cynical about U.S. efforts. This makes it difficult for governments to assist the United States in ways that require the expenditure of political capital at home. This is exacerbated by the prevailing attitude that Washington's behavior is more threatening than the very problems it purports to be tackling. For example, two-thirds of the global public believes that the U.S. military presence in the Middle East provokes more conflict than it prevents (BBC World Service 2007). Most citizens simply do not want their governments to toe the American line; these governments, in turn, are less afraid to challenge Washington.

For most of its history as a great power, the United States has enjoyed a reputation as a relatively benign state whose penchant for isolationism in the early part of the century was replaced by an international profile focused mainly on

32. These numbers are based on the State Department's *Patterns of Global Terrorism* reports for 2003 and 2004 and the National Counterterrorism Center's *Report on Incidents of Terrorism* for 2006.

countering threats and establishing multilateral institutions. President George H. W. Bush, speaking before Congress a month after Iraq invaded Kuwait in August of 1990, took inspiration from this tradition and offered further amplification: "A hundred generations have searched for this elusive path to peace, while a thousand wars raged across the span of human endeavor. Today that new world is struggling to be born, a world quite different from the one we've known. A world where the rule of law supplants the rule of the jungle. A world in which nations recognize the shared responsibility for freedom and justice. A world where the strong respect the rights of the weak."[33] President Bush proceeded to take advantage of the newly unbound Security Council, following its atrophy during the Cold War, seeking approval during every phase of the Gulf War crisis.

His son also made an effort to seek Security Council cover for a war against Saddam Hussein. Once attention turned to Iraq, shortly after 9/11, U.S. statecraft was channeled largely through the UN. In adopting this political strategy, the George W. Bush administration was motivated by a desire to reduce the international political costs of confronting Iraq, with two particular mechanisms in mind. First, it hoped to signal benign intentions to states concerned about U.S. ambitions in the Middle East and about unchecked American power more generally. Second, it hoped to convince domestic publics around the world that military intervention against Iraq was justified and promised benefits for the international community. The imprimatur of an independent institution was the best way to achieve these goals.

By January of 2003, it had become clear that continued diplomacy and inspections would either delay war indefinitely or force the United States to alter its objectives in unacceptable ways. Thus in the end, the costs of working through the UN were deemed too high, and the war was conducted with a small group of like-minded states—a coalition of the willing. The political consequences of acting without IO approval have been multifaceted but almost uniformly negative. The United States has paid a price in terms of soft balancing and a damaged relationship with its European allies, and its image in the world, especially among Muslims, has deteriorated to the point of outright hostility in some countries. These trends complicate the United States' ability to pursue the war on terrorism and other important foreign policy goals.

It is too early to know how long-lasting these effects will be. In their impressive analysis of anti-Americanism around the world, Robert Keohane and Peter Katzenstein (2007) question whether negative attitudes will seriously undermine

33. The text of this address, given on September 11, 1990, is available at http://bushlibrary.tamu.edu/research/papers/1990/90091101.html.

the United States' soft power, though they concede that the long-term effects on U.S. foreign policy are difficult to predict. At the very least, it will take years for the United States to reestablish its former reputation as a relatively benign hegemon. Some progress has already been made in this regard, though, as the post-Iraq confrontations with North Korea and Iran have been orchestrated through the Security Council and with a greater degree of patience. Moreover, early signs indicate that a Barack Obama presidency will help mend international relations and improve public attitudes toward the United States.

7

CONCLUSION: HOW THE SECURITY COUNCIL MATTERS

Despite potentially costly constraints and the luxury of alternatives, even the most powerful states often entangle their foreign relations in international organizations and otherwise choose to operate multilaterally. This is true even for important international security issues where core national interests are at stake and freedom of action is highly valued. Such behavior presents a puzzle for students of international politics, especially those interested in explaining patterns of statecraft and the underexplored relationship between power and institutions. This book uses the case of the United States and its policies toward Iraq to examine these theoretical and policy issues.

There is no question that the presence of a multilateralist norm in the international system, at least since World War II, helps explain this behavior and provides a baseline incentive to operate with other states and through institutions (Finnemore 2003; Ruggie 1993). But this important insight does not explain the substantial variation in the behavior of the United States—sometimes working through IOs, sometimes operating with a multilateral coalition, and sometimes choosing unilateralism. As others have noted, the United States' relationship to multilateral institutions is ambivalent at best (Patrick and Forman 2002; Foot et al. 2003), and foreign security policy in particular has been marked by a mixture of unilateralist and multilateralist outcomes over time (Lake 1999). To a greater or lesser degree, similar variation has been evident for other powerful states as well. The important instrumental and strategic incentives that drive these choices are not well understood.

The appeal of IO-based action is undeniable. In its nearly two-decade confrontation with Iraq, successive American administrations repeatedly turned to the United Nations in spite of the frustrations involved—the painstaking diplomacy and problems of coalition warfare in the Gulf War, the constant difficulties keeping other Security Council members focused on the disarmament task during the interwar period, and the delay and obstruction that preceded the 2003 war, to name but a few examples. It is not surprising that the United States also chose to bypass the UN at crucial points in the saga.

This book helps explain this behavior by offering a theory based on different types of strategic information transmission. When states channel coercive policies through and achieve the approval of independent institutions—those with a diverse membership and the ability to reject undesired actions—this sends politically important information to the international community. Other state leaders are reassured that the coercing state's intentions are not excessively ambitious and threatening to third-party interests, while publics around the world are reassured that the policy provides widespread international benefits. The transmission of these two types of information—intentions information and policy information—augments support of the policy and reduces the international political costs of military interventions and other forms of coercion. While simple multilateralism provides some of these benefits as well, there is no substitute for channeling policy through a formal, standing organization.

While this logic explains the incentives to work through an IO, there are trade-offs: more independent institutions impose costly constraints on states that may not outweigh the political benefits of securing approval. When it comes to statecraft, notes David Baldwin (1985, 119), all choices are inherently costly. Specifying these costs and trade-offs helps us understand how states choose among options on a continuum from pure unilateralism to IO-based action, with multilateral coalitions in between. This suggests yet another way in which the political role of international institutions depends on their design and variation, an important theme of recent international relations scholarship (Hawkins et al. 2006; Haftel and Thompson 2006; Koremenos, Lipson, and Snidal 2004; Goldstein et al. 2001). However, most of the literature on how states design and delegate to institutions treats them as outcomes to be explained, ignoring the question of whether and how states choose to activate institutions in particular episodes—that is, ignoring questions of political strategy and statecraft.[1] This book advances the literature in this direction.

1. An exception is the growing literature on forum shopping among international institutions, especially in the area of trade and commercial disputes (Davis 2008; Busch 2007; Mattli 2001).

Multilateralism in U.S. Foreign Policy

The lessons of the Iraq experience for U.S. foreign policy are varied, and not all are straightforward. What does seem clear is that unilateralism comes with substantial costs and should be reserved for situations that bear directly on important national security interests and threats. Whether the Second Iraq War fits this bill is debatable, though the conventional wisdom has swung substantially in the direction of disapproving of the war in general and of the political approach in particular. Especially in retrospect, the 1998 bombing campaign, Operation Desert Fox, was also quite costly insofar as it made continued inspections impossible and drove the wedge dividing the Security Council and the international community ever deeper. The amount and quality of intelligence on Iraq's weapons never recovered, nor did unity over the appropriate way to manage Iraq. Both factors are arguably indirect causes of the 2003 war.

In the wake of Iraq, foreign policy idealists and realists now converge on a common prescription: the United States cannot succeed without including the UN and other multilateral institutions in its diplomatic and military quiver. Even John Mearsheimer, a realist scholar famous for his skepticism about international institutions, must concede that the UN plays an important political role in the conduct of statecraft. As he told one journalist, "In the Cold War you could argue that American unilateralism had no cost. But as we're finding out with regard to Iraq, Iran and North Korea, we need the Europeans and we need institutions like the UN. The fact is that the United States can't run the world by itself, and the problem is, we've done a lot of damage in our relations with allies, and people are not terribly enthusiastic about helping us now" (Bernstein, *NYT,* September 11, 2003). Upholding the Security Council is not just a matter of principle; it is also a matter of effectiveness and influence.

The Bush administration seems to have adjusted its sails considerably as a result of lessons from Iraq. In its confrontations with North Korea and Iran over nuclear weapons development, the United States has so far worked carefully through the appropriate UN institutions and has also allowed the European Union and relevant governments to play an important diplomatic role. In 2006, the Security Council passed separate resolutions aimed at North Korea and Iran (Resolutions 1718 and 1737, respectively). Both impose sanctions and threaten further coercive measures if the target regimes do not suspend their nuclear activities, with compliance to be verified by International Atomic Energy Agency inspectors and confirmed by the Security Council. North Korea has since halted its nuclear program under international supervision, and Iran is now working with the IAEA to establish a monitoring program. Under the circumstances, the White House (2006) can reasonably argue, "It's not the United States that is saying that the regime needs to fully suspend its enrichment and reprocessing activities, it is the international community." As they play out, these cases will offer an interesting test of whether the Iraq experience has had a real impact on the unilateralism-multilateralism debate in Washington.

By and large, the unilateralism-multilateralism issue is not a partisan one in the United States. Important figures on both sides of the aisle agree that how interventions are conducted by the United States should be a matter of strategic choice dependent on the context at hand. In outlining what he labels a "pragmatic" approach to intervention, George H. W. Bush's secretary of state, James Baker (1996, 32), argues that the form of intervention should be "contingent upon the specific circumstances of the action being contemplated. Sometimes the UN will be the appropriate international vehicle, sometimes regional organizations like NATO, sometimes ad hoc coalitions, and sometimes, as we shall never forget, unilateral action by a great power." Richard Holbrooke, U.S. ambassador to the UN under President Clinton, offers a similar view of the UN's role as part of his vision of a "new realism" that should guide U.S. foreign policy. He recognizes that the UN "can be an important instrument for our foreign policy" but adds, "We must not overlook a basic fact: the U.S. will not always act through the UN. We have other vital instruments of national power at our disposal" (1999). This pragmatic or realistic approach has dominated American foreign policy decisions vis-à-vis multilateral institutions; they are rarely engaged or ignored as a matter of principle.

When U.S. administrations do veer toward excessively ideological or categorical views on the unilateralism-multilateralism question—what we might call knee-jerk unilateralism at one of the continuum and doe-eyed multilateralism on the other—the result is almost always negative. We saw this in Iraq as the scale tipped too far toward unilateralism over time. But it should be noted that the opposite danger has been displayed as well. When President Clinton called for more assertive action in Yugoslavia in the early 1990s (specifically, he proposed lifting the arms embargo on Bosnia and striking Serbian forces), he was unwilling to move without the Europeans and dispatched Secretary of State Warren Christopher to consult with them. The result was deliberation, indecision, and inaction. Robert Jervis (2005, 88) notes, "If the United States had informed the Europeans rather than consulted them, they probably would have complained, but would have gone along; what critics call unilateralism often is effective leadership." The Rwanda case also suggests that inaction—in that event leading to a large-scale, brutal genocide—is a potential risk of multilateral decision making (Barnett 2002). Indeed, in cases of humanitarian emergency, states willing to intervene should not feel constrained by the need for IO approval if doing so will produce delay or impotence.[2]

The Security Council will continue to play an important role in U.S. foreign policy. Inviting Council participation can be costly for the United States because it constrains policy options and sometimes leads to unanticipated outcomes, but it is precisely this independence from American interests that renders the UN—and the Council in particular—so politically important. Former ambassador to the UN Adlai Stevenson captured this logic in testimony before the Senate in 1963:

> The United States does not own or control the United Nations. It is not a wing of the State Department. We are no more or less than the most influential of the 110 members. If we were less, we would be failing to exert the influence of freedom's leader; if we were more, we would destroy the effectiveness of the United Nations, which depends precisely on the fact that it is not an arm of the United States or of any other government, but a truly international organization, no better or worse than the agreements which can be reached by the controlling majorities of its members. (Quoted in Luck 1999, 20)

While there will always be some strain as the United States reconciles its dual roles of hegemonic leader and self-interested superpower (Cronin 2001), American distrust of the UN and fears that it threatens U.S. sovereignty should be kept in perspective. After all, much of the world views the UN as excessively influenced by the United States, not the other way around. And if the Council served U.S. interests all the time, it would lose much of its political usefulness. The constant short-term temptation in Washington to act alone or with a nimble coalition should be balanced against the important and enduring political advantages of working through the UN and other institutions.

In the future as in the past, the United States' intrinsic capabilities will not translate neatly into its *practical* power, and its ability to wield power effectively will depend in part on wise negotiation of the unilateralism-multilateralism trade-offs identified in this book and evidenced in its confrontations with Iraq.

Beyond the Superpower

The Security Council's relevance is arguably magnified with respect to lesser great powers and to the so-called middle powers, that is, states not nearly so

2. This is a major conclusion of the Independent International Commission on Kosovo (2000).

powerful as the United States but capable enough to intervene and coerce and thus to play an important role in international security affairs. For this echelon of states below superpower status—which includes developed countries like Canada, Australia, and the western Europeans, as well as regional powers like India, Brazil, and Nigeria—international organizations have a dual appeal: they provide political benefits through the mechanisms outlined in this book and they also provide some degree of control by restraining the American superpower. IOs can be a sort of "force multiplier" that grants these states more political influence than their material capabilities alone warrant.

For example, when Australia considered intervention to quell government-backed violence and humanitarian suffering in East Timor in 1999, Prime Minister John Howard made Security Council authorization an explicit requirement for any such action (Cole-Adams and Lagan, *Sydney Morning Herald,* September 6, 1999). Whatever modest expeditionary force Australia might have mustered would be no match for Indonesia's two hundred thousand-strong standing army—it would invite a bloody and protracted fight and probably a losing one. On its own, Australia had few options other than to plead with Jakarta. This changed with Security Council backing. Resolution 1264 (September 15, 1999) established a multinational force under Chapter VII, with Australia at the helm. This placed enormous pressure on the Indonesian government, which was forced to relent and to accept the international contingent, and it paved the way for Australia to stabilize the situation, beginning a process that eventually made East Timorese independence possible. Working under the aegis of the Security Council, Australia was able to achieve what it could not on its own.

These political and material advantages help explain why middle powers consistently promote multilateral—and especially IO-based—solutions to international problems. This view is somewhat at odds with the (arguably conventional) view of middle powers as acting "less out of their own interests than out of a belief in international responsibility" (Mingst and Karns 2007, 65). I argue that this normative logic leaves out an important part of the story. When pressed, one senior Canadian official conceded that, while Canadians do feel a principled commitment to multilateralism and the UN in particular, foreign policymakers are also motivated by instrumental calculations. Canada needs multilateralism, this official argued, "because we can't do it ourselves." Canada has made a "pragmatic recognition" that "we're obliged to work multilaterally."[3] Another reported that "we have a national interest in strengthening international legal frameworks. We like to think it's a matter of principle but it really comes out of

3. Author's interview with a deputy director in the Canadian Department of Foreign Affairs, June 16, 2005.

our position in the international system."[4] Among the implications of this position is a need to keep U.S. influence in check, and the UN provides an important vehicle for taming its neighbor's unilateral tendencies (Hampson 2003, 151). In the run-up to the Second Iraq War, this is precisely how Canada attempted to use the Security Council, as a way to buy more time for inspections and to avert war if possible.

India is also very committed to UN peacekeeping and has shown a willingness to participate even in dangerous enforcement operations. As a matter of policy since the end of the Cold War, the Indian government does not intervene militarily in other countries without a UN mandate (with the debatable exception of Kashmir). As with Canada, however, this behavior does not simply flow from a normative commitment to multilateralism; it is driven mainly by practical considerations. As one analyst argues, "India is politically motivated to participate in UN peacekeeping operations. The key sources of its motivation are related to its ambitions for 'great power' recognition in a highly competitive and unpredictable global system." This requires "an increased presence within the UN, with the long-term view of being considered as a favourable candidate for a permanent seat on the Security Council" (Krishnasamy 2003, 264).

The political usefulness of the Security Council helps explain the strong desire among middle powers to seek its approval—and to have other states do so as well. Robust international institutions promise both more influence for smaller states and more predictability when it comes to the behavior of the lone superpower.

The Security Council as a Political Institution

The Security Council today is "unbound" as never before (Matheson 2006). This is true in three senses. First, the end of the Cold War freed the Council from its East-West gridlock, resulting in much more activity over the last two decades (see figure 1.1). This includes expansion in the use of peacekeeping, expansion in the imposition of sanctions, and expansion in the practice of authorizing coalitions of the willing to conduct interventions. Second, the Security Council's peace and security activities have increased in number and scope to include interventions with very complex mandates and often with substantial enforcement elements. The principles of consent and impartiality that were the hallmark of traditional peacekeeping have been diluted in practice, such that the line between peacekeeping and coercive measures under Chapter VII is utterly blurred—hence

4. Author's interview with a senior Canadian diplomat, New York, November 14, 2003.

the reliance today on more accurate concepts such as *peace building* and *peace enforcement*. Indeed, the anachronism of traditional peacekeeping has spurred increased use of delegation to individual states or coalitions to tackle the most stubborn threats and those that require substantial use of force. Third, the Security Council is unbound in the sense of not being dominated by any one state or group of states. None of the P5 governments can expect the other permanent or the nonpermanent members to line up neatly behind its positions. Even the United States, the supposed unipolar power, cannot force consensus, as the Kosovo and Iraq experiences demonstrate.

All of this makes the political study of the Security Council more interesting than ever. While legal scholars have devoted enormous attention to the Council and its relationship to international law, as Ian Hurd (2007, 3) notes, "the practical role of the Council in international relations is not well understood." This is beginning to change, as more sophisticated and nuanced depictions of the UN in international security politics are evident in several recent works (Cronin and Hurd 2008; Hurd 2007; Chapman 2007; Westra 2008; Thompson 2006a; Thakur 2006; Voeten 2005, 2001; Price and Zacher 2004; Barnett 2002). A common theme of these works is that while the Security Council does not always perform as intended, states do have political incentives to work through it for a variety of purposes—to address humanitarian crises, to stem weapons proliferation, to challenge rogue regimes and terrorists, and to establish criminal tribunals.

Of course, the Security Council has a different relationship to weaker states than it does to powerful ones. For the most part, it can impose solutions and enforce decisions when it comes to the former but must persuade and compromise when it comes to the latter. Its legal function as a guarantor of international peace and security is thus highly circumscribed, as the Iraq experience illustrates: the Council was able neither to peacefully disarm Iraq through coercive sanctions and inspections following the Gulf War nor to prevent the United States from launching a preventive war in 2003.

This outcome led many observers to declare the UN dysfunctional and even dead. On the eve of war, in January of 2003, Charles Krauthammer (2003) pronounced the UN "strategically irrelevant" because the United States "is going to disarm Iraq anyway." For Michael Glennon (2003), the lesson from Iraq is that the Security Council is unable to subject the use of force to the rule of law and is thus no longer legally relevant.

But such views fail to understand the Security Council's primary role in international affairs, as a provider of politically useful information. After Iraq's invasion of Kuwait in August of 1990, the Council was able to condemn and isolate Iraq and to facilitate a return to the status quo. Through the different stages of the subsequent conflict, stretching from 1990 to 2003 and beyond, the Council was fairly effective at informing the international community of whether the policies being led by the United States were calibrated to the attendant threats, thereby performing an important "screening" function (Thompson 2006c). From this perspective, the Security Council was equally as effective in 2002–3 as it was in 1990–91. Even when the UN fails to prevent aggression and to otherwise solve security challenges, it provides a forum wherein a diverse set of states produce something approximating a community judgment—one that even the most powerful states cannot escape.

Finally, this book has implications for ongoing, heated debates over reform of the Security Council. Most proposals call for expanding the Council's membership to make it more inclusive and geographically representative.[5] For example, the High-Level Panel on Threats, Challenges and Change (2004) proposed two models for reform, both of which involved increasing the membership from fifteen to twenty-four (but with different combinations of permanent and nonpermanent seats). Another influential proposal, put forward by the so-called Group of Four (Brazil, Germany, India, and Japan), calls for an addition of six permanent and four nonpermanent seats, for a total of twenty-five. In September of 2003, Kofi Annan, addressing the General Assembly, pronounced an "urgent need for the Council to regain the confidence of States and of world public opinion—both by demonstrating its ability to deal effectively with the most difficult issues and by becoming more broadly representative of the international community as a whole" (UN Doc. A/58/PV.7). When it comes to Security Council membership, these various reform templates are united by a sense that bigger is better.

However, the twin goals highlighted by Annan of increased effectiveness and increased representation are not easily reconciled. While it may be true that the Council's legitimacy suffers as a result of its skewed composition and undemocratic procedures, a critique leveled especially by developing countries (Thakur 2004), there are at least three reasons to proceed with caution when it comes to Security Council expansion. First, despite its weaknesses, the Council remains highly authoritative with respect to matters of international security. No other institution has the same ability to confer or withhold legitimacy on state policies at the global level (Hurd 2007), and the presence or absence of a Security Council mandate remains the key factor for most states as they decide whether to support an intervention (Thompson 2006a; Welsh 2004, 184). Second, any increase in the number of members will make agreement harder to reach, especially to the extent that new members wield veto power (Zacher 2004, 221). Nobody has an interest in reviving the paralysis of the Cold War.

5. For an overview and history of various reform proposals, see Luck (2006, chap. 10).

Third and finally, membership expansion simply may not be necessary. If the Council's most important function is as a provider of politically important information to the international community, as this book argues, the real question is whether it is sufficiently independent to provide neutral assessments of state policies and to meaningfully constrain states contemplating intervention. In practice, the Council has demonstrated the willingness and ability—through both the P5 veto and the supermajority voting threshold—to withhold approval of the actions of even its most powerful member, the United States. A larger and more diverse membership risks paralyzing the institution without enhancing its political usefulness.

This suggests that those concerned with augmenting Council legitimacy should perhaps focus on other issues, such as accountability and transparency (Keohane 2006), which are largely a function of its working procedures and the design of relevant resolutions rather than of membership composition. Of course, expanding the Council's size makes sense to the extent that democratic fairness is intrinsically valued. But if the goal is to improve the Council's effectiveness, especially regarding its collective enforcement function, then it is not at all clear that membership expansion is the best path. While it might seem odd to argue against making such an important political institution more democratic, it should be remembered that delegation to nonmajoritarian institutions—including courts, central banks, and countless agencies and commissions—frequently occurs in democracies. These independent institutions serve the public interest precisely because they do not respond to the vicissitudes of popular demand and the interests of powerful political actors.

Appendix

SELECTED SECURITY COUNCIL RESOLUTIONS

660 (1990)
661 (1990)
678 (1990)
687 (1991)
688 (1991)
1134 (1997)
1154 (1998)
1284 (1999)
1441 (2002)

Resolution 660 (1990)

The Security Council,

Alarmed by the invasion of Kuwait on 2 August 1990 by the military forces of Iraq,

Determining that there exists a breach of international peace and security as regards the Iraqi invasion of Kuwait,

Acting under Articles 39 and 40 of the Charter of the United Nations,

1. Condemns the Iraqi invasion of Kuwait;

Adopted by the Security Council at its 2932nd meeting, on 2 August 1990

2. Demands that Iraq withdraw immediately and unconditionally all its forces to the positions in which they were located on 1 August 1990;
3. Calls upon Iraq and Kuwait to begin immediately intensive negotiations for the resolution of their differences and supports all efforts in this regard, and especially those of the League of Arab States;
4. Decides to meet again as necessary to consider further steps to ensure compliance with the present resolution.

Resolution 661 (1990)

The Security Council,

...

Acting under Chapter VII of the Charter of the United Nations,

1. Determines that Iraq so far has failed to comply with paragraph 2 of resolution 660 (1990) and has usurped the authority of the legitimate Government of Kuwait;
2. Decides, as a consequence, to take the following measures to secure compliance of Iraq with paragraph 2 of resolution 660 (1990) and to restore the authority of the legitimate Government of Kuwait;
3. Decides that all States shall prevent:
   (a) The import into their territories of all commodities and products originating in Iraq or Kuwait exported therefrom after the date of the present resolution;
   (b) Any activities by their nationals or in their territories which would promote or are calculated to promote the export or trans-shipment of any commodities or products from Iraq or Kuwait; and any dealings by their nationals or their flag vessels or in their territories in any commodities or products originating in Iraq or Kuwait and exported therefrom after the date of the present resolution, including in particular any transfer of funds to Iraq or Kuwait for the purposes of such activities or dealings;
   (c) The sale or supply by their nationals or from their territories or using their flag vessels of any commodities or products, including weapons or any other military equipment, whether or not originating in their territories but not including supplies intended strictly for medical purposes, and, in humanitarian circumstances, foodstuffs,

---

Adopted by the Security Council at its 2933rd meeting, on 6 August 1990

to any person or body in Iraq or Kuwait or to any person or body for the purposes of any business carried on in or operated from Iraq or Kuwait, and any activities by their nationals or in their territories which promote or are calculated to promote such sale or supply of such commodities or products;

4. Decides that all States shall not make available to the Government of Iraq or to any commercial, industrial or public utility undertaking in Iraq or Kuwait, any funds or any other financial or economic resources and shall prevent their nationals and any persons within their territories from removing from their territories or otherwise making available to that Government or to any such undertaking any such funds or resources and from remitting any other funds to persons or bodies within Iraq or Kuwait, except payments exclusively for strictly medical or humanitarian purposes and, in humanitarian circumstances, foodstuffs;
5. Calls upon all States, including States non-members of the United Nations, to act strictly in accordance with the provisions of the present resolution notwithstanding any contract entered into or licence granted before the date of the present resolution;

...

Resolution 678 (1990)

The Security Council,

Recalling, and reaffirming its resolutions 660 (1990) of 2 August (1990), 661 (1990) of 6 August 1990, 662 (1990) of 9 August 1990, 664 (1990) of 18 August 1990, 665 (1990) of 25 August 1990, 666 (1990) of 13 September 1990, 667 (1990) of 16 September 1990, 669 (1990) of 24 September 1990, 670 (1990) of 25 September 1990, 674 (1990) of of 29 October 1990 and 677 (1990) of 28 November 1990.

Noting that, despite all efforts by the United Nations, Iraq refuses to comply with its obligation to implement resolution 660 (1990) and the above-mentioned subsequent relevant resolutions, in flagrant contempt of the Security Council,

Mindful of its duties and responsibilities under the Charter of the United Nations for the maintenance and preservation of international peace and security,

Determined to secure full compliance with its decisions,

Adopted by the Security Council at its 2963rd meeting, on 29 November 1990

Acting under Chapter VII of the Charter,

1. Demands that Iraq comply fully with resolution 660 (1990) and all subsequent relevant resolutions, and decides, while maintaining all its decisions, to allow Iraq one final opportunity, as a pause of goodwill, to do so;
2. Authorizes Member States co-operating with the Government of Kuwait, unless Iraq on or before 15 January 1991 fully implements, as set forth in paragraph 1 above, the above-mentioned resolutions, to use all necessary means to uphold and implement resolution 660 (1990) and all subsequent relevant resolutions and to restore international peace and security in the area;
3. Requests all States to provide appropriate support for the actions undertaken in pursuance of paragraph 2 of the present resolution;
4. Requests the States concerned to keep the Security Council regularly informed on the progress of actions undertaken pursuant to paragraphs 2 and 3 of the present resolution;
5. Decides to remain seized of the matter.

Resolution 687 (1991)

The Security Council,

Recalling its resolutions 660 (1990) of 2 August 1990, 661 (1990) of 6 August 1990, 662 (1990) of 9 August 1990, 664 (1990) of 18 August 1990, 665 (1990) of 25 August 1990, 666 (1990) of 13 September 1990, 667 (1990) of 16 September 1990, 669 (1990) of 24 September 1990, 670 (1990) of 25 September 1990, 674 (1990) of 29 October 1990, 677 (1990) of 28 November 1990, 678 (1990) of 29 November 1990 and 686 (1991) of 2 March 1991,

Welcoming the restoration to Kuwait of its sovereignty, independence and territorial integrity and the return of its legitimate Government,

. . .

C

7. Invites Iraq to reaffirm unconditionally its obligations under the Geneva Protocol for the Prohibition of the Use in War of Asphyxiating, Poisonous or Other Gases, and of Bacteriological Methods of Warfare, signed at Geneva on 17 June 1925, and to ratify the Convention on the

---

Adopted by the Security Council at its 2981st meeting, on 3 April 1991

Prohibition of the Development, Production and Stockpiling of Bacteriological (Biological) and Toxin Weapons and on Their Destruction, of 10 April 1972;

8. Decides that Iraq shall unconditionally accept the destruction, removal, or rendering harmless, under international supervision, of:
   (a) All chemical and biological weapons and all stocks of agents and all related subsystems and components and all research, development, support and manufacturing facilities;
   (b) All ballistic missiles with a range greater than 150 kilometres and related major parts, and repair and production facilities;
9. Decides, for the implementation of paragraph 8 above, the following:
   (a) Iraq shall submit to the Secretary-General, within fifteen days of the adoption of the present resolution, a declaration of the locations, amounts and types of all items specified in paragraph 8 and agree to urgent, on-site inspection as specified below;
   (b) The Secretary-General, in consultation with the appropriate Governments and, where appropriate, with the Director-General of the World Health Organization, within forty-five days of the passage of the present resolution, shall develop, and submit to the Council for approval, a plan calling for the completion of the following acts within forty-five days of such approval:
      (i) The forming of a Special Commission, which shall carry out immediate on-site inspection of Iraq's biological, chemical and missile capabilities, based on Iraq's declarations and the designation of any additional locations by the Special Commission itself;
      (ii) The yielding by Iraq of possession to the Special Commission for destruction, removal or rendering harmless, taking into account the requirements of public safety, of all items specified under paragraph 8 (a) above, including items at the additional locations designated by the Special Commission under paragraph 9 (b) (i) above and the destruction by Iraq, under the supervision of the Special Commission, of all its missile capabilities, including launchers, as specified under paragraph 8 (b) above;
      (iii) The provision by the Special Commission of the assistance and cooperation to the Director-General of the International Atomic Energy Agency required in paragraphs 12 and 13 below;
10. Decides that Iraq shall unconditionally undertake not to use, develop, construct or acquire any of the items specified in paragraphs 8 and 9 above and requests the Secretary-General, in consultation with the

Special Commission, to develop a plan for the future ongoing monitoring and verification of Iraq's compliance with this paragraph, to be submitted to the Security Council for approval within one hundred and twenty days of the passage of this resolution;

11. Invites Iraq to reaffirm unconditionally its obligations under the Treaty on the Non-Proliferation of Nuclear Weapons of 1 July 1968;
12. Decides that Iraq shall unconditionally agree not to acquire or develop nuclear weapons or nuclear-weapons-usable material or any subsystems or components or any research, development, support or manufacturing facilities related to the above; to submit to the Secretary-General and the Director-General of the International Atomic Energy Agency within fifteen days of the adoption of the present resolution a declaration of the locations, amounts, and types of all items specified above; to place all of its nuclear-weapons-usable materials under the exclusive control, for custody and removal, of the International Atomic Energy Agency, with the assistance and cooperation of the Special Commission as provided for in the plan of the Secretary-General discussed in paragraph 9 (b) above; to accept, in accordance with the arrangements provided for in paragraph 13 below, urgent on-site inspection and the destruction, removal or rendering harmless as appropriate of all items specified above; and to accept the plan discussed in paragraph 13 below for the future ongoing monitoring and verification of its compliance with these undertakings;
13. Requests the Director-General of the International Atomic Energy Agency, through the Secretary-General, with the assistance and cooperation of the Special Commission as provided for in the plan of the Secretary-General in paragraph 9 (b) above, to carry out immediate on-site inspection of Iraq's nuclear capabilities based on Iraq's declarations and the designation of any additional locations by the Special Commission; to develop a plan for submission to the Security Council within forty-five days calling for the destruction, removal, or rendering harmless as appropriate of all items listed in paragraph 12 above; to carry out the plan within forty-five days following approval by the Security Council; and to develop a plan, taking into account the rights and obligations of Iraq under the Treaty on the Non-Proliferation of Nuclear Weapons of 1 July 1968, for the future ongoing monitoring and verification of Iraq's compliance with paragraph 12 above, including an inventory of all nuclear material in Iraq subject to the Agency's verification and inspections to confirm that Agency safeguards cover all relevant nuclear activities in Iraq, to be submitted to the Security Council

for approval within one hundred and twenty days of the passage of the present resolution;

14. Takes note that the actions to be taken by Iraq in paragraphs 8, 9, 10, 11, 12 and 13 of the present resolution represent steps towards the goal of establishing in the Middle East a zone free from weapons of mass destruction and all missiles for their delivery and the objective of a global ban on chemical weapons;

...

F

20. Decides, effective immediately, that the prohibitions against the sale or supply to Iraq of commodities or products, other than medicine and health supplies, and prohibitions against financial transactions related thereto contained in resolution 661 (1990) shall not apply to foodstuffs notified to the Security Council Committee established by resolution 661 (1990) concerning the situation between Iraq and Kuwait or, with the approval of that Committee, under the simplified and accelerated "no-objection" procedure, to materials and supplies for essential civilian needs as identified in the report of the Secretary-General dated 20 March 1991, and in any further findings of humanitarian need by the Committee;
21. Decides that the Security Council shall review the provisions of paragraph 20 above every sixty days in the light of the policies and practices of the Government of Iraq, including the implementation of all relevant resolutions of the Security Council, for the purpose of determining whether to reduce or lift the prohibitions referred to therein;
22. Decides that upon the approval by the Security Council of the programme called for in paragraph 19 above and upon Council agreement that Iraq has completed all actions contemplated in paragraphs 8, 9, 10, 11, 12 and 13 above, the prohibitions against the import of commodities and products originating in Iraq and the prohibitions against financial transactions related thereto contained in resolution 661 (1990) shall have no further force or effect;
23. Decides that, pending action by the Security Council under paragraph 22 above, the Security Council Committee established by resolution 661 (1990) shall be empowered to approve, when required to assure adequate financial resources on the part of Iraq to carry out the activities under paragraph 20 above, exceptions to the prohibition against the import of commodities and products originating in Iraq;

24. Decides that, in accordance with resolution 661 (1990) and subsequent related resolutions and until a further decision is taken by the Security Council, all States shall continue to prevent the sale or supply, or the promotion or facilitation of such sale or supply, to Iraq by their nationals, or from their territories or using their flag vessels or aircraft, of:
    (a) Arms and related materiel of all types, specifically including the sale or transfer through other means of all forms of conventional military equipment, including for paramilitary forces, and spare parts and components and their means of production, for such equipment;
    (b) Items specified and defined in paragraphs 8 and 12 above not otherwise covered above;
    (c) Technology under licensing or other transfer arrangements used in the production, utilization or stockpiling of items specified in subparagraphs (a) and (b) above;
    (d) Personnel or materials for training or technical support services relating to the design, development, manufacture, use, maintenance or support of items specified in subparagraphs (a) and (b) above;

...

I

33. Declares that, upon official notification by Iraq to the Secretary-General and to the Security Council of its acceptance of the provisions above, a formal cease-fire is effective between Iraq and Kuwait and the Member States cooperating with Kuwait in accordance with resolution 678 (1990);
34. Decides to remain seized of the matter and to take such further steps as may be required for the implementation of the present resolution and to secure peace and security in the area.

Resolution 688 (1991)

The Security Council,

...

Gravely concerned by the repression of the Iraqi civilian population in many parts of Iraq, including most recently in Kurdish populated areas, which led

Adopted by the Security Council at its 2982nd meeting, on 5 April 1991 to a massive flow of refugees towards and across international frontiers and to cross-border incursions, which threaten international peace and security in the region,

Deeply disturbed by the magnitude of the human suffering involved, Taking note of the letters sent by the representatives of Turkey and France to the United Nations dated 2 April 1991 and 4 April 1991, respectively (S/22435 and S/22442),

Taking note also of the letters sent by the Permanent Representative of the Islamic Republic of Iran to the United Nations dated 3 and 4 April 1991, respectively (S/22436 and S/22447),

Reaffirming the commitment of all Member States to the sovereignty, territorial integrity and political independence of Iraq and of all States in the area,

Bearing in mind the Secretary-General's report of 20 March 1991 (S/22366),

1. Condemns the repression of the Iraqi civilian population in many parts of Iraq, including most recently in Kurdish populated areas, the consequences of which threaten international peace and security in the region;
2. Demands that Iraq, as a contribution to remove the threat to international peace and security in the region, immediately end this repression, and in that same context expresses the hope that an open dialogue will take place to ensure that the human and political rights of all Iraqi citizens are respected;
3. Insists that Iraq allow immediate access by international humanitarian organizations to all those in need of assistance in all parts of Iraq and to make available all necessary facilities for their operations;
4. Requests the Secretary-General to pursue his humanitarian efforts in Iraq and to report forthwith, if appropriate on the basis of a further mission to the region, on the plight of the Iraqi civilian population, and in particular the Kurdish population, suffering from the repression in all its forms inflicted by the Iraqi authorities;
5. Requests further the Secretary-General to use all the resources at his disposal, including those of the relevant United Nations agencies, to address urgently the critical needs of the refugees and displaced Iraqi population;
6. Appeals to all Member States and to all humanitarian organizations to contribute to these humanitarian relief efforts;
7. Demands that Iraq cooperate with the Secretary-General to these ends;
8. Decides to remain seized of the matter.

Resolution 1134 (1997)

The Security Council,

...

Having considered the report of the Executive Chairman of the Special Commission dated 6 October 1997 (S/1997/774),

Expressing grave concern at the report of additional incidents since the adoption of resolution 1115 (1997) in which access by the Special Commission inspection teams to sites in Iraq designated for inspection by the Commission was again denied by the Iraqi authorities,

Stressing the unacceptability of any attempts by Iraq to deny access to such sites,

Taking note of the progress nevertheless achieved by the Special Commission, as set out in the report of the Executive Chairman, towards the elimination of Iraq's programme of weapons of mass destruction,

Reaffirming its determination to ensure full compliance by Iraq with all its obligations under all previous relevant resolutions and reiterating its demand that Iraq allow immediate, unconditional and unrestricted access to the Special Commission to any site which the Commission wishes to inspect, and in particular allow the Special Commission and its inspection teams to conduct both fixed wing and helicopter flights throughout Iraq for all relevant purposes including inspection, surveillance, aerial surveys, transportation and logistics without interferences of any kind and upon such terms and conditions as may be determined by the Special Commission, and to make use of their own aircraft and such airfields in Iraq as they may determine are most appropriate for the work of the Commission,

Recalling that resolution 1115 (1997) expresses the Council's firm intention, unless the Special Commission has advised the Council that Iraq is in substantial compliance with paragraphs 2 and 3 of that resolution, to impose additional measures on those categories of Iraqi officials responsible for the non-compliance,

Reiterating the commitment of all Member States to the sovereignty, territorial integrity and political independence of Kuwait and Iraq,

Acting under Chapter VII of the Charter of the United Nations,

1. Condemns the repeated refusal of the Iraqi authorities, as detailed in the report of the Executive Chairman of the Special Commission, to allow access to sites designated by the Special Commission, and especially Iraqi actions endangering the safety of Special Commission personnel, the removal and destruction of documents of interest to the Special

Adopted by the Security Council at its 3826th meeting, on 23 October 1997

Commission and interference with the freedom of movement of Special Commission personnel;

2. Decides that such refusals to cooperate constitute a flagrant violation of Security Council resolutions 687 (1991), 707 (1991), 715 (1991) and 1060 (1996), and notes that the Special Commission in the report of the Executive Chairman was unable to advise that Iraq was in substantial compliance with paragraphs 2 and 3 of resolution 1115 (1997);
3. Demands that Iraq cooperate fully with the Special Commission in accordance with the relevant resolutions, which constitute the governing standard of Iraqi compliance;
4. Demands in particular that Iraq without delay allow the Special Commission inspection teams immediate, unconditional and unrestricted access to any and all areas, facilities, equipment, records and means of transportation which they wish to inspect in accordance with the mandate of the Special Commission, as well as to officials and other persons under the authority of the Iraqi Government whom the Special Commission wishes to interview so that the Special Commission may fully discharge its mandate;
5. Requests the Chairman of the Special Commission to include in all future consolidated progress reports prepared under resolution 1051 (1996) an annex evaluating Iraq's compliance with paragraphs 2 and 3 of resolution 1115 (1997);
6. Expresses the firm intention—if the Special Commission reports that Iraq is not in compliance with paragraphs 2 and 3 of resolution 1115 (1997) or if the Special Commission does not advise the Council in the report of the Executive Chairman due on 11 April 1998 that Iraq is in compliance with paragraphs 2 and 3 of resolution 1115 (1997)—to adopt measures which would oblige all States to prevent without delay the entry into or transit through their territories of all Iraqi officials and members of the Iraqi armed forces who are responsible for or participate in instances of non-compliance with paragraphs 2 and 3 of resolution 1115 (1997), provided that the entry of a person into a particular State on a specified date may be authorized by the Committee established by resolution 661 (1990), and provided that nothing in this paragraph shall oblige a State to refuse entry into its own territory to its own nationals or persons carrying out bona fide diplomatic assignments or missions;
7. Decides further, on the basis of all incidents related to the implementation of paragraphs 2 and 3 of resolution 1115 (1997), to begin to designate, in consultation with the Special Commission, individuals whose entry or transit would be prevented upon implementation of the measures set out in paragraph 6 above;

8. Decides not to conduct the reviews provided for in paragraphs 21 and 28 of resolution 687 (1991) until after the next consolidated progress report of the Special Commission, due on 11 April 1998, after which those reviews will resume in accordance with resolution 687 (1991), beginning on 26 April 1998;
9. Reaffirms its full support for the authority of the Special Commission under its Executive Chairman to ensure the implementation of its mandate under the relevant resolutions of the Council;
10. Decides to remain seized of the matter.

Resolution 1154 (1998)

The Security Council,

Recalling all its previous relevant resolutions, which constitute the governing standard of Iraqi compliance,

Determined to ensure immediate and full compliance by Iraq without conditions or restrictions with its obligations under resolution 687 (1991) and the other relevant resolutions,

Reaffirming the commitment of all Member States to the sovereignty, territorial integrity and political independence of Iraq, Kuwait and the neighbouring States,

Acting under Chapter VII of the Charter of the United Nations,

1. Commends the initiative by the Secretary-General to secure commitments from the Government of Iraq on compliance with its obligations under the relevant resolutions, and in this regard endorses the memorandum of understanding signed by the Deputy Prime Minister of Iraq and the Secretary-General on 23 February 1998 (S/1998/166) and looks forward to its early and full implementation;
2. Requests the Secretary-General to report to the Council as soon as possible with regard to the finalization of procedures for Presidential sites in consultation with the Executive Chairman of the United Nations Special Commission and the Director General of the International Atomic Energy Agency (IAEA);
3. Stresses that compliance by the Government of Iraq with its obligations, repeated again in the memorandum of understanding, to accord immediate, unconditional and unrestricted access to the Special Commission

---

Adopted by the Security Council at its 3858th meeting, on 2 March 1998

and the IAEA in conformity with the relevant resolutions is necessary for the implementation of resolution 687 (1991), but that any violation would have severest consequences for Iraq;

4. Reaffirms its intention to act in accordance with the relevant provisions of resolution 687 (1991) on the duration of the prohibitions referred to in that resolution and notes that by its failure so far to comply with its relevant obligations Iraq has delayed the moment when the Council can do so;
5. Decides, in accordance with its responsibility under the Charter, to remain actively seized of the matter, in order to ensure implementation of this resolution, and to secure peace and security in the area.

Resolution 1284 (1999)

The Security Council,

. . .

Acting under Chapter VII of the Charter of the United Nations, and taking into account that operative provisions of this resolution relate to previous resolutions adopted under Chapter VII of the Charter,

A.

1. Decides to establish, as a subsidiary body of the Council, the United Nations Monitoring, Verification and Inspection Commission (UNMOVIC) which replaces the Special Commission established pursuant to paragraph 9 (b) of resolution 687 (1991);
2. Decides also that UNMOVIC will undertake the responsibilities mandated to the Special Commission by the Council with regard to the verification of compliance by Iraq with its obligations under paragraphs 8, 9 and 10 of resolution 687 (1991) and other related resolutions, that UNMOVIC will establish and operate, as was recommended by the panel on disarmament and current and future ongoing monitoring and verification issues, a reinforced system of ongoing monitoring and verification, which will implement the plan approved by the Council in resolution 715 (1991) and address unresolved disarmament issues, and that UNMOVIC will identify, as necessary in accordance with its mandate, additional sites in Iraq to be covered by the reinforced system of ongoing monitoring and verification;

Adopted by the Security Council at its 4084th meeting, on 17 December 1999

3. Reaffirms the provisions of the relevant resolutions with regard to the role of the IAEA in addressing compliance by Iraq with paragraphs 12 and 13 of resolution 687 (1991) and other related resolutions, and requests the Director General of the IAEA to maintain this role with the assistance and cooperation of UNMOVIC;
4. Reaffirms its resolutions 687 (1991), 699 (1991), 707 (1991), 715 (1991), 1051 (1996), 1154 (1998) and all other relevant resolutions and statements of its President, which establish the criteria for Iraqi compliance, affirms that the obligations of Iraq referred to in those resolutions and statements with regard to cooperation with the Special Commission, unrestricted access and provision of information will apply in respect of UNMOVIC, and decides in particular that Iraq shall allow UNMOVIC teams immediate, unconditional and unrestricted access to any and all areas, facilities, equipment, records and means of transport which they wish to inspect in accordance with the mandate of UNMOVIC, as well as to all officials and other persons under the authority of the Iraqi Government whom UNMOVIC wishes to interview so that UNMOVIC may fully discharge its mandate;
5. Requests the Secretary-General, within 30 days of the adoption of this resolution, to appoint, after consultation with and subject to the approval of the Council, an Executive Chairman of UNMOVIC who will take up his mandated tasks as soon as possible, and, in consultation with the Executive Chairman and the Council members, to appoint suitably qualified experts as a College of Commissioners for UNMOVIC which will meet regularly to review the implementation of this and other relevant resolutions and provide professional advice and guidance to the Executive Chairman, including on significant policy decisions and on written reports to be submitted to the Council through the Secretary-General;
6. Requests the Executive Chairman of UNMOVIC, within 45 days of his appointment, to submit to the Council, in consultation with and through the Secretary-General, for its approval an organizational plan for UNMOVIC, including its structure, staffing requirements, management guidelines, recruitment and training procedures, incorporating as appropriate the recommendations of the panel on disarmament and current and future ongoing monitoring and verification issues, and recognizing in particular the need for an effective, cooperative management structure for the new organization, for staffing with suitably qualified and experienced personnel, who would be regarded as international civil servants subject to Article 100 of the Charter of the United Nations, drawn from the broadest possible geographical base, including as he

deems necessary from international arms control organizations, and for the provision of high quality technical and cultural training;

7. Decides that UNMOVIC and the IAEA, not later than 60 days after they have both started work in Iraq, will each draw up, for approval by the Council, a work programme for the discharge of their mandates, which will include both the implementation of the reinforced system of ongoing monitoring and verification, and the key remaining disarmament tasks to be completed by Iraq pursuant to its obligations to comply with the disarmament requirements of resolution 687 (1991) and other related resolutions, which constitute the governing standard of Iraqi compliance, and further decides that what is required of Iraq for the implementation of each task shall be clearly defined and precise;
8. Requests the Executive Chairman of UNMOVIC and the Director General of the IAEA, drawing on the expertise of other international organizations as appropriate, to establish a unit which will have the responsibilities of the joint unit constituted by the Special Commission and the Director General of the IAEA under paragraph 16 of the export/import mechanism approved by resolution 1051 (1996), and also requests the Executive Chairman of UNMOVIC, in consultation with the Director General of the IAEA, to resume the revision and updating of the lists of items and technology to which the mechanism applies;
9. Decides that the Government of Iraq shall be liable for the full costs of UNMOVIC and the IAEA in relation to their work under this and other related resolutions on Iraq;
10. Requests Member States to give full cooperation to UNMOVIC and the IAEA in the discharge of their mandates;
11. Decides that UNMOVIC shall take over all assets, liabilities and archives of the Special Commission, and that it shall assume the Special Commission's part in agreements existing between the Special Commission and Iraq and between the United Nations and Iraq, and affirms that the Executive Chairman, the Commissioners and the personnel serving with UNMOVIC shall have the rights, privileges, facilities and immunities of the Special Commission;
12. Requests the Executive Chairman of UNMOVIC to report, through the Secretary-General, to the Council, following consultation with the Commissioners, every three months on the work of UNMOVIC, pending submission of the first reports referred to in paragraph 33 below, and to report immediately when the reinforced system of ongoing monitoring and verification is fully operational in Iraq;

...

Resolution 1441 (2002)

The Security Council,

...

Determined to secure full compliance with its decisions, Acting under Chapter VII of the Charter of the United Nations,

1. Decides that Iraq has been and remains in material breach of its obligations under relevant resolutions, including resolution 687 (1991), in particular through Iraq's failure to cooperate with United Nations inspectors and the IAEA, and to complete the actions required under paragraphs 8 to 13 of resolution 687 (1991);
2. Decides, while acknowledging paragraph 1 above, to afford Iraq, by this resolution, a final opportunity to comply with its disarmament obligations under relevant resolutions of the Council; and accordingly decides to set up an enhanced inspection regime with the aim of bringing to full and verified completion the disarmament process established by resolution 687 (1991) and subsequent resolutions of the Council;
3. Decides that, in order to begin to comply with its disarmament obligations, in addition to submitting the required biannual declarations, the Government of Iraq shall provide to UNMOVIC, the IAEA, and the Council, not later than 30 days from the date of this resolution, a currently accurate, full, and complete declaration of all aspects of its programmes to develop chemical, biological, and nuclear weapons, ballistic missiles, and other delivery systems such as unmanned aerial vehicles and dispersal systems designed for use on aircraft, including any holdings and precise locations of such weapons, components, subcomponents, stocks of agents, and related material and equipment, the locations and work of its research, development and production facilities, as well as all other chemical, biological, and nuclear programmes, including any which it claims are for purposes not related to weapon production or material;
4. Decides that false statements or omissions in the declarations submitted by Iraq pursuant to this resolution and failure by Iraq at any time to comply with, and cooperate fully in the implementation of, this resolution shall constitute a further material breach of Iraq's obligations and will be reported to the Council for assessment in accordance with paragraphs 11 and 12 below;

Adopted by the Security Council at its 4644th meeting, on 8 November 2002

5. Decides that Iraq shall provide UNMOVIC and the IAEA immediate, unimpeded, unconditional, and unrestricted access to any and all, including underground, areas, facilities, buildings, equipment, records, and means of transport which they wish to inspect, as well as immediate, unimpeded, unrestricted, and private access to all officials and other persons whom UNMOVIC or the IAEA wish to interview in the mode or location of UNMOVIC's or the IAEA's choice pursuant to any aspect of their mandates; further decides that UNMOVIC and the IAEA may at their discretion conduct interviews inside or outside of Iraq, may facilitate the travel of those interviewed and family members outside of Iraq, and that, at the sole discretion of UNMOVIC and the IAEA, such interviews may occur without the presence of observers from the Iraqi Government; and instructs UNMOVIC and requests the IAEA to resume inspections no later than 45 days following adoption of this resolution and to update the Council 60 days thereafter;
6. Endorses the 8 October 2002 letter from the Executive Chairman of UNMOVIC and the Director-General of the IAEA to General Al-Saadi of the Government of Iraq, which is annexed hereto, and decides that the contents of the letter shall be binding upon Iraq;
7. Decides further that, in view of the prolonged interruption by Iraq of the presence of UNMOVIC and the IAEA and in order for them to accomplish the tasks set forth in this resolution and all previous relevant resolutions and notwithstanding prior understandings, the Council hereby establishes the following revised or additional authorities, which shall be binding upon Iraq, to facilitate their work in Iraq:
   —UNMOVIC and the IAEA shall determine the composition of their inspection teams and ensure that these teams are composed of the most qualified and experienced experts available;
   —All UNMOVIC and IAEA personnel shall enjoy the privileges and immunities, corresponding to those of experts on mission, provided in the Convention on Privileges and Immunities of the United Nations and the Agreement on the Privileges and Immunities of the IAEA;
   —UNMOVIC and the IAEA shall have unrestricted rights of entry into and out of Iraq, the right to free, unrestricted, and immediate movement to and from inspection sites, and the right to inspect any sites and buildings, including immediate, unimpeded, unconditional, and unrestricted access to Presidential Sites equal to that at other sites, notwithstanding the provisions of resolution 1154 (1998) of 2 March 1998;

—UNMOVIC and the IAEA shall have the right to be provided by Iraq the names of all personnel currently and formerly associated with Iraq's chemical, biological, nuclear, and ballistic missile programmes and the associated research, development, and production facilities;
—Security of UNMOVIC and IAEA facilities shall be ensured by sufficient United Nations security guards;
—UNMOVIC and the IAEA shall have the right to declare, for the purposes of freezing a site to be inspected, exclusion zones, including surrounding areas and transit corridors, in which Iraq will suspend ground and aerial movement so that nothing is changed in or taken out of a site being inspected;
—UNMOVIC and the IAEA shall have the free and unrestricted use and landing of fixed- and rotary-winged aircraft, including manned and unmanned reconnaissance vehicles;
—UNMOVIC and the IAEA shall have the right at their sole discretion verifiably to remove, destroy, or render harmless all prohibited weapons, subsystems, components, records, materials, and other related items, and the right to impound or close any facilities or equipment for the production thereof; and
—UNMOVIC and the IAEA shall have the right to free import and use of equipment or materials for inspections and to seize and export any equipment, materials, or documents taken during inspections, without search of UNMOVIC or IAEA personnel or official or personal baggage;

8. Decides further that Iraq shall not take or threaten hostile acts directed against any representative or personnel of the United Nations or the IAEA or of any Member State taking action to uphold any Council resolution;
9. Requests the Secretary-General immediately to notify Iraq of this resolution, which is binding on Iraq; demands that Iraq confirm within seven days of that notification its intention to comply fully with this resolution; and demands further that Iraq cooperate immediately, unconditionally, and actively with UNMOVIC and the IAEA;
10. Requests all Member States to give full support to UNMOVIC and the IAEA in the discharge of their mandates, including by providing any information related to prohibited programmes or other aspects of their mandates, including on Iraqi attempts since 1998 to acquire prohibited items, and by recommending sites to be inspected, persons to be interviewed, conditions of such interviews, and data to be collected, the results of which shall be reported to the Council by UNMOVIC and the IAEA;

11. Directs the Executive Chairman of UNMOVIC and the Director-General of the IAEA to report immediately to the Council any interference by Iraq with inspection activities, as well as any failure by Iraq to comply with its disarmament obligations, including its obligations regarding inspections under this resolution;
12. Decides to convene immediately upon receipt of a report in accordance with paragraphs 4 or 11 above, in order to consider the situation and the need for full compliance with all of the relevant Council resolutions in order to secure international peace and security;
13. Recalls, in that context, that the Council has repeatedly warned Iraq that it will face serious consequences as a result of its continued violations of its obligations;
14. Decides to remain seized of the matter.

Bibliography

Abbott, Kenneth, and Duncan Snidal. 1998. "Why States Act through Formal International Organizations." *Journal of Conflict Resolution* 42 (1): 3–32.

——. 2000. "Hard and Soft Law in International Governance." *International Organization* 54 (3): 421–56.

Adams, Paul. 2003. "'Shock and Awe'—An Inevitable Victory." In *The Battle for Iraq*, ed. Sara Beck and Malcolm Downing, 105–20. Baltimore: Johns Hopkins University Press.

Albright, Madeleine. 1998. Remarks on Air Strikes against Iraq, December 16. Washington, D.C.: Office of the Spokesman, U.S. Department of State. http://secretary.state.gov/www/statements/1998/981216.html.

——. 2003. *Madam Secretary.* New York: Miramax.

Aldrich-Moodie, Benjamin. 1998. "Negotiating Coalition: Winning Soviet Consent to Resolution 678 Against Iraq." WWS Case Study 1/98, Woodrow Wilson School of Public and International Affairs.

Alexander, Michael, and Timothy Garden. 2001. "The Arithmetic of Defence Policy." *International Affairs* 77 (3): 121–36.

Alexandrova, Olga. 1991. "Soviet Policy in the Gulf Conflict." *Aussenpolitik* 42 (3): 231–40.

Allison, Graham. 2004. *Nuclear Terrorism: The Ultimate Preventable Catastrophe.* New York: Times Books.

Andrews, David M. 2005. "The United States and Its Atlantic Partners." In *The Atlantic Alliance under Stress: U.S.—European Relations after Iraq*, ed. David M. Andrews, 56–78. New York: Cambridge University Press.

Asmus, Ronald D. 2003. "Rebuilding the Atlantic Alliance." *Foreign Affairs* 82 (5): 20–31.

Asmus, Ronald, Philip Everts, and Pierangelo Isernia. 2004. "Power, War and Public Opinion: Looking behind the Transatlantic Divide." *Policy Review,* no. 123: 73–88.

Atkinson, Rick. 1993. *Crusade: The Untold Story of the Persian Gulf War.* New York: Houghton Mifflin.

Azzam, Maha. 1991. "The Gulf Crisis: Perceptions in the Muslim World." *International Affairs* 67 (3): 473–85.

Badsey, Stephen. 1992. "The Media War." In *The Gulf War Assessed*, ed. John Pimlott and Stephen Badsey, 219–45. London: Arms and Armour.

Baldwin, David A. 1979. "Power Analysis and World Politics: New Trends versus Old Tendencies." *World Politics* 31 (2): 161–94.

——. 1985. *Economic Statecraft.* Princeton: Princeton University Press.

Baker, James, with Thomas DeFrank. 1995. *The Politics of Diplomacy.* New York: G.P. Putnam's Sons.

Baker, James. 1996. "Intervention the Post-Cold War Era: The Case for Pragmatism." In *Managing Conflict in the Post-Cold War World: The Role of Intervention*, 29–34. Washington, D.C.: Aspen Institute.

Baram, Amatzia. 1998. *Building toward Crisis: Saddam Husayn's Strategy for Survival.* Washington. D.C.: Washington Institute for Near East Policy.

Barnett, Michael. 1997. "Bringing in the New World Order: Liberalism, Legitimacy, and the United Nations." *World Politics* 49 (4): 526–51.

——. 2002. *Eyewitness to Genocide: The United Nations and Rwanda.* Ithaca: Cornell University Press.

Barnett, Michael, and Martha Finnemore. 2004. *Rules for the World: International Organizations in World Politics.* Ithaca: Cornell University Press.

Bawn, Kathleen. 1995. "Political Control versus Expertise: Congressional Choices about Administrative Procedures." *American Political Science Review* 89 (1): 62–73.

Bayard, Thomas, and Kimberly Elliott. 1994. *Reciprocity and Retaliation in U.S. Trade Policy.* Washington, D.C.: Institute for International Economics.

BBC News. 1998. "Opposition Grows against Use of Force." February 9. http://news.bbc.co.uk/2/hi/54985.stm.

——. 2003a. "France Treads Carefully on Iraq." February 6. http://news.bbc.co.uk/2/hi/middle_east/2732939.stm.

——. 2003b. "Polls Find Europeans Oppose Iraq War." February 11. http://news.bbc.co.uk/1/hi/world/europe/2747175.stm.

——. 2003c. "Tiptoeing along the Tightrope." February 15. http://news.bbc.co.uk/2/low/americas/2765123.stm.

BBC World Service. 2007. "World View of US Role Goes from Bad to Worse." January 23. http://www.globescan.com/news_archives/bbcusop.

Beard, Jack M. 2002. "America's New War on Terror: The Case for Self-Defense under International Law." *Harvard Journal of Law and Public Policy* 25 (2): 559–90.

Bennett, Andrew, Joseph Lepgold, and Danny Unger. 1994. "Burden-Sharing in the Persian Gulf War." *International Organization* 48 (1): 39–75.

——, eds. 1997. *Friends in Need: Burden Sharing in the Gulf War.* New York: St. Martin's.

Bennett, W. Lance. 1990. "Toward a Theory of Press-State Relations in the United States." *Journal of Communication* 40 (2): 103–25.

Bennett, W. Lance, and David L. Paletz, eds. 1994. *Taken by Storm: The Media, Public Opinion, and U.S. Foreign Policy in the Gulf War.* Chicago: University of Chicago Press.

Bernhard, William. 1998. "A Political Explanation of Variation in Central Bank Independence." *American Political Science Review* 92 (2): 311–27.

Beschloss, Michael, and Strobe Talbott. 1993. *At the Highest Levels.* Boston: Little, Brown.

Beste, Ralf, Dirk Koch, Romain Leick, Gabor Steingart, and Alexander Szandar. 2003. "More Europe." *Spiegel Online,* March 31. http://www.spiegel.de/international/spiegel/0,1518,242828,00.html.

Blair, Tony. 1998. Prime Minister's Statement to Parliament concerning Iraq, December 17. http://www.number-10.gov.uk/output/Page1169.asp.

——. 2003. Prime Minister's Statement Opening Iraq Debate, March 18. Prime Minister's Speeches 2003. http://www.number-10.gov.uk/output/Page3294.asp.

Blix, Hans. 2004. *Disarming Iraq.* New York: Pantheon.

Boehmer, Charles, Erik Gartzke, and Timothy Nordstrom. 2004. "Do Intergovernmental Organizations Promote Peace?" *World Politics* 57 (1): 1–38.

Boileau, Alain E. 1997. "To the Suburbs of Baghdad: Clinton's Extension of the Southern Iraqi No-Fly Zone." *ILSA Journal of International and Comparative Law* 3:875–94.

Boyer, Yves, Serge Sur, and Olivier Fleurence. 2003. "France: Security Council Legitimacy and Executive Primacy." In *Democratic Accountability and the Use of Force in International Law,* ed. Charlotte Ku and Harold K. Jacobson, 280–99. New York: Cambridge University Press.

Brands, H. W. 2004. "George Bush and the Gulf War of 1991." *Presidential Studies Quarterly* 34:113–31.

Brumberg, Daniel. 1997. "From Strategic Surprise to Strategic Gain: Egypt's Role in the Gulf Coalition." In *Friends in Need,* ed. Andrew Bennett, Joseph Lepgold, and Danny Unger, 91–112. New York: St. Martin's.

Busch, Marc L. 2007. "Overlapping Institutions, Forum Shopping, and Dispute Settlement in International Trade." *International Organization* 61 (4): 735–61.

Bush, George. 1990a. "The Persian Gulf: Pursuing Multinational Objectives." *Dispatch* 1 (1): 57.

——. 1990b. The President's News Conference, November 30. http://bushlibrary.tamu.edu/papers/1990.

——. 1991. Radio Address to the Nation on the Persian Gulf Crisis, January 5. http://bushlibrary.tamu.edu/research/papers/1991/91010500.html.

Bush, George, and Mikhail Gorbachev. 1990. "US-USSR Statement, September 9, 1990." *Dispatch* 1 (3): 2.

Bush, George, and Brent Scowcroft. 1998. *A World Transformed.* New York: Knopf.

Butler, Richard. 2000. *The Greatest Threat: Iraq, Weapons of Mass Destruction, and the Crisis of Global Security.* New York: Public Affairs.

BVA. 1998. "Sondages à la Une: Les Risques d'Intervention Militaire en Irak." February 26. http://www.bva.fr/fr/archives/irak2.html.

Byers, Michael. 2002. "Terrorism, the Use of Force and International Law after 11 September." *International Relations* 16 (2): 155–70.

——. 2004. "Agreeing to Disagree: Security Council Resolution 1441 and Intentional Ambiguity." *Global Governance* 10 (2): 165–86.

Byman, Daniel L., and Matthew C. Waxman. 2000. *Confronting Iraq: U.S. Policy and the Use of Force since the Gulf War.* Santa Monica: RAND.

——. 2002. *The Dynamics of Coercion: American Foreign Policy and the Limits of Military Might.* New York: Cambridge University Press.

Calvert, Randall. 1985. "The Value of Biased Information: A Rational Choice Model of Political Advice." *Journal of Politics* 47 (2): 530–55.

Carney, James, and John F. Dickerson. 2001. "Inside the War Room." *Time,* December 31.

Caron, David. 1993. "The Legitimacy of the Collective Authority of the Security Council." *American Journal of International Law* 87 (4): 552–88.

Carpenter, Daniel. 2001. *The Forging of Bureaucratic Autonomy.* Princeton: Princeton University Press.

Carr, Edward Hallett. 1946. *The Twenty Years' Crisis, 1919–1939.* 2nd ed. New York: St. Martin's.

CBC News. 2003. "Canada Proposing Middle Ground in UN Dispute over Iraq." February 26. http://www.cbc.ca/world/story/2003/02/26/can_unsecurity030226.html.

Center for Public Opinion and Democracy. 2003a. "Indians Reject War against Iraq." March 30. http://www.cpod.ubc.ca/polls/index.cfm?fuseaction=viewItem&itemID=56.

——. 2003b. "Spaniards Reject War on Iraq." March 29. http://www.cpod.ubc.ca/polls/index.cfm?fuseaction=viewItem&itemID=52.

Champion, Marc, Charles Fleming, Ian Johnson, and Carla Anne Robins. 2003. "Allies at Odds: Behind U.S. Rift with Europeans." *Wall Street Journal,* March 27, A1.

Chan, Steve, and William Safran. 2006. "Public Opinion as a Constraint against War: Democracies' Responses to Operation Iraqi Freedom." *Foreign Policy Analysis* 2:137–56.

Chapman, Terrence L. 2007. "International Security Institutions, Domestic Politics, and Institutional Legitimacy." *Journal of Conflict Resolution* 51 (1): 134–66.

Chapman, Terrence L., and Dan Reiter. 2004. "The United Nations Security Council and the Rally 'Round the Flag Effect." *Journal of Conflict Resolution* 48 (6): 886–909.

Chayes, Abram. 1974. *The Cuban Missile Crisis: International Crises and the Rule of Law.* London: Oxford University Press.

Chayes, Abram, and Antonia Handler Chayes. 1995. *The New Sovereignty.* Cambridge: Harvard University Press.

Checkel, Jeffrey T. 2001. "Why Comply? Social Learning and European Identity Change." *International Organization* 55 (3): 553–88.

Cheney, Richard. 2002. "Vice President Speaks at VFW 103rd National Convention." http://www.whitehouse.gov/news/releases/2002/08/20020826.html.

Chicago Council on Foreign Relations and German Marshall Fund. 2002. "Worldviews 2002: American and European Public Opinion and Foreign Policy." http://www.worldviews.org/detailreports/compreport/index.htm.

Cirincione, Joseph. 2003. "How Will the Iraq War Change Global Nonproliferation Strategies?" *Arms Control Today* 33 (3): 3–6.

Clark, Wesley. 2001. *Waging Modern War: Bosnia, Kosovo, and the Future of Combat.* New York: Public Affairs.

Claude, Inis. 1966. "Collective Legitimization as a Political Function of the United Nations." *International Organization* 20 (3): 367–79.

CNN. 2002. "Bush: U.S. Will Move on Iraq if UN Won't." September 13. http://archives.cnn.com/2002/US/09/12/bush.speech.un.

——. 2003a. "Chirac, Putin: No Need for War." February 10. http://www.cnn.com/2003/WORLD/meast/02/10/sprj.irq.france.putin.

——. 2003b. "Rice, Blix Meet on Iraq Inspections." January 14. http://www.cnn.com/2003/WORLD/meast/01/14/sproject.irq.blix/index.html.

——. 2003c. "Spain: No Combat Role in Iraq War." http://www.cnn.com/2003/WORLD/meast/03/18/sprj.irq.spain.

——. 2005. *The Situation Room,* transcript of show aired on November 2, 2005. http://transcripts.cnn.com/TRANSCRIPTS/0511/02/sitroom.03.html.

CNN/Angus Reid Group. 1998. "International Reaction to the U.S.-Led Military Attack against Iraq." CNN/Angus Reid Group International Monitor, December 22.

Cockburn, Andrew, and Patrick Cockburn. 1999. *Out of the Ashes: The Resurrection of Saddam Hussein.* New York: HarperCollins.

Collier, David. 1991. "The Comparative Method: Two Decades of Change." In *Comparative Political Dynamics: Global Research Perspectives,* ed. Dankwart A. Rustow and Kenneth Paul Erickson, 7–31. New York: HarperCollins.

Collier, David, James Mahoney, and Jason Seawright. 2004. "Claiming Too Much: Warnings about Selection Bias." In *Rethinking Social Inquiry,* ed. Henry E. Brady and David Collier, 85–102. Lanham, Md.: Rowman & Littlefield.

Conetta, Carl. 2003. "Disarming Iraq: What Did the UN Missions Accomplish?" Project on Defense Alternatives, Briefing Memo #27. Cambridge, Mass. http://www.comw.org/pda/fulltext/0304bm27.pdf.

Connaughton, Richard. 1992. *Military Intervention in the 1990s.* New York: Routledge.

Conte, Alex. 2005. *Security in the 21st Century: The United Nations, Afghanistan and Iraq.* Burlington, Vt.: Ashgate.

Cooley, John K. 1991. "Pre-War Gulf Diplomacy." *Survival* 33 (2): 125–39.
Cooper, Andrew F., and Kim Richard Nossal. 1997. "The Middle Powers in the Gulf Coalition: Australia, Canada, and the Nordics Compared." In *Friends in Need,* ed. Andrew Bennett, Joseph Lepgold, and Danny Unger, 269–95. New York: St. Martin's.
Cordesman, Anthony H. 1999. *Iraq in Crisis: A History from Desert Fox to June 1999.* Washington, D.C.: Center for Strategic and International Studies.
——. 2001. *The Lessons and Non-Lessons of the Air and Missile Campaign in Kosovo.* Westport, Conn.: Praeger.
——. 2003. *The Iraq War: Strategy, Tactics, and Military Lessons.* Westport, Conn: Praeger.
Cortell, Andrew P., and James Davis. 1996. "How Do International Institutions Matter? The Domestic Impact of International Rules and Norms." *International Studies Quarterly* 40 (4): 451–78.
Cortell, Andrew P., and Susan Peterson. 2006. "Dutiful Agent, Rogue Actors, or Both? Staffing, Voting Rules, and Slack in the WHO and WTO." In *Delegation and Agency in International Organizations,* ed. Darren G. Hawkins, David A. Lake, Daniel L. Nielson, and Michael J. Tierney, 255–80. New York: Cambridge University Press.
Cortright, David, and George A. Lopez. 1999. "Are Sanctions Just?" *Journal of International Affairs* 52 (2): 735–55.
Cox, Michael. 2006. "The Transatlantic Crisis: The Wolf Is at the Door." *European Political Science* 5 (1): 34–40.
Craven, Matthew. 2002. "Humanitarianism and the Quest for Smarter Sanctions." *European Journal of International Law* 13 (1): 43–61.
Crawford, Vincent, and Joel Sobel. 1982. "Strategic Information Transmission." *Econometrica* 50:1431–51.
Cronin, Bruce. 2001. "The Paradox of Hegemony: American's Ambiguous Relationship with the United Nations." *European Journal of International Relations* 7 (1): 103–30.
Cronin, Bruce, and Ian Hurd, eds. 2008. *The UN Security Council and the Politics of International Authority.* New York: Routledge.
Cukierman, Alex, and Mariano Tommasi. 1998. "When Does It Take a Nixon to Go to China?" *American Economic Review* 88 (1): 180–97.
Daalder, Ivo H. 2003. "The Coalition That Isn't." *Brookings Daily War Report,* March 24. http://www.brook.edu/printme.wbs?page=/pagedefs/04bdf0f4830cff3c78f3d6460a1415cb.xml.
Daalder, Ivo H., and James M. Lindsay. 2003. *American Unbound: The Bush Revolution in Foreign Policy.* Washington, D.C.: Brookings Institution Press.
Daalder, Ivo H., and Michael E. O'Hanlon. 2000. *Winning Ugly: NATO's War to Save Kosovo.* Washington, D.C.: Brookings Institution Press.
Dahl, Robert. 1999. "Can International Organizations Be Democratic? A Skeptic's View." In *Democracy's Edges,* ed. Ian Shaprio and Casiano Hacker-Cordón, 19–36. New York: Cambridge University Press.
Dannreuther, Roland. 1991–92. *The Gulf Conflict: A Political and Strategic Analysis.* Adelphi Paper 264. London: International Institute for Strategic Studies.
Davis, Christina L. 2008. "Forum Choice in Trade Disputes." Paper presented at the workshop on Globalization, Institutions and Economic Security, Ohio State University, February 25.
Davis, John. 2006. "The Ideology of War: The Neoconservatives and the Hijacking of US Policy in Iraq." In *Presidential Policies and the Road to the Second Iraq War,* ed. John Davis, 29–61. Burlington, Vt.: Ashgate.

de Jonge Oudraat, Chantal. 2002. "UNSCOM: Between Iraq and a Hard Place." *European Journal of International Law* 13 (1): 139–52.

——. 2004. "The Future of U.S.-European Relations." In *Wars on Terrorism and Iraq,* ed. Thomas G. Weiss, Margaret E. Crahan, and John Goering, 174–87. New York: Routledge.

de La Gorce, Paul-Marie. 1997. "A Setback for America's Anti-Saddam Crusade." *Le Monde Diplomatique,* December.

Department of Defense. 2000. *Kosovo/Operation Allied Forces After-Action Report.* Report to Congress, January 31. Washington: Department of Defense.

Diamond, Howard. 1998. "UNSCOM Future Uncertain after Strikes on Iraq." *Arms Control Today,* November/December.

——. 1999. "Security Council Remains Divided over Iraqi Arms Regime, Sanctions." *Arms Control Today,* April/May.

Diamond, Larry. 2005. *Squandered Victory: The American Occupation and the Bungled Effort to Bring Democracy to Iraq.* New York: Owl Books.

Diehl, Paul F., Jennifer Reifschneider, and Paul R. Hensel. 1996. "United Nations Intervention and Recurring Conflict." *International Organization* 50 (4): 683–700.

Dobbins, James, John G. McGinn, Keith Crane, Seth G. Jones, Rollie Lal, Andrew Rathmell, Rachel Swanger, and Anga Timilsina. 2005. *America's Role in Nation-Building: From Germany to Iraq.* Santa Monica: RAND Corporation.

Downs, Anthony. 1957. *An Economic Theory of Democracy.* New York: Harper & Row.

Downs, George W., David M. Rocke, and Randolph Siverson. 1985. "Cooperation and Arms Races." *World Politics* 38 (1): 118–46.

Dreher, Axel, and Nathan M. Jensen. 2007. "Independent Actor or Agent? An Empirical Analysis of the Impact of U.S. Interests on IMF Conditions." *Journal of Law and Economics* 50 (1): 105–24.

Drezner, Daniel W. 2000. "Bargaining, Enforcement, and Multilateral Sanctions: When Is Cooperation Counterproductive?" *International Organization* 54 (1): 73–102.

——, ed. 2003. *Locating the Proper Authorities: The Interaction of Domestic and International Institutions.* Ann Arbor: University of Michigan Press.

——. 2007. *All Politics Is Global: Explaining International Regulatory Regimes.* Princeton: Princeton University Press.

Duelfer, Charles. 2004. Transmittal Message, September 23, 2004, accompanying the *Comprehensive Report of the Special Advisor to the DCI on Iraq's WMD.* http://www.foia.cia.gov/duelfer/Iraqs_WMD_Vol1.pdf.

Dunnigan, James, and Austin Bay. 1992. *From Shield to Storm: High-Tech Weapons, Military Strategy, and Coalition Warfare in the Persian Gulf.* New York: William Morrow.

Edelstein, David M. 2004. "Occupational Hazards: Why Military Occupations Succeed or Fail." *International Security* 29 (1): 49–91.

Eichenberg, Richard C. 2005. "Victory Has Many Friends: U.S. Public Opinion and the Use of Military Force, 1981–2005." *International Security* 30 (1): 140–77.

Elster, Jon. 1979. *Ulysses and the Sirens.* Cambridge: Cambridge University Press.

Embassy of France. 2003. Statements made by M. Chirac during his joint press conference with Mr. Blix and Mr. ElBaradei following their meeting, Paris 17.01.2003. http://www.ambafrance-uk.org/statements-made-by-M-Chirac-during,4990.html.

EOS Gallup Europe. 2003. "International Crisis Survey: Public Opinion Survey in 30 European Countries." Report released January 29, 2003. On file with author.

Epstein, David, and Sharyn O'Halloran. 1999. *Delegating Powers.* Cambridge: Cambridge University Press.

Evans, Peter, Harold Jacobson, and Robert Putnam, eds. *Double-Edged Diplomacy: International Bargaining and Domestic Politics.* Berkeley: University of California Press.

Ezzat, Dina. 1999. "A Monster Far Worse than UNSCOM." *Al-Ahram Weekly On-Line,* 5–11 August 1999. http://weekly.ahram.org.eg/1999/441/intervw.htm.

Farer, Tom J. 2004. "The Interplay of Domestic Politics, Human Rights, and U.S. Foreign Policy." In *Wars on Terrorism and Iraq,* ed. Thomas G. Weiss, Margaret E. Crahan, and John Goering, 29–60. New York: Routledge.

Fearon, James. 1994. "Domestic Political Audiences and the Escalation of International Disputes." *American Political Science Review* 88 (3): 577–92.

Fearon, James. 1997. "Signaling Foreign Policy Interests: Tying Hands versus Sinking Costs." *Journal of Conflict Resolution* 41 (1): 68–90.

Fenton, Neil. 2004. *Understanding the UN Security Council: Coercion or Consent?* Burlington, Vt.: Ashgate.

Finnemore, Martha. 1998. "Military Intervention and the Organization of International Politics." In *Collective Conflict Management and Changing World Politics,* ed. Joseph Lepgold and Thomas G. Weiss, 181–204. Albany: SUNY Press.

——. 2003. *The Purpose of Intervention: Changing Beliefs about the Use of Force.* Ithaca: Cornell University Press.

Finnemore, Martha, and Kathryn Sikkink. 1998. "International Norm Dynamics and Political Change." *International Organization* 52 (4): 887–917.

Foot, Rosemary, S. Neil MacFarlane, and Michael Mastanduno, eds. 2003. *U.S. Hegemony and International Organizations.* New York: Oxford University Press.

Franck, Thomas M. 1990. *The Power of Legitimacy among Nations.* New York: Oxford University Press.

——. 1995. *Fairness in International Law and Institutions.* New York: Oxford University Press.

Freedman, Lawrence, and Efraim Karsh. 1993. *The Gulf Conflict, 1990–1991.* Princeton: Princeton University Press.

Freedman, Robert. 2002. Putin in the Middle East. *Middle East Review of International Affairs* 6 (2): 1–16.

Friedman, Norman. 1991. *Desert Victory.* Annapolis: Naval Institute Press.

Frum, David. 2003. *The Right Man: An Inside Account of the Bush White House.* New York: Random House.

Fukuyama, Francis. 2006. *America at the Crossroads: Democracy, Power, and the Neoconservative Legacy.* New Haven: Yale University Press.

Fuller, Graham. 1991. "Moscow and the Gulf War." *Foreign Affairs* 70 (3): 55–76.

Gaddis, John Lewis. 1997. *We Now Know: Rethinking Cold War History.* New York: Oxford University Press.

Gallup International. 2003a. "Iraq Poll 2003." http://www.gallup-international.com/ContentFiles/survey.asp?id=10.

——. 2003b. "Post War Iraq Poll." http://www.gallup-international.com/ContentFiles/survey.asp?id=9.

Gardiner, Nile. 2002. "Tony Blair's Challenge in Securing British Support for a War against Iraq." Backgrounder #1596, September 27. Washington, D.C.: Heritage Foundation.

Gause, F. Gregory, III. 1999. "Getting It Backward on Iraq." *Foreign Affairs* 78 (3): 54–65.

George, Alexander, and Andrew Bennett. 2005. *Case Studies and Theory Development in the Social Sciences.* Cambridge, Mass.: MIT Press.

George, Alexander, and Timothy McKeown. 1985. "Case Studies and Theories of Organizational Decision-Making." In *Advances in Information Processing in*

Organizations, vol. 2., ed. Robert F. Coulam and Richard A. Smith, 21–58. Greenwich, Conn.: JAI Press.

George, Alexander, and William Simons, eds. 1994. *The Limits of Coercive Diplomacy.* 2nd ed. Boulder: Westview.

German Marshall Fund. 2003. "Transatlantic Trends 2003." http://www.transatlantictrends.org/trends/doc/2003_english_top.pdf.

Gilligan, Thomas, and Keith Krehbiel. 1989. "Asymmetric Information and Leigislative Rules with a Heterogeneous Committee." *American Journal of Political Science* 33: 459–90.

——. 1990. "Organization of Informative Committees by Rational Legislatures." *American Journal of Political Science* 34:531–64.

Glennon, Michael. 2001. *Limits of Law, Prerogatives of Power.* New York: Palgrave.

Glennon, Michael J. 2003. "Why the Security Council Failed." *Foreign Affairs* 82 (3): 16–35.

Goldstein, Judith, Miles Kahler, Robert Keohane, and Anne-Marie Slaughter, eds. 2001. *Legalization and World Politics.* Cambridge, Mass: MIT Press.

Gordon, Michael R., and Bernard E. Trainor. 2006. *Cobra II: The Inside Story of the Invasion and Occupation of Iraq.* New York: Pantheon.

Gordon, Philip. 2001–2. "NATO after 11 September." *Survival* 43 (4): 89–106.

Gordon, Philip, and Jeremy Shapiro. 2004. *Allies at War: America, Europe and the Crisis over Iraq.* New York: McGraw-Hill.

Graham-Brown, Sarah. 1999. *Sanctioning Saddam: The Politics of Intervention in Iraq.* New York: I.B. Tauris.

Gray, Christine. 2002. "From Unity to Polarization: International Law and the Use of Force against Iraq." *European Journal of International Law* 13 (1): 1–19.

Gruber, Lloyd. 2000. *Ruling the World: Power Politics and the Rise of Supranational Institutions.* Princeton: Princeton University Press.

Grunberg, Isabelle. 1997. "Still a Reluctant Ally? France's Participation in the Gulf War Coalition." In *Friends in Need,* ed. Andrew Bennett, Joseph Lepgold, and Danny Unger, 113–34. New York: St. Martin's.

Haass, Richard. 1994. "Military Force: A User's Guide." *Foreign Policy,* no. 96:21–37.

Haftel, Yoram Z., and Alexander Thompson. 2006. "The Independence of International Organizations: Concept and Applications." *Journal of Conflict Resolution* 50 (2): 253–75.

Hale, William. 1992. "Turkey, the Middle East and the Gulf Crisis." *International Affairs* 68 (4): 679–92.

Hall, Peter, and Robert Franzese Jr. 1998. "Mixed Signals: Central Bank Independence, Coordinated Wage Bargaining, and European Monetary Union." *International Organization* 52 (3): 505–35.

Hampson, Fen Olser. 2003. "Canada: Committed Contributor of Ideas and Forces, but with Growing Doubts and Problems." In *Democratic Accountability and the Use of Force in International Law,* ed. Charlotte Ku and Harold K. Jacobson, 127–53. New York: Cambridge University Press.

Hannah, John B. 1997. "Soviet Contributions to the Gulf War Coalition." In *Friends in Need,* ed. Andrew Bennett, Joseph Lepgold, and Danny Unger, 241–68. New York: St. Martin's.

Hastings, Elizabeth Hann, and Philip K. Hastings, eds. 1992. *Index to International Public Opinion, 1990–1991.* Westport, Conn.: Greenwood.

Hawkins, Darren, David A. Lake, Daniel Nielson, and Michael J. Tierney, eds. 2006a. *Delegation and Agency in International Organizations.* New York: Cambridge University Press.

——. 2006b. "States, International Organizations, and Principal-Agent Theory." In *Delegation and Agency in International Organizations,* ed. Hawkins et al., 3–38. New York: Cambridge University Press.

Hawkins, Darren G., and Joshua Lloyd. 2003. "Questioning Comprehensive Sanctions: The Birth of a Norm." *Journal of Human Rights* 2 (3): 441–54.

Hayward, Malcolm. 1994. "The Making of the New World Order: The Role of the Media." In *The Gulf War and the New World Order,* ed. Tareq Ismael and Jacqueline Ismael, 224–41. Miami: University Press of Florida.

Heikal, Mohamed. 1992. *Illusions of Triumph: An Arab View of the Gulf War.* London: HarperCollins.

Hellman, Gunther. 1997. "Absorbing Shocks and Mounting Checks: Germany and Alliance Burden Sharing in the Gulf War." In *Friends in Need,* ed. Andrew Bennett, Joseph Lepgold, and Danny Unger, 165–94. New York: St. Martin's.

Herrmann, Richard K., and Vaughn P. Shannon. 2001. "Defending International Norms: The Role of Obligation, Material Interest, and Perception in Decision Making." *International Organization* 55 (3): 621–54.

High-Level Panel on Threats, Challenges and Change. 2004. *A More Secure World: Our Shared Responsibility.* UN Doc. A/59/565.

Hinnebusch, Raymond A. 1997. "Syria's Role in the Gulf War Coalition." In *Friends in Need,* ed. Andrew Bennett, Joseph Lepgold, and Danny Unger, 219–39. New York: St. Martin's.

Hiro, Dilip. 1992. *Desert Shield to Desert Storm: The Second Gulf War.* New York: Routledge.

Hoffmann, Stanley, with Frédéric Bozo. 2004. *Gulliver Unbound: America's Imperial Temptation and the War in Iraq.* Lanham, Md.: Rowman & Littlefield.

Holbrooke, Richard. 1999. "A New Realism for a New Era: The U.S. and the UN in the 21st Century." Address to the National Press Club. USUN Press Release #103-(99), November 2.

Hopf, Ted. 2005. "Dissipating Hegemony: US Unilateralism and European Counter-Hegemony." In *Partners or Rivals? European-American Relations after Iraq,* ed. Matthew Evangelista and Vittorio Emanuele Parsi, 39–59. Milan: Vita e Pensiero.

Housego, Kim. 2003. "Paris, Moscow and Berlin Issue Declaration against Iraq War, Call for Ministers' Gathering." Associated Press, March 15.

Howell, William G., and Jon C. Pevehouse. 2007. *While Dangers Gather: Congressional Checks on Presidential War Powers.* Princeton: Princeton University Press.

Huber, John, and Charles Shipan. 2002. *Deliberate Discretion? The Institutional Foundations of Bureaucratic Autonomy.* Cambridge: Cambridge University Press.

Hurd, Ian. 1999. "Legitimacy and Authority in International Politics." *International Organization* 53 (2): 379–408.

——. 2002. "Legitimacy, Power, and the Symbolic Life of the UN Security Council." *Global Governance* 8:35–51.

——. 2007. *After Anarchy: Legitimacy and Power in the United Nations Security Council.* Princeton: Princeton University Press.

Hurwitz, Jonathan. 1989. "Presidential Leadership and Public Followership." In *Manipulating Public Opinion,* ed. Michael Margolis and Gary A. Mauser, 222–49. Pacific Grove, Calif.: Brooks/Cole.

ICRC. 1999. *Iraq: 1989–1999, A Decade of Sanctions.* Geneva: International Committee of the Red Cross.

IISS (International Institute for Strategic Studies). 2004. *Strategic Survey 2003/4.* London: Oxford University Press.

Ikenberry, G. John. 2001. *After Victory: Institutions, Strategic Restraint, and the Rebuilding of Order after Major Wars.* Princeton University Press.
Independent International Commission on Kosovo. 2000. *The Kosovo Report: Conflict, International Response, Lessons Learned.* New York: Oxford University Press.
"Ingrates." 1999. *New Republic* 220 (3):9.
Iraq Study Group. 2006. *The Iraq Study Group Report.* New York: Vintage Books.
Ismael, Tareq Y., and Andrej Kreutz. 2001. "Russian-Iraqi Relations: A Historical and Political Analysis." *Arab Studies Quarterly* 23 (4): 87–115.
Jervis, Robert. 1976. *Perception and Misperception in International Politics.* Princeton: Princeton University Press.
——. 2005. *American Foreign Policy in a New Era.* New York: Routledge.
Johnston, Alastair Iain. 2001. "Treating International Institutions as Social Environments." *International Studies Quarterly* 45 (4): 487–515.
Johnstone, Ian. 2003. "Security Council Deliberation: The Power of the Better Argument." *European Journal of International Law* 14 (3): 437–80.
Kahler, Miles. 2000. "Conclusion: The Causes and Consequences of Legalization." *International Organization* 54 (3): 661–83.
Kampfner, John. 2003. *Blair's Wars.* London: Simon & Schuster.
Katzenstein, Peter J., ed. 1997. *Tamed Power: Germany in Europe.* Ithaca: Cornell University Press.
Kay, Sean. 2004. "NATO, the Kosovo War and Neoliberal Theory." *Contemporary Security Policy* 25 (2): 252–79.
Kearney, Martha. 2003. "Blair's Gamble." In *The Battle for Iraq,* ed. Sara Beck and Malcolm Downing, 79–91. Baltimore: Johns Hopkins University Press.
Keefer, Philip, and David Stasavage. 2002. "Checks and Balances, Private Information, and the Credibility of Monetary Commitments." *International Organization* 56 (4): 751–74.
Keegan, John. 2004. *The Iraq War.* New York: Knopf.
Keohane, Robert O. 1984. *After Hegemony: Cooperation and Discord in the World Political Economy.* Princeton University Press.
——. 2006. "The Contingent Legitimacy of Multilateralism." In *Multilateralism under Challenge? Power, International Structure, and World Order,* ed. Edward Newman, Ramesh Thakur, and John Tirman, 56–76. Tokyo: United Nations University Press.
Keohane, Robert O., and Peter J. Katzenstein. 2007. "The Political Consequences of Anti-Americanism." In *Anti-Americanism in World Politics,* ed. Peter J. Katzenstein and Robert O. Keohane. Ithaca: Cornell University Press.
Keohane, Robert O., and Joseph S. Nye. 1989. *Power and Interdependence.* 2nd ed. New York: HarperCollins.
——. 2004. "Redefining Accountability for Global Governance." In *Governance in a Global Economy,* ed. Miles Kahler and David A. Lake, 386–411. Princeton: Princeton University Press.
Khalidi, Washid. 1991. "Why Some Arabs Support Saddam." In *The Gulf War Reader,* ed. Micah Sifry and Christopher Cerf, 161–71. New York: Random House.
Kiewiet, Roderick, and Mathew McCubbins. 1991. *The Logic of Delegation.* Chicago: University of Chicago Press.
King, Gary, Robert O. Keohane, and Sidney Verba. 1994. *Designing Social Inquiry.* Princeton: Princeton University Press.
Kirschner, Jonathan. 1995. *Currency and Coercion: The Political Economy of International Monetary Power.* Princeton: Princeton University Press.
Kissinger, Henry. 2003. "NATO's Split; Atlantic Alliance Is in Its Gravest Crisis." *San Diego Union-Tribune,* February 16, G1.

Kitfield, James. 2003. "Damage Control." *National Journal,* July 19, 2336–41.
Koh, Harold Hongju. 2003. "On American Exceptionalism." *Stanford Law Review* 55 (5): 1479–1527.
Koremenos, Barbara, Charles Lipson, and Duncan Snidal. 2001. "The Rational Design of International Institutions." *International Organization* 55 (4): 761–99.
——. 2004. *The Rational Design of International Institutions.* New York: Cambridge University Press.
Koskenniemi, Martti. 1996. "The Place of Law in Collective Security." *Michigan Journal of International Law* 17 (2): 455–90.
Krasner, Stephen. 1991. "Global Communications and National Power: Life on the Pareto Frontier." *World Politics* 43 (2): 336–66.
Krasner, Stephen D., ed. 1983. *International Regimes.* Ithaca: Cornell University Press.
Krasno, Jean E., and James S. Sutterlin. 2003. *The United Nations and Iraq: Defanging the Viper.* Westport, Conn.: Praeger.
Krauthammer, Charles. 2003. "UN, R.I.P." *Washington Post,* January 31, A27.
Krehbiel, Keith. 1991. *Information and Legislative Organization.* Ann Arbor: University of Michigan Press.
Krishna, Vijay, and John Morgan. 2001. "Asymmetric Information and Legislative Rules: Some Amendments." *American Political Science Review* 95 (2): 435–52.
Krishnasamy, Kabilan. 2003. "The Paradox of India's Peacekeeping." *Contemporary South Asia* 12 (2): 263–80.
Ku, Charlotte, and Harold K. Jacobson. 2003. "Toward a Mixed System of Democratic Accountability." In *Democratic Accountability and the Use of Force in International Law,* ed. Charlotte Ku and Harold K. Jacobson, 349–83. New York: Cambridge University Press.
Kull, Stephen, and I. M. Destler. 1999. *Misreading the Public: The Myth of a New Isolationism.* Washington, D.C.: Brookings Institution Press.
Kydd, Andrew. 2000. "Trust, Reassurance and Cooperation." *International Organization* 54 (2): 325–57.
Kydd, Andrew. 2003. "Which Side Are You On? Bias, Credibility, and Mediation." *American Journal of Political Science* 47 (4): 597–611.
Kydland, Finn, and Edward Prescott. 1977. "Rules Rather Than Discretion: The Inconsistency of Optimal Plans." *Journal of Political Economy* 85:473–86.
Lake, Anthony. 1993. "From Containment to Enlargement." *U.S. Department of State Dispatch* 4 (39): 658–64.
Lake, David. 1999. *Entangling Relations: American Foreign Policy in Its Century.* Princeton: Princeton University Press.
Lantis, Jeffrey S., and Eric Moskowitz. 2005. "The Return of the Imperial Presidency? The Bush Doctrine and U.S. Intervention in Iraq." In *Contemporary Cases in U.S. Foreign Policy: From Terrorism to Trade,* 2nd ed., ed. Ralph G. Carter, 89–121. Washington, D.C.: CQ Press.
Lemann, Nicholas. 2003. "How It Came to War." *New Yorker,* March 31, 36–40.
LeoGrande, William M. 1990. "From Reagan to Bush: The Transition in US Policy Towards Central America." *Journal of Latin American Studies* 22 (3): 595–621.
Lepgold, Joseph. 1997. "Britain in Desert Storm: The Most Enthusiastic Junior Partner." In *Friends in Need,* ed. Andrew Bennett, Joseph Lepgold, and Danny Unger, 69–89. New York: St. Martin's.
Lesch, Ann Mosely. 1991. "Contrasting Reactions to the Persian Gulf Crisis: Egypt, Syria, Jordan and the Palestinians." *Middle East Journal* 45 (1): 30–50.
Lindley, Dan. 2007. *Promoting Peace with Information: Transparency as a Tool of Security Regimes.* Princeton: Princeton University Press.

Lipson, Charles. 1984. "International Cooperation in Economic and Security Affairs." *World Politics* 37 (1): 1–23.
Lipson, Michael. 2006. "Between Iraq and a Hard Place: UN Arms Inspections and the Politics of Security Council Resolution 1441." Paper presented at the annual convention of the Midwest Political Science Association, Chicago, April 20–23.
Lobel, Jules, and Michael Ratner. 1999. "Bypassing the Security Council: Ambiguous Authorizations to Use Force, Cease-Fires and the Iraqi Inspections Regime." *American Journal of International Law* 93 (1): 124–54.
Los Angeles Times Poll. 2002. "Nation: Bush, Economy and Iraq." Study #480, conducted December 12–15. http://www.latimesinteractive.com/pdfarchive/stat_sheets/la-timespoll480ss.pdf.
Luard, Evan. 1984. "Collective Intervention." In *Intervention in World Politics,* ed. Hedley Bull, 157–79. Oxford: Clarendon Press.
Luck, Edward. 2002. "The United States, International Organizations, and the Quest for Legitimacy." In *Multilateralism and U.S. Foreign Policy,* ed. Stewart Patrick and Shepard Forman, 47–74. Boulder: Lynne Rienner.
Luck, Edward C. 1999. *Mixed Messages: American Politics and International Organization, 1919–1999.* Washington, D.C.: Brookings Institution Press.
——. 2006. *UN Security Council: Practice and Promise.* New York: Routledge.
Lundestad, Geir. 2005. "Toward Transatlantic Drift?" In *The Atlantic Alliance under Stress: U.S.-European Relations after Iraq,* ed. David M. Andrews, 9–29. New York: Cambridge University Press.
Lupia, Arthur, and Mathew McCubbins. 1994. "Who Controls? Information and the Structure of Legislative Decision Making." *Legislative Studies Quarterly* 29 (3): 361–84.
Majone, Giandomenico. 2001. "Two Logics of Delegation: Agency and Fiduciary Relations in EU Governance." *European Union Politics* 2:103–21.
Malanczuk, Peter. 1991. "The Kurdish Crisis and Allied Intervention in the Aftermath of the Second Gulf War." *European Journal of International Law* 2 (2): 114–32.
——. 1997. *Akehurst's Modern Introduction to International Law.* 7th rev. ed. New York: Routledge.
Malone, David M. 1998. *Decision-Making in the UN Security Council.* Oxford: Clarendon Press.
——. 1999. "Goodbye UNSCOM: A Sorry Tale in US-UN Relations." *Security Dialogue* 30 (4): 393–411.
——, ed. 2004. *The UN Security Council: From the Cold War to the 21st Century.* Boulder: Lynne Rienner.
——. 2006. *The International Struggle over Iraq: Politics in the UN Security Council.* New York: Oxford University Press.
Malone, David M., and Yuen Foong Khong, eds. 2003. *Unilateralism and U.S. Foreign Policy: International Perspectives.* Boulder: Lynne Rienner.
Manheim, Jarol B., and Robert B. Albritton. 1984. "Changing National Images: International Public Relations and Media Agenda Setting." *American Political Science Review* 78 (3): 641–57.
March, James G., and Johan P. Olsen. 1989. *Rediscovering Institutions: The Organizational Basis of Politics.* New York: Free Press.
Martin, Lisa. 1992a. *Coercive Cooperation: Explaining Multilateral Economic Sanctions.* Princeton: Princeton University Press.
——. 1992b. "Interests, Power, and Multilateralism." *International Organization* 46 (4): 765–92.

——. 2000. *Democratic Commitments: Legislatures and International Cooperation.* Princeton: Princeton University Press.

Matheson, Michael J. 2006. *Council Unbound: The Growth of UN Decision Making on Conflict and Postconflict Issues after the Cold War.* Washington, D.C.: United States Institute of Peace Press.

Matthews, Ken. 1993. *The Gulf Conflict and International Relations.* New York: Routledge.

Mattli, Walter. 2001. "Private Justice in a Global Economy." *International Organization* 55 (4): 919–47.

Maxfield, Sylvia. 1997. *Gatekeepers of Growth.* Princeton: Princeton University Press.

McKay, James. 2005. "Fear of the Unknown: The Coalition from Operation Desert Fox to Operation Iraqi Freedom." *Defense & Security Analysis* 21 (2): 143–58.

McWilliams, Wayne C., and Harry Piotrowski. 1997. *The World since 1945: A History of International Relations.* Boulder: Lynne Rienner.

Mearsheimer, John J. 1983. *Conventional Deterrence.* Ithaca: Cornell University Press.

Meital, Yoram. 1993. "Egypt in the Gulf Crisis." In *Iraq's Road to War,* ed. Amatzia Baram and Barry Rubin, 191–202. New York: St. Martin's.

Miers, Anne, and T. Clifton Morgan. 2002. "Multilateral Sanctions and Foreign Policy Success: Can Too Many Cooks Spoil the Broth?" *International Interactions* 28 (2): 117–36.

Milgrom, Paul, and John Roberts. 1990. "Bargaining Costs, Influence Costs, and the Organization of Economic Activity." In *Perspectives on Positive Political Economy,* ed. James Alt and Kenneth Shepsle, 57–89. Cambridge: Cambridge University Press.

Milner, Helen V. 1997. *Interests, Institutions, and Information: Domestic Politics and International Relations.* Princeton: Princeton University Press.

Mingst, Karen. 2003. "Domestic Political Factors and Decisions to Use Military Force." In *Democratic Accountability and the Use of Military Force in International Law,* ed. Charlotte Ku and Harold Jacobson, 61–80. Cambridge: Cambridge University Press.

Mingst, Karen A., and Margaret P. Karns. 2007. *The United Nations in the 21st Century.* 3rd ed. Boulder: Westview.

Mitzen, Jennifer. 2005. "Reading Habermas in Anarchy: Multilateral Diplomacy and Global Public Spheres." *American Political Science Review* 99 (3): 401–17.

Moe, Terry M. 2005. "Power and Political Institutions." *Perspectives on Politics* 3 (2): 215–33.

Moens, Alexander. 2004. *The Foreign Policy of George W. Bush: Values, Strategy, and Loyalty.* Burlington, Vt.: Ashgate.

Moisi, Dominique. 1999. "Iraq." In *Transatlantic Tensions,* ed. Richard Haass, 124–39. Washington, D.C.: Brookings Institution Press.

Morgenthau, Hans. 1985. *Politics among Nations.* 6th ed. New York: Knopf.

Morrow, James. 1999. "The Strategic Setting of Choices: Signaling, Commitment and Negotiation in International Politics." In *Strategic Choice and International Relations,* ed. David A. Lake and Robert Powell, 77–114. Princeton: Princeton University Press.

Mueller, John. 1994. *Policy and Opinion in the Gulf War.* Chicago: University of Chicago Press.

——. 2005. "Force, Legitimacy, Success, and Iraq." In *Force and Legitimacy in World Politics,* ed. David Armstrong, Theo Farrell, and Bice Maiguashca, 109–25. New York: Cambridge University Press.

Mueller, John, and Karl Mueller. 1999. "Sanctions of Mass Destruction." *Foreign Affairs* 78 (May/June): 43–53.

Murphy, John F. 2004. *The United States and the Rule of Law in International Affairs.* New York: Cambridge University Press.
Murray, Williamson, and Robert H. Scales. 2003. *The Iraq War: A Military History.* Cambridge, Mass: Belknap.
Newnham, Randall. 2008. "'Coalition of the Bribed and Bullied?' U.S. Economic Linkage and the Iraq War Coalition." *International Studies Perspectives* 9 (2): 183–200.
News Conference. 1990. "News Conference of President Bush and President Mikhail Gorbachev of the Soviet Union, September 9, 1990." *Weekly Compilation of Presidential Documents.* Vol. 26. Washington, D.C.: Government Printing Office.
Nielson, Daniel, and Michael Tierney. 2003. "Delegation to International Organizations: Agency Theory and World Bank Environmental Reform." *International Organization* 57: 241–76.
Nolte, Georg. 2003. "Germany: Ensuring Political Legitimacy for the Use of Military Forces by Requiring Constitutional Accountability." In *Democratic Accountability and the Use of Force in International Law,* ed. Charlotte Ku and Harold K. Jacobson, 127–53. New York: Cambridge University Press.
North, Douglass, and Barry Weingast. 1989. "Constitutions and Commitment: The Evolution of Institutions Governing Public Choice in 17th Century England." *Journal of Economic History* 49 (4): 803–32.
Nuruzzaman, Mohammed. 2006. "Beyond Realist Theories: "Neo-Conservative Realism" and the American Invasion of Iraq." *International Studies Perspectives* 7 (3): 239–53.
Nuti, Leopoldo. 2005. "The Richest and Farthest Master Is Always Best: U.S.-Italian Relations in Historical Perspective." In *The Transatlantic Alliance under Stress,* ed. David M. Andrews, 177–98. New York: Cambridge University Press.
Nye, Joseph S. 2004. *Soft Power: The Means to Success in World Politics.* New York: Public Affairs.
Office of the President. 1990. "Remarks and a Question-and-Answer Session with Reporters in Aspen, Colorado, August 6, 1990." *Weekly Compilation of Presidential Documents.* Vol. 26. Washington, D.C.: Government Printing Office.
Olson, Mancur. 1965. *The Logic of Collective Action.* Cambridge, Mass: Harvard University Press.
O'Neill, Barry. 1997. "Power and Satisfaction in the Security Council." In *The Once and Future Security Council,* ed. Bruce Russett, 59–82. New York: St. Martin's.
OPEC. 2005. *Annual Statistical Bulletin 2005.* Vienna: Organization of the Petroleum Exporting Countries.
O'Sullivan, Meghan. 2003. *Shrewd Sanctions: Statecraft and State Sponsors of Terrorism.* Washington, D.C.: Brookings Institution Press.
Packer, George. 2005. *The Assassins' Gate: America in Iraq.* New York: Farrar, Straus & Giroux.
Papayoanou, Paul. 1997. "Intra-Alliance Bargaining and U.S. Bosnia Policy." *Journal of Conflict Resolution* 41 (1): 91–116.
Pape, Robert. 1996. *Bombing to Win.* Ithaca: Cornell University Press.
——. 2003. "The World Pushes Back." *Boston Globe,* March 23, H1.
——. 2005. "Soft Balancing against the United States." *International Security* 30 (1): 7–45.
Parasiliti, Andrew. 1994. "Defeating the Vietnam Syndrome: The Military, the Media, and the Gulf War." In *The Gulf War and the New World Order* ed. Tareq Ismael and Jacqueline Ismael, 242–63. Gainesville: University Press of Florida.

Paul, T. V. 2005. "Soft Balancing in the Age of U.S. Primacy." *International Security* 30 (1): 46–71.

Paret, Peter. 1986. "Introduction." In *Makers of Modern Strategy from Machiavelli to the Nuclear Age*, ed. Peter Paret, 3–8. Princeton: Princeton University Press.

Patrick, Stewart, and Shepard Forman, eds. 2002. *Multilateralism and U.S. Foreign Policy: Ambivalent Engagement.* Boulder: Lynne Rienner.

Pauly, Robert J., Jr., and Tom Lansford. 2005. *Strategic Preemption: U.S. Foreign Policy and the Second Iraq War.* Burlington, Vt.: Ashgate.

PBS. 1997. *Frontline: The Gulf War: Part B.* Documentary aired on February 4, 1997. Transcript available at www.pbs.org/wgbh/pages/frontline/gulf/script_b.html.

Pearson, Graham. 1999. *The UNSCOM Saga.* New York: St. Martin's.

Peterson, John. 2003. "The U.S. and Europe in the Balkans." In *Europe, America, Bush*, ed. John Peterson and Mark Pollack. New York: Routledge.

Pew Research Center. 2002. *What the World Thinks in 2002.* Washington, D.C.: Pew Research Center for the People and the Press.

——. 2003a. "America's Image Further Erodes, Europeans Want Weaker Ties." Report released March 18. Washington, D.C.: Pew Research Center for the People and the Press.

——. 2003b. "Bush's Ratings Rose Last Night." Report released April 10. Washington, D.C.: Pew Research Center for the People and the Press.

——. 2003c. "Views of a Changing World 2003: War with Iraq Further Divides Global Publics." Report released June 3. Washington, D.C.: Pew Research Center for the People and the Press.

Pickering, Thomas. 1991. Pickering Testifies on Gulf Cease-Fire Implementation. Statement by Thomas Pickering, U.S. ambassador to the UN, in testimony before the House Foreign Affairs Committee, July 18. http://www.fas.org/news/iraq/1991/910718-190813.htm.

——. 1998. "Iraq and the Security Council Vote." USIA Foreign Press Center Briefing, March 3. Federal News Service. http://www.fnsg.com/transcripta.htm?id=19980303t6268&query=.

PIPA. 2003. "Americans on the Iraq War and the Future of the United Nations." The PIPA/Knowledge Networks Poll, March 31.

Pollack, Kenneth. 2002. "Next Stop Baghdad?" *Foreign Affairs* 81 (2): 32–47.

Pollack, Mark. 2003. *The Engines of European Integration.* New York: Oxford University Press.

Pollock, David. 1992. "The 'Arab Street'? Public Opinion in the Arab World." Policy Paper No. 32, Washington Institute for Near East Policy.

Pond, Elizabeth. 2005. "The Dynamics of the Feud over Iraq." In *The Atlantic Alliance under Stress*, ed. David M. Andrews, 30–55. New York: Cambridge University Press.

Popkin, Samuel. 1991. *The Reasoning Voter.* Chicago: University of Chicago Press.

Powell, Colin, with Joseph Persico. 1995. *My American Journey.* New York: Random House.

Price, Richard M. 1997. *The Chemical Weapons Taboo.* Ithaca: Cornell University Press.

Price, Richard M. and Mark W. Zacher, eds. 2004. *The United Nations and Global Security.* New York: Palgrave.

Purrington, Courtney, and A. K. 1991. "Tokyo's Policy Responses during the Gulf Crisis." *Asian Survey* 31 (4): 307–23.

Putnam, Robert. 1988. "Diplomacy and Domestic Politics: The Logic of Two-Level Games." *International Organization* 42 (3): 427–60.

Reinalda, Bob, and Bertjan Verbeek, eds. 1998. *Autonomous Policy Making by International Organizations.* New York: Routledge.

Risse-Kappen, Thomas. 1995. *Cooperation among Democracies: The European Influence on U.S. Foreign Policy.* Princeton: Princeton University Press.

Ritter, Scott. 1999. *Endgame: Solving the Iraq Crisis.* New York: Simon & Schuster.

——. 2005. *Iraq Confidential: The Untold Story of the Intelligence Conspiracy to Undermine the UN and Overthrow Saddam Hussein.* New York: Nation Books.

Roberts, Adam. 2004. "The Use of Force." In *The UN Security Council: From the Cold War to the 21st Century,* ed. David M. Malone, 133–52. Boulder: Lynne Rienner.

Rogoff, Kenneth. 1985. "The Optimal Design of Commitment to an Intermediate Monetary Target." *Quarterly Journal of Economics* 100 (4): 1169–89.

Ross, Carne. 2007. *Independent Diplomat: Dispatches from an Unaccountable Elite.* Cornell University Press.

Ross, Dennis. 2007. *Statecraft: And How to Restore America's Standing in the World.* New York: Farrar, Straus & Giroux.

Roy Morgan Research. 2003. "Is the U.S. Too Keen to Use Military Force in Other Countries?" Finding No. 3627, May 16. http://www.roymorgan.com/news/polls/2003/3627.

Rubin, James P. 2003. "Stumbling into War: A Diplomatic Postmortem." *Foreign Affairs* 82 (5): 46–66.

Ruggie, John G, ed. 1993. *Multilateralism Matters: The Theory and Praxis of an Institutional Form.* New York: Columbia University Press.

Ruiz Fabri, Hélène. 2002. "The UNSCOM Experience: Lessons from an Experiment." *European Journal of International Law* 13 (1): 153–59.

Rumsfeld, Donald. 2005. Remarks Delivered at the Shangri-La Hotel, Singapore, June 4. http://www.defenselink.mil/speeches/speech.aspx?speechid=77.

Russett, Bruce, ed. 1997. *The Once and Future Security Council.* New York: St. Martin's.

Sarkees, Meredith Reid. 2000. "The Correlates of War Data on War: An Update to 1997." *Conflict Management and Peace Science* 18 (1): 123–44.

Sarooshi, Danesh. 1999. *The United Nations and the Development of Collective Security.* Oxford: Oxford University Press.

Sartori, Anne E. 2005. *Deterrence by Diplomacy.* Princeton: Princeton University Press.

Sayari, Sabri. 1997. "Between Allies and Neighbors: Turkey's Burden Sharing Policy in the Gulf Conflict." In *Friends in Need,* ed. Andrew Bennett, Joseph Lepgold, and Danny Unger, 197–217. New York: St. Martin's.

Schachter, Oscar. 1984. "The Right of States to Use Armed Force." *Michigan Law Review* 82:1620–46.

——. 1989. "Self-Defense and the Rule of Law." *American Journal of International Law* 83 (2): 259–77.

Schelling, Thomas. 1966. *Arms and Influence.* New Haven: Yale University Press.

Schimmelfennig, Frank. 1998. "NATO Enlargement: A Constructivist Explanation." *Security Studies* 8 (2): 198–234.

Schofield, Richard. 1993. *Kuwait and Iraq: Historical Claims and Territorial Disputes.* London: Royal Institute of International Affairs.

Schultz, Kenneth. 2001. *Democracy and Coercive Diplomacy.* Cambridge: Cambridge University Press.

——. 2003. "Tying Hands and Washing Hands: The U.S. Congress and Multilateral Humanitarian Intervention." In *Locating the Proper Authorities,* ed. Daniel W. Drezner, 105–42. Ann Arbor: University of Michigan Press.

Schuster, Jürgen, and Herbert Maier. 2006. "The Rift: Explaining Europe's Divergent Iraq Policies in the Run-Up of the American-led War on Iraq." *Foreign Policy Analysis* 2:223–44.

Shapiro, Robert, and Lawrence Jacobs. 2000. "Who Leads and Who Follows? U.S. Presidents, Public Opinion, and Foreign Policy." In *Decisionmaking in a Glass House,* ed. Brigitte Nacos, Robert Shapiro, and Pierangelo Isernia, 223–45. New York: Rowman & Littlefield.

Sharp, Jane M.O. 2005. "Debunking the Myth: The US-UK "Special Relationship" after Iraq." In *Partners or Rivals? European-American Relations after Iraq,* ed. Evangelista and Vittorio Emanuele Parsi, 109–37. Milan: Vita e Pensiero.

Shevardnadze, Eduard. 1991. *The Future Belongs to Freedom.* London: Sinclair Stevenson.

Sifry, Micah, and Christopher Cerf, eds. 1991. *The Gulf War Reader: History, Documents, Opinions.* New York: Random House.

Simmons, Beth A. 2000. "International Law and State Behavior: Commitment and Compliance in International Monetary Affairs." *American Political Science Review* 94 (4): 819–35.

Slater, Jerome. 1969. "The Limits of Legitimization in International Organizations." *International Organization* 23 (1): 48–72.

Smith, Edwin M. 2003. "Collective Security, Peacekeeping, and Ad Hoc Multilateralism." In *Democratic Accountability and the Use of Force in International Law,* ed. Charlotte Ku and Harold K. Jacobson, 81–103. New York: Cambridge University Press.

Smith, James McCall. 2000. "The Politics of Dispute Settlement Design: Explaining Legalism in Regional Trade Pacts." *International Organization* 54 (1): 137–80.

Sobel, Richard. 1996. "U.S. and European Attitudes toward Intervention in the Former Yugoslavia: *Mourir pour la Bosnie*?" In *The World and Yugoslavia's Wars,* ed. Richard Ullman, 145–81. New York: Council on Foreign Relations Press.

Soutou, Georges-Henri. 2005. "Three Rifts, Two Reconciliations: Franco-American Relations During the Fifth Republic." In *The Atlantic Alliance under Stress,* ed. David M. Andrews, 102–27. New York: Cambridge University Press.

Stanfield, Rochelle L. 1990. "Looking Beyond the Guns of August." *National Journal* 22:1959–60.

Stein, Arthur A. 1982. "Coordination and Collaboration: Regimes in an Anarchic World." *International Organization* 36 (2): 299–324.

Sterner, Michael. 1997. "Closing the Gate: The Persian Gulf War Revisited." *Current History* 96 (January): 13–19.

Stone, Randall W. 2002. *Lending Credibility: The International Monetary Fund and the Post-Communist Transition.* Princeton: Princeton University Press.

Stothard, Peter. 2003. *Thirty Days: Tony Blair and the Test of History.* New York: HarperCollins.

Styan, David. 2004. "Jacques Chirac's 'Non': France, Iraq and the United Nations, 1991–2003." *Modern and Contemporary France* 12 (2): 371–85.

"Survival as Victory." 1998. *Al-Ahram Weekly On-line,* no. 409, December 24–30. http://weekly.ahram.org.eg/1998/409/ir10.htm.

Suskin, Ron. 2004. *The Price of Loyalty: George W. Bush, The White House, and the Education of Paul O'Neill.* New York: Simon & Schuster.

Swedberg, Richard. 1986. "The Doctrine of Economic Neutrality of the IMF and the World Bank." *Journal of Peace Research* 23 (4): 377–90.

Taft, William H. IV, and Todd F. Buchwald. 2003. "Preemption, Iraq, and International Law." *American Journal of International Law* 97 (3): 557–63.

Tago, Atsushi. 2005. "Determinants of Multilateralism in U.S. Use of Force: State of Economy, Election Cycle, and Divided Government." *Journal of Peace Research* 42 (5): 585–604.

Tannenwald, Nina. 2008. *The Nuclear Taboo: The United States and the Non-Use of Nuclear Weapons since 1945.* New York: Cambridge University Press.

Teixeira da Silva, Pascal. 2004. "Weapons of Mass Destruction: The Iraqi Case." In *The UN Security Council: From the Cold War to the 21st Century,* ed. David Malone, 205–18. Boulder: Lynne Rienner.

Telhami, Shibley. 1993. "Arab Public Opinion and the Gulf War." In *The Political Psychology of the Gulf War,* ed. Stanley Renshon, 183–97. Pittsburgh: University of Pittsburgh Press.

——. 2003. "Aftereffects of the Iraq War in the Middle East." *In the National Interest* 2 (17). Online at www.inthenationalinterest.com/archives/Volume02/Vol2Issue17.html.

Terasawa, Katsuaki, and William Gates. 1993. "Burden-Sharing in the Persian Gulf: Lessons Learned and Implications for the Future." *Defense Analysis* 9 (2): 171–95.

Thacker, Strom C. 1999. "The High Politics of IMF Lending." *World Politics* 52 (1): 38–75.

Thakur, Ramesh. 2004. "Developing Countries and the Intervention-Sovereignty Debate." In *The United Nations and Global Security,* ed. Richard M. Price and Mark W. Zacher, 193–208. New York: Palgrave.

——. 2006. *The United Nations, Peace and Security.* New York: Cambridge University Press.

Thatcher, Margaret. 1993. *The Downing Street Years, 1979–1990.* New York: Harper-Collins.

Thomas, Hugh. 1967. *Suez.* New York: Harper & Row.

Thomas, James P. 2000. *The Military Challenges of Transatlantic Coalitions.* London: International Institute for Strategic Studies.

Thomas, Ward. 2001. *The Ethics of Destruction.* Ithaca: Cornell University Press.

Thompson, Alexander. 2002. "Applying Rational Choice Theory to International Law: The Promise and Pitfalls." *Journal of Legal Studies* 31:S285–S306.

——. 2005. "Understanding IO Legitimation." Paper presented at the annual convention of the International Studies Association, Honolulu, September 1–5.

——. 2006a. "Coercion through IOs: The Security Council and the Logic of Information Transmission." *International Organization* 60 (1): 1–34.

——. 2006b. "Principal Problems: The Rise and Fall of UN Weapons Inspections in Iraq." Paper presented at the annual convention of the International Studies Association, San Diego, March 2–5.

——. 2006c. "Screening Power: International Organizations as Informative Agents." In *Delegation and Agency in International Organizations,* ed. Darren Hawkins, David A. Lake, Daniel Nielson, and Michael J. Tierney, 229–54. New York: Cambridge University Press.

"Those Awkward Hearts and Minds." 2003. *Global Agenda,* April 1.

Trachtenberg, Marc. 2005. "The Iraq Crisis and the Future of the Western Alliance." In *The Atlantic Alliance under Stress,* ed. David M. Andrews, 201–31. New York: Cambridge University Press.

Trevan, Tim. 1999. *Saddam's Secrets: The Hunt for Iraq's Hidden Weapons.* London: HarperCollins.

United Nations. 1996. *The United Nations and the Iraq-Kuwait Conflict, 1990–1996.* New York: UN Department of Public Information.

United Nations, Department of Public Affairs. 1998. Daily Highlights, February 22. http://www.un.org/NewLinks/sg_iraq.htm.

Unger, Danny. 1997. "Japan and the Gulf War: Making the World Safe for Japan-U.S. Relations." In *Friends in Need,* ed. Andrew Bennett, Joseph Lepgold, and Danny Unger, 137–63. New York: St. Martin's.

U.S. Congress. 1991. *The Persian Gulf Crisis: Relevant Documents, Correspondence, Reports.* Washington, D.C.: Government Printing Office.

U.S. House of Representatives. Committee on Foreign Affairs. 1991. *U.N. Role in the Persian Gulf and Iraqi Compliance with U.N. Resolutions: Hearings before the Committee on Foreign Affairs.* 102nd Cong., 1st sess., April 23, July 18, and October 21.

——. 1992. U.N. Role in the Persian Gulf and Iraqi Compliance with U.N. Resolutions: Hearings before the Committee on Foreign Affairs. 102nd Cong., 2nd sess., April 1 and July 29.

U.S. House of Representatives. Committee on International Relations. 1999. *Iraq's Compliance the U.N. Security Council: Communication from the President of the United States to the Committee on International Relations.* 106th Cong., 1st sess, March 4.

U.S. News & World Report. 1992. *Triumph without Victory: The Unreported History of the Persian Gulf War.* New York: Random House.

Verbeek, Bertjan. 1998. "International Organizations: The Ugly Duckling of International Relations Theory?" In *Autonomous Policy Making by International Organizations,* ed. Bob Reinalda and Bertjan Verbeek, 11–26. New York: Routledge.

Voeten, Erik. 2001. "Outside Options and the Logic of Security Council Action." *American Political Science Review* 95 (4): 845–58.

——. 2005. "The Political Origins of the UN Security Council's Ability to Legitimize the Use of Force." *International Organization* 59 (3): 527–57.

Wallace, William and Tim Oliver. 2005. "A Bridge Too Far: The United Kingdom and the Transatlantic Relationship." In *The Atlantic Alliance under Stress,* ed. David M. Andrews, 152–76. New York: Cambridge University Press.

Wallander, Celeste. 1999. *Mortal Friends, Best Enemies: German-Russian Cooperation after the Cold War.* Ithaca: Cornell University Press.

Wallensteen, Peter, and Patrik Johansson. 2004. "Security Council Decisions in Perspective." In *The UN Security Council: From the Cold War to the 21st Century,* ed. David M. Malone, 17–33. Boulder: Lynne Rienner.

Walt, Stephen M. 1987. *The Origins of Alliances.* Ithaca: Cornell University Press.

——. 2005. *Taming American Power: The Global Response to U.S. Primacy.* New York: Norton.

Waltz, Kenneth N. 1979. *Theory of International Politics.* New York: McGraw-Hill.

Watson, Bruce W., Bruce George, Peter Tsouras, and B. L. Cyr. 1991. *Military Lessons of the Gulf War.* Novato, Calif.: Presidio.

Watson, Russell, with John Barry, Douglas Waller, and Margaret Garrard Warner. 1990. "The Price of Success." *Newsweek,* October 1, 20–22.

Wedgwood, Ruth. 2002. "Unilateral Action in a Multilateral World." In *Multilateralism and U.S. Foreign Policy,* ed. Stewart Patrick and Shepard Forman, 167–89. Boulder: Lynne Rienner.

Welsh, Jennifer M. 2004. "Authorizing Humanitarian Intervention." In *The United Nations and Global Security,* ed. Richard M. Price and Mark W. Zacher, 177–92. New York: Palgrave.

Western, Jon. 2005. *Selling Intervention and War: The Presidency, the Media, and the American Public.* Baltimore: Johns Hopkins University Press.

Weston, Burns H. 1991. "Security Council Resolution 678 and Persian Gulf Decision Making: Precarious Legitimacy." *American Journal of International Law* 85 (3): 515–35.

Westra, Joel. 2007. *International Law and the Use of Armed Force: The UN Charter and the Major Powers.* New York: Routledge.

Wheeler, Nicholas J. 2000. *Saving Strangers: Humanitarian Intervention in International Society.* New York: Oxford University Press.
White, Nigel D. 2003. "The United Kingdom: Increasing Commitment Requires Greater Parliamentary Involvement." In *Democratic Accountability and the Use of Force in International Law,* ed. Charlotte Ku and Harold K. Jacobson, 231–53. New York: Cambridge University Press.
White, Nigel D. and Robert Cryer. 1999. "Unilateral Enforcement of Resolution 687: A Threat Too Far?" *California Western International Law Journal* 29:243–82.
White House. 1998. Statement by the President. Office of the Press Secretary, December 16.
——. 2002. "The National Security Strategy of the United States of America." September 2002. http://www.whitehouse.gov/nsc/nss.pdf.
——. 2006. Press Briefing by Scott McClellan, April 12. http://www.whitehouse.gov/news/releases/2006/04/20060412-4.html.
Woodward, Bob. 1991. *The Commanders.* New York: Simon & Schuster.
——. 2002. *Bush at War.* New York: Simon & Schuster.
——. 2004. *Plan of Attack.* New York: Simon & Schuster.
——. 2006. *State of Denial: Bush at War, Part III.* New York: Simon & Schuster.
Yarbrough, Beth, and Robert Yarbrough. 1997. "Dispute Settlement in International Trade: Regionalism and Procedural Coordination." In *The Political Economy of Regionalism,* ed. Edward Mansfield and Helen Milner, 134–63. New York: Columbia University Press.
Yetiv, Steve A. 2004. *Explaining Foreign Policy: U.S. Decision-Making and the Persian Gulf War.* Baltimore: Johns Hopkins University Press.
Young, Oran. 1994. *International Governance.* Ithaca: Cornell University Press.
Zacher, Mark W. 2004. "The Conundrums of International Power Sharing: The Politics of Security Council Reform." In *The United Nations and Global Security,* ed. Richard M. Price and Mark W. Zacher, 211–25. New York: Palgrave.
Zakaria, Fareed. 2002. "Our Way: The Trouble with Being the World's Only Superpower." *New Yorker,* October 14.
——. 2003. "The Arrogant Empire." *Newsweek,* March 24.
Zaller, John. 1994. "Strategic Politicians, Public Opinion, and the Gulf Crisis." In *Taken by Storm: The Media, Public Opinion, and U.S. Foreign Policy in the Gulf War,* ed. W. Lance Bennett and David L. Paletz, 250–74. Chicago: University of Chicago Press.
Zaller, John, and Dennis Chiu. 1996. "Government's Little Helper: U.S. Press Coverage of Foreign Policy Crises, 1946–1991." *Political Communication* 13 (4): 385–405.
Zanini, Michele, and Jennifer Morrison Taw. 2000. *The Army and Multinational Force Compatibility.* Santa Monica: RAND.

Index

Page numbers with an *f* indicate figures; page numbers with a *t* indicate tables.